No is Not a Lonely Utterance

No is Not a Lonely Utterance

The Art and Activism of Complaining

SARA AHMED

ALLEN LANE
an imprint of
PENGUIN BOOKS

ALLEN LANE

UK | USA | Canada | Ireland | Australia
India | New Zealand | South Africa

Allen Lane is part of the Penguin Random House group of companies whose addresses can be found at global.penguinrandomhouse.com

Penguin Random House UK
One Embassy Gardens, 8 Viaduct Gardens, London SW11 7BW

penguin.co.uk

First published 2025
001

Copyright © Sara Ahmed, 2025

The moral right of the author has been asserted

Penguin Random House values and supports copyright.
Copyright fuels creativity, encourages diverse voices, promotes freedom of expression and supports a vibrant culture. Thank you for purchasing an authorized edition of this book and for respecting intellectual property laws by not reproducing, scanning or distributing any part of it by any means without permission. You are supporting authors and enabling Penguin Random House to continue to publish books for everyone.
No part of this book may be used or reproduced in any manner for the purpose of training artificial intelligence technologies or systems. In accordance with Article 4(3) of the DSM Directive 2019/790, Penguin Random House expressly reserves this work from the text and data mining exception.

Set in 11.5/15.25pt Crimson Text
Typeset by Six Red Marbles UK, Thetford, Norfolk
Printed and bound in Great Britain by Clays Ltd, Elcograf S.p.A.

The authorized representative in the EEA is Penguin Random House Ireland, Morrison Chambers, 32 Nassau Street, Dublin D02 YH68

A CIP catalogue record for this book is available from the British Library

ISBN: 978-0-241-75927-1

Penguin Random House is committed to a sustainable future for our business, our readers and our planet. This book is made from Forest Stewardship Council® certified paper.

Contents

Preface: A Complaint Biography — ix
Introduction: A Feminist Ear — 1

PART ONE
Making Complaints

1/ Complaints as Coming Out Stories — 39
   Letting it In, Hitting the Doors, Unintentional Complaints, After Complaint

2/ A Complainer as an Institutional Plumber — 71
   From Informality to Formality, From Warnings to Threats, From Bribes to Blanks, Administrative Violence

PART TWO
Changing Institutions

3/ Complaint as Feminist Pedagogy — 111
   Institutional Power, Loyalties and Legacies, Policing the Critic, A Will to Power

4/ Complaint as Diversity Work — 159
   Diversity Workers, Hostile Environments, Changing Policies, Forced Change

PART THREE
Dismantling and World Building

5/ **Complaints as Activism**   215
Becoming Complaint Activists, Complaint Collectives, Research and Activism, Complaint to Protest

6/ **Complaint as a Queer Method**   259
False Positives, Institutional Closets, Communicating Complaints, Survival as Complaint

A Complainer's Survival Kit   309
A Complaint Curriculum   317

Acknowledgements   327
Notes   331

This content warning is a dedication.

No is Not a Lonely Utterance is dedicated to everyone who needs to take care in reading it because of what they have been through.

It tells stories of harassment, bullying, assault and hostile environments from the point of view of those who have said *no* to them.

Preface: A Complaint Biography

A complaint can change your life. It does not even have to be your own complaint – the complaint that changed my life was made by students where I used to work. What I learnt about the institution from what happened to their complaint, what it did and did not do, where it did and did not go, led me to leave not just my post but my profession.

I shared my reasons for resigning on my blog. I wrote that I was leaving because the university had failed to address sexual harassment as an 'institutional problem'. I called my resignation 'an act of feminist protest'. If it sounds dramatic, it was. If I sound bold, I wasn't. I also wrote that I resigned 'because the costs of doing this work have been too high'. I did not feel bold, more sad and tired and shattered.

I remember the day I moved out of my office. I chose a day I knew colleagues were less likely to be there because I was not sure I would be able to sustain a conversation. I sat in my office and packed my books, files and papers quietly, boxing my work up, getting it ready to be removed. Getting myself ready. I felt myself begin to fall apart when an administrator asked me how I was doing, her kindness almost unbearable. I left through the back door, quietly, trying not to look behind me.

Well, that's one way of telling the story.

There are other ways.

A complaint, in leading me to leave one profession, is how I took up another. A complaint is how I became a writer. By withdrawing my labour from an institution, I became freer to express myself. I think of leaving and I think not just of those boxes, all packed up, but of the connections I formed, the collectives I became part of, the urgency we felt in taking up the task of trying to change the institution. I think of how that urgency travelled into my writing, my communications, my world. When I left, I took so much with me – not just knowledge, but a sharpened sense of the point and the purpose of fighting for change.

There are many ways of telling the story of a complaint.

They can all be true.

A back door, an opening to another path.

For those of you who picked up this book because of your own experiences of complaint, how would you tell the story? Would you begin with the moment you first felt something was wrong, or when you consciously recognized something was wrong, or when you decided to complain after not being sure whether to or not, or when you found the right forms, or when you filled them in, or when you began to express your complaint by putting words on paper or by saying them out loud to yourself or to others? It is hard to know how to begin the story of a complaint when it is hard to know when a complaint begins.

The word *complaint* might bring to mind a formal

and bureaucratic process; forms filled in and submitted in accordance with procedures laid out in advance. Many complaints take form in this way. You might be obliged to follow the procedures in order for your complaint to be registered as one. But a complaint can also be an expression of grief, pain or dissatisfaction as well as a bodily ailment (especially a minor one). A complaint can be how you let other people know something is wrong. Or how your body lets you know. A complaint can be that pain in your neck. Or a lump in your throat.

There can be an art to how we express our complaints. There can be art in where we express them. Take, for example, the Guerrilla Girls, a group of anonymous artist activists formed in 1985, who used 'disruptive headlines, outrageous visuals and killer statistics to expose gender and ethnic bias and corruption in art, film, politics and pop culture'.[1] Curator Sarah Urist Green called the Guerrilla Girls 'expert complainers'.[2] I would call them creative complainers. They ran an exhibition titled *Complaints Department* at the Tate Modern in London, in October 2016, in which participants were invited to 'post their complaints', or to make their complaints 'face to face' during office hours.[3] The Guerrilla Girls teach us the art of complaining, how we can create our own platforms, by evoking the typically banal settings in which complaints are made, whether that's a specially designated department or a faculty of Human Resources.

I hope to show in this book that more creative forms of complaining do not necessarily take place in a separate sphere

Guerrilla Girls, *Complaints Department*
(Tate, London, 2016, copyright © Guerrilla Girls)

from administration. A formal complaint can require you to keep telling the story, to explain what happened that led you to complain. And you might have to keep telling that story to the different people tasked by the organization to receive complaints. The need to keep complaining can be exhausting; it might feel far from creative. Some people compare complaining to talking to a brick wall. We can still turn that wall into a testimonial. One member of the Guerrilla Girls describes how they took their 'complaint departments all over the world' and would 'paint a wall and invite people to come in and complain about anything they want'. They then gathered these complaints together to create 'a time capsule of discontent at a certain time and in a certain place'.[4]

The creativity of complaint is more apparent when we bring our complaints together. Since I left my post in 2016, that is what I have been doing: collecting complaints and bringing them together. This book is itself a collection of other people's complaints. Some of you might find your complaints in here. Or you might hear in other people's complaints something of your own.

In the past few years, I have been sharing stories of complaints in lectures and in an academic monograph with the pithy title *Complaint!* (the exclamation point capturing something of the intensity of the work).[5] I am sharing them again in a more accessible form because of what I learnt from sharing them before: hearing about other people's complaints helps us to handle our own. Other people can best explain why. One person wrote on social media, '[it] makes me (and probably a gazillion other people, sadly) feel as if you've been listening at my door/reading my texts/being copied on the email I sent, gosh, just this morning, to say, "Uh, the guy I've been reporting for the past six years is still at it, surprise."' It helps to know that our complaints are not so singular. Otherwise, it is hard not to feel that we are the problem, that when the same things keep happening, we made them happen.

Another person wrote to me, 'I thought that I had had a unique experience. It's so therapeutic to know what I experienced is real – that it actually happens to other people ... that it wasn't just in my head. But it's also infuriating that my experience is generalizable, and it feels disillusioning as hell that I'd never heard about this happening to other people.' It helps to know that the problems you are having are not mental, just in your head. Reality can be therapy, at least sometimes. It can still be infuriating to learn that what happened when you complained happened to other people.

You might recognize yourself in someone else's complaint or you might recognize an institution. A reviewer of my monograph on complaint wrote, 'I kept thinking, "She's writing about me, about my former institution." It made it even more painful that she wasn't.' It can be more painful to hear yourself and your institution in other people's complaints because it tells you there is more *to* what you experienced; more people, more violence, more pain.

That we *don't know* the continuity of other people's complaints with our own is why we need to share our stories. Complaints are mostly confidential; they are made behind closed doors. In listening to each other's stories of complaint, we put our *ears to the door*, overhearing conversations that would otherwise be kept secret ('it makes me . . . feel as if you've been listening at my door').

Complaints, once made, have their own lives. But their lives remain entangled with ours. I use the term *complaint biography* to describe this entanglement. I kept noticing how people would begin by telling me about a specific complaint they had made, the one that had brought them to be in conversation with me, but would then digress, telling me about other complaints they had or had not made before. I learnt something about complaint from this tendency to digress. A story of one complaint ends up as a story of another because their lives are as messy as ours. I invite each of you reading this book to put your ear to your own past, to think about your own complaints, those you made, those you didn't make, so they can join the stories collected here.

Do you remember the first complaint you made? I remember mine. I was at school. School had always been a difficult space for me; the lessons seemed to be more about the power of those who taught them than the content of what they taught. In primary school, I had a teacher who would repeatedly hit students on their hands with his ruler. He singled out those of us who did not give him the respect he did not deserve. I remember another teacher who would insist she was right even when she was wrong. I was being taught authority meant the right to be wrong.

Mostly, I did not complain about the teachers, just catalogued instances in the firmness of my resolve about who I did not want to become. But there was one time I did complain. It was after a physical education class. The teacher did not think we were paying attention to her properly. She suspected some students were causing a disruption. Some of us probably were. Her punishment was to cancel the whole class. We were sent from an outdoor sports field to the library and told to write essays about sport instead. I happened to prefer the new activity to the cancelled one. I wrote an essay on horse riding; the books piling up around me, shiny pictures of horses. I could hear the sounds of annoyance, shuffled papers, and sensed sideways glances, directed at those of us who had deprived others of an activity they would have enjoyed. I am not sure who was being disruptive on that day. I am not sure anyone was sure. So, the sideways glances fell on those assumed to be the likely cause.

I felt them fall on me. I knew I was supposed to feel ashamed. And I did. I also felt a sense of indignation. The annoyance of my classmates helped me to understand how discipline is achieved by encouraging people to adopt the attitude that those who disobey are in the way, stopping them from getting what they want. It was not just that the other students were *not* annoyed with the teacher but that they identified with her, sharing her annoyance with the students who were disruptive. I did not identify with the teacher because I thought she was wrong. So, in a paragraph in the middle of the essay, I made a complaint. I wrote that it was unjust to punish everyone for the misdemeanours, whether real or perceived, of a few.

The teacher read the essay and found the complaint. I was sent to the headmistress's office. When I think back to this experience, my first experience of complaining, or at least the first complaint I remember making, it is the feeling I recall mostly, how it *felt* to be sent to the headmistress's office, which was not just, at least in the consciousness of students, an actual room but a dreaded destination. Complaints can be a story of where we end up, those dreaded destinations, offices with closed doors, the conversations that happen inside of them; atmospheres, stern, solemn. The headmistress asked me to explain my actions, perhaps also myself. I said that I had complied with the punishment, but that I thought it was wrong and that I had a right to say what was wrong. She said I would not be allowed to go to an art class unless I apologized to the teacher. I really wanted to go to the art class; it was where I could best express myself.

And so, I apologized to the teacher. And then, I was allowed to go to that class. I was learning how compliance works; we are told to protect our relationship to those with authority, or to be willing to repair any damage to those relationships, to get where we want to go.

Looking back, I am struck by how I inserted my critique of the teacher's action into the essay. My complaint was *almost* hidden in an act of compliance. Perhaps I did not expect anyone to find it. Perhaps the point was just to express myself, to put on paper what I felt and thought. Or perhaps I did not have the confidence to be more direct, to confront the teacher. That we express our complaints obliquely or indirectly, not quite coming out with them, is a consequence of a central problem addressed in this book: those receiving our complaints are often who we are complaining about.

And by *those* I am not just referring to a person or persons but to institutions. Complaint procedures designed by institutions seem to be used primarily to protect them and those whom they value most, their most senior employees. This problem of institutions handling complaints made about them is the origin of the *ombudsman*. That word was borrowed from Sweden, the first country to appoint an independent official to investigate complaints made against government officials and agencies. The existence of an ombudsman does not resolve the problem of complaints remaining internal to organizations for the many complaints that don't make it to one.

We can complain at work without filling in forms or addressing institutions. And it is because complaints can be made in so many different ways that it is not always clear whether an action is a complaint. You might think of yourself as making one – perhaps you complained about a sexist or racist comment made during a meeting – and be laughed off as if you don't really mean it. Or you might think of yourself as not complaining but be heard as if you are – perhaps you answered the question 'Is that Miss or Mrs?' with a polite but firm 'Ms', or asked a colleague not to keep calling you 'darling'. Requests for change, including in the informal ways we address each other, are often heard as being negative or mean-spirited.

In this book, I use the term *complainer* rather than the more legalistic term *complainant* because of how it is filled by negativity as well as feeling. The negativity of a complaint is directed outwards: it is how we say *no* to an existing state of affairs or refuse to accept things as they are. But when you become a complainer, negativity is assumed to come from within. The word *complainer* is thus rather akin to *killjoy*; in fact, *killjoy* is typically listed as a synonym for *complainer*. The killjoy and the complainer are both used to diagnose a problem as being one of character: as if you complain *because* you are a complainer or kill joy *because* you are joyless.

I have written about killjoys, specifically feminist killjoys, many times before. In *The Promise of Happiness*, published in 2010, they had a chapter of their own. In *The Feminist Killjoy Handbook*, published thirteen years later, I gave them a whole book. I began that book by setting a scene: I am at a table with my family, having polite conversations, trying hard not to react to sexist comments made by my father.

Invariably I would fail and end up saying I had a problem with what he said. And then, the atmosphere would change, becoming tense, as if I had created a problem rather than pointed one out. I heard these words often: 'Sara, another dinner ruined!'

If I was a complainer at school, I was a killjoy at home, not quite willing or able to be silent or compliant in order to keep the peace with a patriarch or to sustain the illusion that all was well. I did not call myself a feminist killjoy back then. The feminist killjoy is, in fact, a stereotype of feminists: those miserable feminists who make misery their mission. Misery is not our mission. So why claim the name? A conversation I had with Patricia, a professor, gives clues as to why. Patricia had supported students who made a collective complaint about sexual harassment by another lecturer in her department. She explains how their complaint was framed: 'You feminists come along, and you just spoil the fun.' We claim the name *feminist killjoy* not because we intend to cause misery. That's the stereotype. We claim that name because if doing our work causes misery, that is what we might need to cause.

I now think of becoming a feminist killjoy as another thread in my complaint biography. *No is Not a Lonely Utterance* can thus be read as a companion text to *The Feminist Killjoy Handbook* not least because the complainer and the killjoy are themselves companions; their stories, our stories, tangled together. Claiming the name *feminist killjoy* means being willing to be heard as a complainer, heard as negative for not wanting to reproduce the same things, heard as destructive for the same reason.

To complain is to be a *killjoy at work*. I mean by this: complaining is both a job we end up doing, and what we learn on the job. That's why, in this book, I make use of some **killjoy truths** and **killjoy commitments** introduced in *The Feminist Killjoy Handbook*, as well as offer some new ones. They appear throughout as sentences written in bold. **Killjoy truths** are what we learn from our efforts to change institutions. They are flashes of insight, which often come from encountering resistance to change (and that can include our own resistance). **Killjoy commitments** are what we are willing to do to bring about change. We might need to be willing to say *no*, whatever the consequences.

You would be right to ask: *no* to what? *No* can be a simple utterance, an answer to a question, yes or no. But, as you will hear in the chapters that follow, saying *no* within an institution, or to one, is no simple matter. When we say *no* to institutions and the conduct they enable, often in contradiction with their own policies, and are called killjoys or complainers, that *no* is dismissed as deriving from ill intent. We learn on the job how hard it is to say *no* or how hard it is made to say it. We learn from what comes back at us when we say it. We hear how we are not heard.

To be heard as complaining is not to be heard.

If you became a complainer in one situation, you might become rather cautious about complaining in another. Let me return to Patricia's experience. She told me what happened in her next job when she tried to complain about sexism and misogyny she experienced at an away-day. She made an informal complaint, but when nothing happened, she let it drop. 'It does shake you,' Patricia said. 'You think, oh, I am making a fuss.' She turned that worry into a question: 'Should I make a fuss?' She worried all the more because she had 'already made a massive fuss at my previous institution'. Still, she regrets not pursuing it: 'That's why I am so cross now, I didn't say anything.'

If you can regret not complaining, you can regret complaining. One student, Andrea, told me about her experience of making a complaint about harassment and bullying by a professor in her department. Her complaint did not get anywhere. She said, 'Maybe you could make an argument that somehow it is therapeutic to air one's woes, but, to be perfectly frank, I haven't found it therapeutic at all and it continues, and I am finding it difficult to move on with my life.' It is hard to put a complaint behind you when what you complained about continues. Experiences of complaining or not complaining can have knock-on effects on our sense of ourselves. But not just on our sense of ourselves. Andrea left the institution with a sharp critique of how it 'weeded out anyone who thinks a bit differently'.

A complaint biography can thus be about our changing relationship to institutions. That's why my first complaint (or at least the first one I remember making) was not the beginning but in the middle of my complaint biography. What led me to complain at that moment was more structure than event, how I had come to feel alienated from the school as one of only a few students of colour. All my teachers at the school were white; in fact, I have never had a teacher who wasn't. I was not only schooled in whiteness by teachers. When I answered my peers' questions about why I had a 'funny' surname by explaining my father was from Pakistan, I was left feeling it was 'funny' to come from somewhere else.[6] Their parents would make anxious references to colour; I remember one saying, 'Well, at least you must tan easily, dear,' another saying it was such a shame I was not given more lines in *The King and I* (that Orientalist play set in Thailand) because I 'looked the part'. Yes, these were little comments, not worth complaining about. But in adding up, they might have had something to do with why I eventually complained, albeit about something else.

As a university student, I complained more. I complained about how our courses were organized around a narrow body of work (I called it: 'all white men until week ten'). I did not use formal procedures but complained informally through what I said in and out of seminars. I probably became known as a complainer during this time. And there were consequences, as you would probably expect: more resources were given to my peers who had more positive relationships with the senior people in the department.

My first academic job was in Women's Studies. It felt rather like a feminist bubble. I had less to complain about because we were creating our own feminist courses, our own resources. When I became co-director of the Institute for Women's Studies in the year 2000, I began to attend more university committees. Some of them took place in the top room of the fanciest building on campus. I remember my feeling of alienation as I entered that room and saw what was on the walls, who was on them, paintings of old white men, former vice-chancellors; they were modern in style but not content. I remember women coming around in uniforms serving tea and cake. But what really stood out was how the secretary and the chair of the board engaged in sexual innuendo throughout the meeting. I remember feeling shocked by how everyone else seemed to be laughing along.

My feminist bubble had burst. Our complaint biographies can include moments like this, when reality intrudes, and illusions shatter. We do not always make complaints at those moments, which is why our complaint biographies include the times we don't complain.

You can have a complaint without making one.

If I didn't complain back then, the critiques I've offered of institutions since might be how I made that complaint later in another way. I did not make these critiques on my own but in conversation with others.

How I ended up in these conversations is another story of complaint, involving yet more meetings. I became co-director of Women's Studies the year before the Amendment of the Race Relations Act (2001) came into force. The Act required all public authorities to have a race equality policy and action plan. Many of the meetings during the year 2000 involved discussions of how our university was going to write its policy (and who would write it). Usually, I was the only person of colour in these meetings. In one, a professor from another department claimed the whiteness of the university 'was just about geography'. In another, the dean said that racism was 'too difficult to deal with'.

I knew enough to realize I would become a problem person if I said anything and did not yet have the confidence to become that person. So, I sent the dean an email, in which I argued that racism is reproduced by being treated as 'too difficult to deal with'. I also said that the whiteness of the university was an achievement (I probably had that statement about geography in mind). In response to this informal complaint, the dean put me forward to be a member of a new group, which had been set up to write our Race Equality and Action Plan. A complaint, whether made formally or not, can be how you end up taking on an institutional role that is about (or seems to be about) institutional change.

Whatever this role was about, I learnt so much from taking it on. It was how I ended up in conversation with diversity practitioners about the work of trying to change institutions. I was so fascinated by these conversations that I ended up doing an empirical study of diversity work based on interviews with practitioners. It remains interesting to me that some of the strongest critiques of institutions I've heard have come from diversity practitioners who, in the UK, are usually administrators. Practitioners, tasked by institutions to bring about change within them, collect evidence of resistance to change.

That is how, over a long period of time, in one way or another, I have been listening to people's stories about trying to change institutions. It wasn't until my second and last job as an academic that I participated in a formal complaint process. That I had already been involved in the effort to change institutions *before* participating in that process mattered. It helped me to realize that complaining is how we gather even more information about the institution we are complaining about, most of which is never revealed by it. Complaints are *missing data*. To collect that data creates a very different picture of the institution. As soon as I began to release the data, people told me that the picture it was creating was not *specific* to universities; that the same kinds of things were happening in other workplaces. At a recent event, someone came up to me and said, 'It doesn't *just* happen at universities, you know.'

I did not have to share stories of complaint to be reminded of this. One time, I was dropping off our dogs to our sitter, Sally. I was on route to give some lectures in the US. Sally asked me what I was lecturing on. I told her: complaint. She then shared with me what happened when she made a complaint about bullying at her former workplace. She said, 'They locked the door, and I knew I was in trouble.' I did not tell her my lecture was entitled, 'Closing the Door'. Sally kept her hands on her face when she shared what happened, showing as well as telling me how hot and bothered it still made her feel to talk about it, even though it had happened a long time ago. Whenever I've talked about complaints, difficult experiences like this have been shared with me, brought into the conversation and also my consciousness.

In the past decade, I have collected many fragments of different complaints. And I have learnt from each sharp piece. But people need dedicated time to tell the story, to explain how different pieces fit together. So, in this book, the stories of making complaints at universities, shared with me in detail and in confidence, retain an exemplary status. Rather than focus on what they tell us about universities, I pull out their significance for an understanding of institutional power and institutional change. I make connections between these stories and those that have entered the public domain because they ended up in courts or were shared by whistle-blowers or investigative journalists.

In sharing stories of complaint, I have taken care not to turn them into a moral message. My task is not to tell you to complain or how to complain. Complaints can be used in problematic ways, and they are not always the right course of action. Instead, I listen to each *no*, each utterance. I think again of one reader who said it felt as if I had 'been listening at [their] door'. I hadn't, of course. But we learn from how much of our own experiences we can hear in each other's stories. I call the task of listening to complaint *becoming a feminist ear*.

Introduction: A Feminist Ear

On 14 June 2017, Grenfell Tower, in west London, caught fire. Seventy-two people lost their lives that day. Seventy-two people had their lives stolen. Prior to the fire, the residents of Grenfell Tower had formed a collective, the Grenfell Action Group, because their individual complaints about fire safety had either been ignored or treated as malicious. In 2013, the Westminster council threatened one resident, Francis O'Connor with legal action, accusing him of 'defamatory behaviour' and 'harassment' after he blogged about fire safety concerns. Another resident, Edward Daffarn, observed, 'Most people would engage with KCTMO's [Kensington and Chelsea Tenant Management Association] complaints process once, and they would find out it wasn't worth complaining.'[1] Whilst some residents stopped complaining because of what happened (or did not happen) when they did, Mr Daffarn persisted; he made seven complaints about fire safety before that fatal fire. He said he was 'stigmatized as a troublemaker'.[2]

Behind many disasters are unheard complaints.

Journalist Peter Apps begins his vital book *Show Me the Bodies: How Grenfell Happened* with a scene of devastation. 'It should have been a normal flat fire,' he writes, but 'this fire would be different.' Most readers probably assume at this point that Apps is referring to Grenfell. He is not. He is referring to a fire that destroyed another tower block in Southwark, south-east London, eight years earlier on 3 July 2009. Six people died in that fire. Residents had also raised concerns about fire safety: there were no communal fire alarms, no sprinkler systems. One resident was quoted by the *Evening Standard*: 'Every time we complained, they told us they had taken our concerns on board, but nothing ever happened.'

When 'nothing ever happened' in response to residents' complaints, the same thing happened. Grenfell happened. Apps stresses that Grenfell was not just an accident waiting to happen. It was *allowed* to happen or *let happen*. That's why Grenfell 'tells us something about how we are governed', demonstrating the lack of priority given to 'human life, especially when those lives are likely to be poor, immigrant and from ethnic minority backgrounds'.[3] When the residents' complaints were not heard, they were told their lives did not matter. And when their complaints were not heard, history was repeated.

It can be a disaster not to hear complaints.

Having your complaints heard is not just about getting your opinions validated or stories acknowledged. It is about more than being given a voice or a say. Having your complaints heard is about being able to change the conditions in which you live or work.

Unheard complaints mean unchanged conditions. You don't have to complain about unsafe conditions unless you have them. If this seems too obvious to say, the obvious needs to be said. This is why it is important we don't *neutralize* complaints as if they are just tools that do different things for different people. Some people do not have to complain to get what they need. You don't have to complain about not being able to access the building when you can access the building. You don't have to complain about being harassed and bullied when you are not harassed or bullied. You don't have to complain about not being promoted when you are promoted. You don't have to complain about not being protected when your neighbourhoods are as protected as you are. To be more valued is to have less need to complain. But when those who are more valued complain, their complaints might also be more valued.

It is the people who have more need to complain who are more likely to be stigmatized as troublemakers. The stigma relates not only to the complaints but the conditions that make them necessary.

The people who make these complaints still end up stuck

with the sign 'troublemaker'. Or by it. Catherine Mayer, co-founder of the Women's Equality Party, who made a complaint about age and sex discrimination at *Time Magazine*, describes 'troublemaker' as 'the sign you're hanging around your neck'.[4] Cricketer Azeem Rafiq described how he was 'labelled a troublemaker' after complaining about bullying from another player on his team.[5] Elizabeth Taylor, interviewed for *Panorama* special 'Is this Church Racist?', comments: 'The issue that came up again and again and again was the feeling that [church members] were not safe within the Church, that it was not safe to complain, that, in taking that complaint of racism further, that will mark them out as a troublemaker.'[6] When you have been told that it is not safe to complain, or when you have internalized that message as a feeling of risk or danger, you hear another instruction: to accept the conditions, to suffer them in silence.

And yet some complaints are encouraged or just relatively routine. Consumer complaints, for instance, a familiar genre, are usually quite easy to make, however much we might experience having to make them as a source of frustration. The earliest recorded written complaint, from about 1750 BCE, a tablet addressed to Ea-nāṣir, was in fact a consumer complaint. It was from a customer named Nanni who complained about the quality of copper delivered to his servant (and also about the rudeness of the merchant).[7] Consumer complaints can be treated as a useful form of feedback or a nuisance. They can be ignored or dealt with. This book is more focused on workplace complaints than consumer complaints, although I discuss how complaints about harassment and discrimination are managed and filtered by being treated *as* consumer complaints, as if not wanting to be harassed or discriminated against is the same thing as not liking a product or finding it faulty.

Not all complaints are made *to* someone. Complaints can be made *with* someone. They can be how we interact with each other, shared rather cheerfully. Complaints about the weather, for instance, can be a form of social bonding. We might rather enjoy grumbling about another cold and rainy day because it gives us the feeling of being in it together. It does not follow that we are all in it together. If some people are given permission to complain, or even a right to complain, other people, those who are not from here, or assumed not to be from here, complaining about *anything*, even the weather, risks being heard as being ungrateful.

You might complain, only to be told to go back to where you came from. I remember another fire, that took place at the Yarl's Wood detention centre on 14 February 2002. The centre had opened the previous year. Emma Ginn, from the Campaign to Stop Arbitrary Detentions at Yarl's Wood, stated, 'Since the camp opened there have been daily complaints about the delays in access to medical treatment and delays in moving people to hospital. There have also been complaints about limited association times, bad food, delay of incoming phone calls, the use of handcuffs when detainees are taken to court, the dentist's or to hospital, unequal distribution of a weekly £2 telephone card to all detainees. Neither detainees nor visitors are allowed pen and paper during visits and children's access to education is very poor.'[8]

Before and after the fire, multiple complaints had been made about sexual harassment, sexual assault and intimidation by guards, the invasion of privacy and unsanitary conditions.

The fire caused extensive damage to the building. Harmit Athwal, from the Institute for Race Relations, wrote that 'the Fire Brigades' Union criticized the decision to keep the remaining 250 asylum seekers at the centre in "unsafe" conditions and it also criticized the Home Office's original decision not to fit sprinklers at the centre.' Athwal also noted that the officers were ordered to 'lock the detainees in the burning building', concluding, 'Maintaining the "security" of the site was, apparently, more important than the lives of asylum seekers detained at the centre.'[9] So, how was the fire reported in the press? The headline from the *Sun* was: 'This Is How They Thank Us'.

The fire is framed not only as caused by the asylum seekers but as a consequence of ingratitude. The trope of the ungrateful asylum seeker is still with us. Take an exchange between Tory MP Lee Anderson and the then Home Secretary Suella Braverman in 2022. They both used the language of 'invasion' to describe the impact of those seeking asylum in the UK. Anderson claimed that 'Albanian criminals' were leaving safe countries only to complain about their accommodation. He asked, 'Does the Home Secretary agree with me that if the accommodation is not good enough for them, they can get on a dinghy and go straight back to France?' Braverman agreed and replied, 'Any complaints that the accommodation isn't good enough is frankly absolutely indulgent and ungrateful.'[10]

The ungrateful asylum seeker is assumed to be bogus, falsely receiving benefits, taking what is ours. Such stories could be called complaints about complaints. These complaints (about complaints) do not tend to be heard *as* complaints, becoming instead a stock of oft-made statements about how things are, or who we are, or who they are. We can and do challenge that stock, statement by statement. But they surround us like an atmosphere. Many people who enter a country as migrants or refugees do not feel that they can complain because of how it would be used against them as yet more evidence they do not belong here.

You can be born in the UK and still feel like this. Those of us whose parents come from other countries (especially countries formerly colonized by Britain) are constantly reminded that our acceptance is conditional on our conduct. Black British writer Musa Okwonga describes how, as the child of refugees from Uganda, he had initially internalized the expectation of gratitude but then began 'to notice more and more that the very moment immigrants were seen as contributing anything less than wholesomely to the national effort, they were viewed with contempt.'[11]

The harder it is to complain about living or working conditions, the more vulnerable people are to exploitation. And the more vulnerable people are, the harder it is for them to complain. This feedback loop between vulnerability and complaint is another hard lesson of the Covid pandemic. As Zubaida Haque, then deputy director of the Runneymede Trust declared, 'We know that BME [Black and Minority Ethnic] NHS staff can't complain as much because they're worried about the recriminations of complaining. They're much more likely to be harassed and face discrimination compared to their white counterparts. There is the question of, did they have the appropriate PPE equipment? If they didn't, did they feel they could complain or were they worried about the recriminations from complaining.'[12] The expectation of gratitude can be turned into a demand for sacrifice. I think of the title of the powerful poem 'You Clap For Me Now', by artist Darren James Smith, a 'coronavirus poem on racism and immigration in Britain'.[13] You might be cheered when you are useful, only to be told to go home when you are not. To hear a complaint is to hear through *that* cheer, to what it covers over, the toil.

I call listening to a complaint *becoming a feminist ear*. I first used the term *feminist ear* to capture what I could hear from being in an audience for the screening of the feminist film *A Question of Silence* (1982, dir. Marlene Gorris). It was shown during the London Feminist Film Festival at the Hackney Picturehouse on 30 November 2012. It was so cathartic to be in that audience. It was so loud! There was one scene when the audience became especially rowdy. It is a meeting. A woman is seated at a table of men; she is the secretary. She makes a point and is ignored. And then a man makes the same point and is congratulated loudly by the other men. She sits there in silence. Silence can be a space we fill. And the audience filled it, groaning loudly; a sound that increased until it became a feminist roar.

There was one other time I heard a feminist audience be that loud. It was during an academic talk by anthropologist

Sarah Franklin at the inaugural conference for the Centre for Feminist Research at Goldsmiths, in London, on 9 May 2014. She was exploring sexism in the academy by discussing a professor's rather extreme response to one of her essays, a feminist critique of the sociologist Émile Durkheim. The professor's scrawling marks were mostly made with red pen, turning her essay into a 'bloody document'. Franklin had kept the essay at least in part because it is a time-piece, telling us not just about the past but how it endures, 'a reminder of a problem the academy has yet even to acknowledge fully: the everyday institutional sexism that grows like grass all over campus – unchecked, unacknowledged, and indeed largely unchanged *because* it is ignored'.[14] When Franklin showed that 'bloody document' on a PowerPoint slide, with some of her sentences vehemently crossed out and his words scrawled in large print, some capitalized, in the margins (such as 'slovenly' and 'dreadful' and 'WRONG!'), the audience shouted out in recognition. The atmosphere was riotous. There was a palpable sense of energy as well as relief.

Why relief? Maybe it is because when our work elicits extreme reactions like this, the sexism that tells us we are wrong, we often sit with them on our own. Or maybe it is because sexism can be so subtle that even when it stops us from doing something, or being something, it is hard to put our finger on it. It can be a relief to have displayed right in front of us what usually works by not being so visible or audible. To shout out in recognition is to be released from the prism of our experience. We are louder not only when we are heard together, but when we hear together. Feminist recognition is loud.

It can also be hard to put your finger on racism. Sociologist Shirley Anne Tate uses this exact expression for the way racism 'melts into thin air' in organizations even as it 'permeates their very spaces, their very walls', how Black and brown people come to know we are not meant to be here.[15] We can know it, feel it in our bones, without always being able to show it. It is cathartic to be with others who know it without needing to be shown it. When recognition is loud, so too is solidarity. Mary, an Indigenous academic, told me how she and other women of colour created a space for themselves in the middle of their very white department; their voices were louder (her own 'a little louder' still as she is hard of hearing) with 'expletives coming out of our mouths all the time'. Raising the volume of our voices might be how we hear each other over the racism that permeates 'their very walls'.

To listen to a complaint might mean to become more attuned to our differences, some of which manifest in sound. Many meanings of the word *complaint* relate to sound. In early uses, to complain had the sense of 'to cry out', a complaint as a lament, a lament as 'wailing, moaning, weeping'. To complain can be to seep as well as weep. It is not only humans that are heard as complaining. The creak of a ship has been called complaint, in the sense of 'to strain or groan from over-straining'. Complaints can be the sound of being over-stressed or under pressure. To listen to a complaint is to hear these sounds, these moans, these groans as speech, as saying something, or doing something.

Complaints can be expressed without words. I think of a conversation I had with Stephanie, a lesbian professor, about the complaints she made and did not make over her career. She could hear herself complaining as she was talking about complaining. She said, 'I am moaning now, I can feel that whining in my voice [*makes whining sound*].' I replied, 'We have plenty to moan about.' We can hear the complainer arrive in our own voices as well as each other's. Stephanie also said, 'If you have a situation and you make a complaint, then you are the woman who complains, the lesbian who complains.' The situations she kept ending up in were hard to untangle from who she was and how she was seen, as a woman, as a lesbian. The negativity of complaint is sticky; it sticks to some people more than others. Stephanie added, 'And you can feel the change in your voice and the dynamic in meetings. And you don't like to hear yourself talking like that, but you end up being in that situation, again.'

I hear so much in that 'again'. To be a feminist ear is *to hear again*. A complainer is heard as a *broken record*, as if she is stuck on the same point.[16] We learn to hear repetition not as beginning with the complaint but with what the complaint is *about*.

You have to keep making the same complaints when the same things keep happening.

I became a feminist ear by listening to the students' complaints.

Let me share a little more of that story.

I heard about the students' complaints before I heard from the students. I was sitting in my office with a colleague on the afternoon of 6 July 2013. We were chatting whilst our PhD student was having a viva in the department's meeting room. My colleague asked me if I had heard about what had been going on in another department. I said I had no idea. She shared with me what she had been told by a student, who was being sexually harassed by an academic in that department. I felt myself sinking into my chair. She told me incident after incident, involving more students and more professors. One still stands out: a professor had assaulted a student on a bus on their way back from an event. It was especially disturbing to hear that other people, staff and students, had been on that bus, had seen him force himself on her, without saying anything or doing anything.

I knew I needed to say something. I could not sit with this information like I was on that bloody bus. I emailed my head of department. She told me to get in touch with a senior administrator. That is what I did. The administrator emailed me back. 'There is an ongoing inquiry,' she said. We spoke on the phone. I told her what I had been told, conscious of my role in relaying information, that I was sharing stories of what had happened to other people without having spoken to them. She was not surprised. It turned out that stories like this were coming out all over the place. But there was something in her response that disturbed me, as if what was happening was not noteworthy, was even to be expected.

Later that year on 3 November, I was called to a meeting

with students from that department. The inquiry that had taken place over the summer had not found enough evidence of sexual harassment. The students wanted to meet with a feminist academic about what to do next.

The meeting was held in my department's main room. You had to have a key to get into it, so I waited outside in the corridor for the students to arrive along with another academic from their department. I felt nervous. I knew I was being called upon not only to listen but to participate in an action, to find a way to get their complaint moving again. I worried about becoming upset. I knew I had to hold myself together, to give the students a chance to express themselves.

We sat down together. And then, the students spoke. They told us not only what happened that had led them to complain but what had happened when they complained. They told us about previous inquiries, how they had been put under pressure not to complain or to withdraw their complaints. When I sat there, listening to the students, so eloquent and clear in their delivery despite their trauma, possibly even because of it, I knew that my relation to my place of work would not be the same. It should not be. It could not be.

It would not be. The day after I met with the students, I talked to the other academic who had been at the meeting. She explained that when she became director of Postgraduate Studies, young women started coming to her office with their complaints. She told me that there had been even earlier inquiries, involving yet more academics from the same department. To complain is often to go back: you hear about other complaints, earlier complaints. It is like discovering a secret room, full of untold stories.

The week after I met with the students, another feminist colleague came to my office. I shared with her some of what the students had disclosed to me. She burst into tears. She said something like, 'After all of our work this still happens.' There was so much feminist grief in this *still*, that the same things happen, despite everything, all that work, our feminist work, to try to change the culture of sexual harassment. We need time, also space, to express this grief, to turn it out and, sometimes, to turn it into complaint.

Many more students came to my office in the weeks that followed. One student wrote to me, 'We're all concerned that your office has become something of an emergency drop-in centre for women in various states of crisis. I hope you're all right.' I am still touched by her concern. The students did not come to me because I had any special training or skills. I didn't and I don't. They came to me because I said I was willing to listen. They came to me because they had nowhere else to go.

They had already tried to hold the institution to account, combining their knowledge and experiences to make a collective complaint. Leila Whitley, Tiffany Page, Alice Corble, Chryssa Sdrolia and Heidi Hasbrouck (as well as others who remained anonymous) have since shared their story, explaining how the complaint brought them together. They began their studies 'at different times and in different year groups'. They did not 'all have the same experience of harassment'. They came together because of what they faced, working as they did in a department where 'sexualized abuses happened in the open', where they were 'grabbed at and touched', or watched others 'be grabbed at and touched'.

They came together to try and stop what was happening, complaining not about a person but the culture, refusing to accept that culture as inevitable. 'We did not want future cohorts of students to be confronted with what happened to us,' they stated. 'We knew this couldn't continue to be the way things were.'[17] But the institution did not recognize their complaint because it did not come from a named individual, and nor was it about an individual perpetrator. It was because of how sexual harassment had been institutionalized that they were reluctant to put forward their complaints in this form. To name themselves would be to make themselves vulnerable to retaliation, to name just one perpetrator would make the problem individual, not institutional.

The requirement to give complaints a certain form stops many from being made. Together we pushed for a change of form so that students could make complaints individually but anonymously. When the requirements for the form of complaint were loosened, more students came forward to testify in the inquiries. There was nothing automatic about this process. The students still had to find a way to make complaints that would be 'legible to the university'. They explained, 'These complaints often did not sound like us: we had such a narrow channel in which to describe what happened to us, what it meant, and what it did.'[18] To make formal complaints often means being channelled in a certain direction by the institution. The more chance you have of getting the complaint through, the less the complaint sounds like you. But the complaint was still *theirs*.

As a result of the students' efforts, the university reopened the inquiry. It was a new inquiry really, with a new team responsible for gathering evidence. At this time, my feeling was that the complaints were being taken seriously. I felt like we were getting somewhere. Or that we were going to get somewhere.

I was interviewed at 9 a.m. on 4 March 2014 for this new inquiry, before my first lecture, at the beginning of a busy workday. The interview was held in a room in the main administrative building; I had been there before for conferences or for more formal departmental meetings, but it was not where I usually went. Complaints can lead you to the less-used rooms; they might feel shadowy, at the edges of your environment. I sat down on one side of the table and was interviewed by two people on the other side. An administrator was next to me, taking minutes. I was reporting mainly on what the students had told me. What had gone into my ears needed to come out again in a way that was respectful of confidences shared.

I went straight from the meeting to give a lecture on 'The Idea of Race'. It is always emotional to give this lecture. For some of us, race is not an abstraction. We embody it. This time I am shaking. Everything pours out. I only just manage to hold myself together. I think of how we have to hold ourselves together. When you are doing the work of complaint, you are usually still at work. After that inquiry, there were two more, which happened in quick succession. Each inquiry meant having to testify again, letting the complaints travel through me.

It was such an intense and also queer experience, and I mean *queer* in the old sense of odd. I had to keep switching dimensions. We were having so many meetings, not just about the complaints but about what they revealed; the harassment, the scale of it. But most people in my department did not know what was going on. And I had to keep going back to that job, my day job, to so many more meetings; and that world, which was supposed to be the real world, the upright, brightly lit world, felt increasingly unreal; topsy-turvy, upside down. Words typically used to describe experiences of complaint are odd, disorientating, strange, weird, bizarre and surreal.

We began to meet regularly as a working group, myself, five PhD students and Beverley Skeggs, another feminist academic, that spring. We had a reading group on sexism, which was also attended by MA students. We began doing an audit of the college curriculum (another way of reading about sexism). Whilst our work exceeded the form of a complaint, complaint gave it urgency.

But it was getting harder. The more we tried to raise the issue of sexual harassment as an institutional problem, the more resistance we encountered. We heard ourselves being addressed as the problem.

To locate a problem is to become the location of a problem.

A colleague attended a university meeting where the students were described by a senior manager as 'always complaining', as if they were a bunch of troublesome children using complaint to get what they want. We began to hear the term 'vicarious trauma' floating around; it popped up in discussions and documents. I think it was used to imply we had infected each other with misery, rather than worked purposefully together to address the role of the institution in enabling sexual harassment.

The more we spoke of institutional harassment, the more we began to experience it. The students who participated in the complaint were made a problem by their peers, blamed for the suspension of some of the professors, who were quickly turned into victims. I was accused on email threads and public posts of organizing a witch-hunt, of wanting the department for myself. I began to receive more and more accusatory and threatening messages. The students and I shared the communications with each other, so we did not have to sit with them on our own.

The university was busy appearing to do something at the same time as we were being targeted. They appointed someone new to write a new policy. We talked to him. He had *no idea* of what had happened, of why we needed a new policy. We tried to tell him. We were told off for communicating the way we did. We kept being told that confidentiality was necessary to protect the students. But they were not being protected, because the silence left a vacuum in which accusations could fly more freely. Confidentiality protected the institution.

So much of our efforts end up being focused on getting a public acknowledgement that these inquiries into sexual harassment had taken place. It was like they had not even happened, which might have been the effect the institution was looking for. We began the process of drafting a letter to the warden requesting that acknowledgement. After receiving feedback from colleagues, the language of the letter gradually became less confrontational, more appealing, referencing the risk to the university's reputation as 'a progressive and critical institution'. We called for the warden to make a public statement recognizing the problem of sexual harassment at the college, stating, 'It is possible to acknowledge that the problem of sexual harassment has come up in a number of recent inquiries without breaching confidentiality agreements.' We asked for resources to support 'a series of events on sexual harassment', including the conference the students had already begun organizing.

We sent the letter on 1 October 2015. We received a reply from the warden soon after. He wrote, 'I will continue to have conversations with colleagues and ensure [sexual harassment] remains high up on the agenda, but in the meantime, I wanted to drop you a note to assure you of my support and to show my appreciation for your positive and proactive approach.' It was a positive reply, matching the tone of our positive letter. The warden did not promise to make a public statement; there was no reference made to that request by any senior manager at any point.

The university gave the students money for the conference – £1752, much less than what they had asked for. Later, they turned the amount they had been given into the name of a new lobby group, the '1752 group'.[19] They found out that the money had come from the existing Equality and Diversity budget: there had been no new allocation of funds. No new commitment. One of my heads of department wrote to me; he was supportive and sympathetic: 'Sara, are you OK with the warden's reply?' I told him about the budget and said, 'Diversity work is all about "not OK". This is an example of commitment being said more than being done.' I can hear my resignation.

Later that year, on 2 December, the conference on sexual harassment took place. It was powerful; it was moving. The students led. They taught. But the audience that needed to be there was missing. Only one senior manager turned up for that event – and she left after the first panel. After my talk she asked a question that showed she did not get it, would not get it, referencing everything that was being done by the college. Another of my heads of department, who was also supportive and sympathetic, did not go because, he said, it would be too depressing. He probably needed to be depressed. We all did. It was depressing. In my talk I alluded to 'the problems here' but was not explicit about what they were. I felt like I was circling around the issue, never quite landing on it. I posted the talk on my blog that evening.[20] I used the word **here** twice, both times in bold. I was not feeling bold.

The following year, on 9 March 2016, we held a panel on sexism, to launch the special issue of a journal on sexism that came out of the inaugural conference I mentioned earlier. After the panel, a student who had begun her MA that academic year approached Tiffany Page and Leila Whitley, who had presented their work. She was considering whether to complain about harassment and bullying from a professor based in the same department. She told them that until she had been listening to this panel on that day, she had no idea that there had been any previous inquiries. *No idea.* I think that was the moment when it really hit me, the true costs of confidentiality. *No idea.* The failure to be public about the problem of sexual harassment meant it would keep being reproduced despite everything, all that work, over so many years.

After the event, a feminist colleague expressed concern to me in private that to go public about the problem would lead to people overlooking the feminist work that had been done at the college. She wasn't saying we should be silent. But I realized how silence can be turned into a feminist instruction, the same silence that led to the violence of *no idea*. If we are silent about sexual harassment to protect the feminist reputation of an institution, we are not working for a feminist institution.

The final straw was something small, the failure to find a way to give me the support I needed to take a period of unpaid leave. I had taken too much on. I just couldn't do it any more. I sent my resignation letter to my heads of department on 28 April 2016. I wrote a clear statement. All that was clear to me was my need to get out.

When I think of my need to get out, my mind goes back to that first meeting in that room. I would walk by it on the way to my office: it was the first room on the corridor after the administrator's room. We would have other meetings in that room, academic meetings, so much shuffling, papers and persons rearranged. I reached a point when I could not go back to it, turning up at the same old meetings, doing the same old things. The room was occupied by a history that felt as tangible as the walls.

I shared news of my resignation on my blog on 30 May 2016. It was the first reference in public to the inquiries into sexual harassment that had taken place. I suspect if I hadn't posted about them, they would still be a secret. I did not resign in order to make this disclosure. But resigning meant I could make it. Yes, I became a troublemaker. We become troublemakers because of what our complaints threaten to reveal. Disclosure is treated as damage.

I am willing to cause damage.

I did not think my resignation would mean much to anyone but me and those I worked with. But there was no point resigning in silence when I was resigning because of it. I was totally unprepared for the reaction. The story got picked up by a newspaper. It was turned into a sex scandal. One reporter from the *Sun* got my partner's mobile phone number and rang her while we were out walking our dog. I was asked to share my story on television. There is no way

I would have done that. I did not want the story to become about me, to turn the students' complaint into my platform.

The college responded quickly, launching a PR statement that did not reference my resignation and made liberal use of the language of equality and diversity. They announced they did not tolerate sexual harassment. And yet they had. These statements were empty; made *because they have no force*.[21] They knew we knew this, but the statement still circulated; busier for being emptier. It mentioned the Centre for Feminist Research and the conference organized by students as evidence of what the college had done, yes, all that work we had to do because of what they were not doing.

Our effort to change institutions can be used by them as evidence they have changed.

We began to receive more disclosures, including some very distressing accounts, from former students. Disclosures were not coming just to me. One of the students emailed, 'I also had a disclosure yesterday from a member of staff who has been subject to serious harassment and bullying there and was previously a student [in the department], so all the stuff coming out now both internally and externally to the college has triggered a further breakdown in her through these repetitions. "Can of worms" doesn't even begin to describe the lid that has been lifted here.'

On 15 June 2016, I went into work for my last proper

day. I was there for our Departmental Board, the final meeting I was to attend in my department. It was also the date of a meeting scheduled with the warden and the students. I did not make the latter meeting. A caring colleague got my resignation on the agenda, which meant he got sexual harassment on the agenda. It is mentioned along with another item. When the other item was picked up and discussed at length, I heard what was not discussed; how sexual harassment was passed over. Again. I felt sick to my stomach. I rushed out of the room I was in, only just making it to the toilet in time. I left the college early that day, missing the final meeting with the students and the warden. Months later, as I shared in my preface, I returned to my office to pack up my things, leaving through the back door. I didn't put that date in my diary.

I could add to the timeline. I could say something about how it went, the meeting between the warden and the students on that day. Not all members of our collective attended. One member said she wouldn't attend because if she did she would 'most likely vomit all over his table'. Later that day, another member of our collective gave an account of the meeting for those of us who could not make it. She said the warden had been briefed to listen, 'And he did.' She added, 'He obviously found this difficult and kept verbally telling himself off for talking. But he did listen for an hour and a half to what we had to say. Essentially it felt like as a group we got to say everything that we've wanted to say. And it felt like we were finally, after so many, many years, listened to.'

I could describe how that euphoria was short-lived; despite all the activity, the new policies, new groups set up, everything seemed to be done with an eye on repairing the college's reputation. I could describe how our complaints were quickly called *historic*. We knew what they wanted to make history; and who. I could describe how, in one workshop on sexual harassment, colleagues were told what to do in order not to be accused of it rather than not to do it. I could describe how the students were stopped from talking about the problem openly; one student was even told by a feminist head of department that it would 'undermine her authority', for them to talk freely. I could describe how a story in a broadsheet newspaper in which one of the students was going to be named, to share her experiences, was pulled by the newspaper at the very last minute and how a puff PR piece on how well the university had responded to sexual harassment came out in the same newspaper a little later.

I could describe all of *this*. I have just described all of *this*. *This* led me here. I began to get statements of solidarity, letters from people all over the world telling me what happened when they complained about sexual harassment or what it meant to them to know we had. These messages were a lifeline. They helped me to pull myself out of the institution, and the trauma of that experience.

I decided to research complaint before I resigned. That I resigned enabled me to do it because it led people, many of whom had also left or lost their jobs as a result of complaining, to me. To become a feminist ear is to give complaints somewhere to go. One person wrote, 'I want the complaint to go somewhere, rather than round and round in my head.' When a complaint goes round and round in your head, it is a lot of movement not to get very far. In the two years after leaving my post, I conducted forty interviews with students, academics and administrators, most of whom were based in the UK.[22] I describe these interviews as testimonies not just because they testify to difficult experiences but because of how they took the form of what they described: long stories about long stories. I asked participants to share the experiences that led them to complain as well as their experiences of complaint. So much came out in response to that request.

The longer it takes to make a complaint, the longer it takes to tell the story. I wanted to give people the time they needed to take. It can take time even to get started. Anne, a senior researcher, spoke of how just 'by starting' her story, she could 'feel emotion coming out'. She had to find a way to hold herself together to share an experience of breaking apart. When emotions come out in telling a story, it is harder to tell it. The difficulty of telling the story is part of the story.

Once people had told me their stories, or as much of them as they could, I offered to be in dialogue, to share and compare our different experiences. That is also what becoming a feminist ear means: to open a space for conversation. One person said at the end of her testimony, 'It helped me to talk to you. It made me feel less alone.' It helped me to talk to you, too. Leaving institutions can be how we communicate more easily about experiences we have within them. It mattered that I understood what the institution was like from having been in it but was no longer there. It meant that the complaint was being heard not just by someone else but from somewhere else.

It was an intense time. That intensity seemed to fill the rooms, whether virtual or actual. I was listening to other people talk about complaint whilst working through the trauma of leaving my post as a result of one. There was something about that time and space that would be hard to capture again.

The point of receiving these stories was to send them back out again. Another student sent me a message: 'I am writing because I need a feminist ear. Perhaps you can use this complaint in your work.' To become a feminist ear is not only to be willing to receive complaints but to make use of them. Just as I could not sit with the information shared with me about my former workplace as if I was just another person on that bus, I could not sit with these stories as if I was just another filing cabinet.

I am still receiving complaints. And I am still sending them out. That's why I have written this book, sharing more stories of complaint from my research, pulling them together with other stories, so that you can know you are not alone. I quote at length from participants in my study. These quotes are important, giving a sense of texture, quality and feeling; how it feels to be *that* person with *that* problem making *that* complaint. I know how it feels to be *that* person with *that* problem making *that* complaint. Although my role is primarily a collector of other people's complaints, at times I will come into the text with stories of my own.

There is a typical cycle in how stories of complaints and grievances in workplaces come out: a scandal is reported in the press about bullying or harassment in this institution or that. Behind many disasters are unheard complaints, yes. Behind many scandals, also. Then, an inquiry. Then, a report. In these reports, based as they are on qualitative research, including interviews and focus groups, you will find quotes from individuals. These quotes are presented as a list, sometimes put in text boxes, cut off from the analysis almost as if they speak for themselves.[23] It is made too easy to slip past them, not to hear them. In the chapters that follow, I do not put quotes in boxes. My task is to get them out of boxes (and not just text boxes). I work with all the quotes as closely as I can, using details in them, from them, words and images, finding significance, making connections, pointing to patterns. I am still moved by the power of the testimonies shared with me, their beauty, even poetry. That too is what it means to become a feminist ear, being moved. That ear is not mine nor yours but *ours*, a space of reciprocity, to-and-fro, what we pick up from each other.

I have structured this book into three parts. I start simply, with individual stories of making formal complaints, before gradually stepping out, creating a more complex picture of institutions, explaining why they are difficult to change and why we need them to. By describing the same phenomena across different chapters, I offer more complex interpretations of what is going on. One example is warnings: you will hear how many people are warned about the consequences of complaining. Each time warnings come up, I develop the diagnosis of what they are doing or what they are telling us. Another example is nods: I begin by observing how nods seem to surround those who complain before showing how nods can be a technique of power – so much can be achieved by a nod.

Stories of complaint are thus more than a common thread. They are how we deepen our understanding of institutional power. We come up with our own concepts to make sense of what is going on. A concept is often understood as something abstract, what we drag away from a concrete situation through mental labour. In *Living a Feminist Life* (2017), thinking with Audre Lorde's work, I described concepts as *sweaty*, created *by* physical as well as mental labour, *from* the effort to make room in a world that does not give us room. I was influenced too by Angela Y. Davis, who points to how concepts (such as intersectionality) are not invented in academic articles but come from 'rich histories of struggle'.[24]

Many of the concepts I have developed in my work came from listening to other people talk about their struggles to change institutions. One example is 'the complaint collective', a sweaty term for sweaty work. When we were working as a collective on complaint, we did not call ourselves a 'complaint collective'. That term came to mind as I was listening to another student talk about how she worked as a member of a group. Hearing about other collectives taught me about our own. Since then, I have been hearing from more groups calling themselves 'complaint collectives'. That term, which came *from* other feminists, goes out *to* other feminists, a way of communicating something about our shared struggles.

A term that arrived in a similar way is 'complaint activism'. That term came to mind as Esther, a student, was reflecting on her experience of complaining about disability discrimination. She said, 'That's the nutshell of my complaint experiences: the things I have found not helpful are long complaint processes, writing letters and asking nicely and doing things for no pay. I don't do that anymore.' I responded, 'It almost sounds like you have a style of "complaint activism". Is that how you would describe it?' Esther answered, 'Yes, it is how I would describe it.' The term *complaint activism* helped me to hear something in other people's stories that I might not have otherwise heard – how so much of the activism around complaints is necessary because of what they fail to do.

That work of trying to build less-hostile institutions is *how* we learn the scale of the problem. Why use the term *hostile* to denote that scale? The term *hostile environment* is definitional for workplace harassment. Carrie N. Baker, in her history of the women's movement against sexual harassment in the United States, explains how the term 'hostile environment' entered into the law through the activism of working-class women, informed by the labour movement and backed by the unions. She writes, 'Blue-collar women urged courts and policymakers to broaden their definition of sexual harassment to include not just sexual demands by a supervisor of a subordinate employee but also hostile environment harassment – when supervisors or co-workers create a hostile working environment through sexual or nonsexual behavior.' These behaviours are intended to make the working life intolerable, as 'an attempt to discourage women from staying in the trade because they were taking a "man's job"'. Baker quotes from Sue Doro, a machinist in Milwaukee, who described how a co-worker sabotaged her machine: 'Dick would loosen stuff on it, which could kill you. Like, he would loosen a big drill, a huge part. If it's not right, and it hits, it will shatter in your face . . . He did stuff like that.'[25]

A hostile environment is about the creation of a workplace that is so intimidating, offensive and even dangerous that people leave of their own accord. In the UK, the Equality Act (2010) renders harassment, including a hostile environment, against the law for all groups with protected characteristics. Most organizational policies on harassment now use this term. However, 'hostile environment' was also a term used by the British government as a name for a policy. Theresa May, when Home Secretary in 2012, described its intention as 'to create here in Britain a really hostile environment for illegal migration'.[26] The use of a term that was already definitional of harassment was in fact instructive, teaching us how harassment became a national policy, or to be more precise, given that the category of *illegal immigrant* is a racializing category, how racial harassment became a national policy. May's hostile environment policy included a controversial advertising campaign. Vans were sent into areas with high immigrant populations bearing the message, 'In the UK illegally? Go home or face arrest'.[27] Those of us who are not white are often told to 'go home' or 'go back'. So, when *that* was the message we saw, we knew who it was addressed to.

More recently, the British government turned the hostile environment policy into a pledge to 'Stop the boats'. That pledge did more than reference the smalls boats in which asylum seekers make desperate journeys across harsh seas; so many losing their lives, losses that remain unmourned by the nations that ought to be giving asylum. We learnt this when 'Stop the boats' was turned into a racist chant alongside 'Pakis out' in the fascist demonstrations that took place in the UK in August 2024.

We hear the hostility when it is directed against us. I have been writing this book in an increasingly hostile environment, with more and more messages sent out to some people that say: you do not belong here; you have taken what is ours. I have been writing whilst those of us who use the word *queer* to describe ourselves or our projects are called *groomers* and *paedophiles*. I have been writing whilst many people in government and the media have been campaigning to dismantle the rights of trans people, with report after report, article after article, representing trans people as *dangerous* and *deluded*. I have been writing whilst politicians describe the reform of the welfare system to make it harder to access benefits as 'a moral mission', labelling those who need benefits, including disabled people, the poor and the unemployed, *fraudsters*.[28] I have been writing whilst Israel has been conducting a genocide in Gaza and when those of us who have protested that genocide, and who are fighting for a free Palestine, are labelled *extremists*.

At times, it has been hard to pick up my pen and to keep writing through all of this. But I know that by writing *through* hostile environments, I write *against* them. Being a feminist ear means being willing to take it in, as much as we can, to digest these messages in order to contest them. Sometimes, the hostility that is already there comes out more explicitly, giving us a chance to protest, to mobilize collectively, to say *no*, loudly together. But hostile environments are often masked by the very policies we have against them. It is harder to fight against what many people do not see (and might even be invested in not seeing). That is why it remains important to show that, for many of us, Black people, people of colour, undocumented workers, working-class people, women, disabled people, LGBTQIA+ people, institutions remain hostile environments even when they appear committed to change. To complain, and to learn from complaint, is how we acquire the skills and knowledge we need to make institutions less hostile. Lessening hostility might sound unambitious. It is not.

Part One

Making Complaints

In this part of the book, I take you through some people's experiences of making formal complaints in their workplaces. Most employers have complaint procedures, laying out a path that the person with a complaint would need to follow, typically written as a series of stages. These procedures are often visualized as a flow chart with arrows and straight lines.

It all looks rather clear. And that is what a good complaint procedure should be: rather clear. It should be accessible and easy to find. It should not only exist in paper or virtual form but be the subject of ongoing discussion within the organization. Many organizations have policies and procedures that 'just sit there on a website', to borrow the words from one participant in my study. Good practice for organizations in handling complaints would be rather like good practice in handling pretty much everything else: they should communicate well, respond in a timely fashion to concerns raised, follow their own timelines, and ensure the process is as transparent as possible.

If a complaint procedure is a picture of good practice,

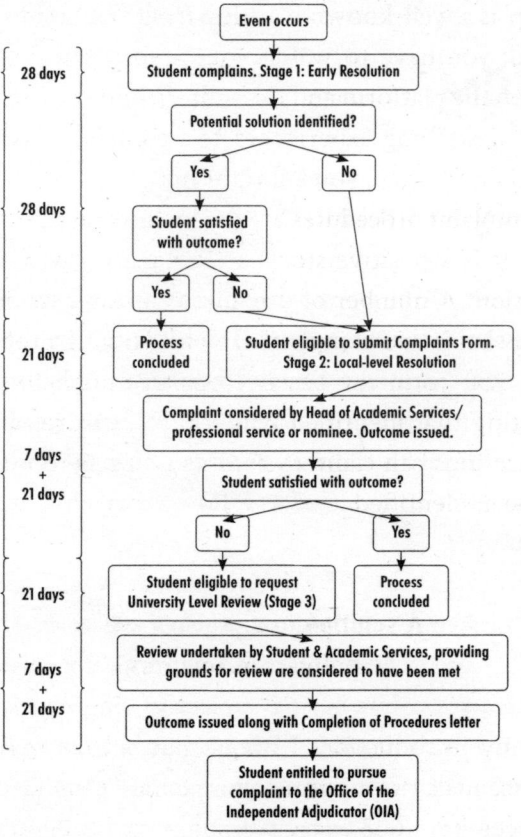

A complaint procedure.

that is not what complaints look like (or feel like) for many people. This might not surprise you. Life does not look like a procedure! So why would a complaint? Procedures are about what is supposed to happen. But the gap between what is supposed to happen when you complain and what does happen is one that many end up falling through. 'Mind the gap' is a well-known warning from the London Underground; you have to watch your step because of the gap between the platform and the train. 'Mind the gap' is a good way of describing experiences of a complaint: you mind a gap, you find a gap, you fall right in it.

Complaint procedures are the institution's story of complaint. It is a positive story: a clear path towards a happy resolution. A number of organizations have made the following claim: that complaints, by identifying problems and issues, will 'form the basis of positive publicity, in demonstrating that identified issues have been resolved'. Yes, organizations can claim to resolve issues before they have even been identified.

A solution to a problem can be a problem in new form.

In my introduction, I noted that behind many workplace scandals are unheard complaints. One example: on 16 November 2023, sixty women wrote a letter that was leaked to the *Guardian* about the widespread 'toxic culture' and 'hostile behaviour', including sexual harassment and sexual assault, at the Ministry of Defence.[1] The letter 'called for immediate action to change the department's policies and address the issues identified with its internal culture'. The group of women insisted the 'scale of this problem and the extent to which it affects defence merits a properly resourced external intervention'. In the final part of the book, we consider letters such as this a form of complaint activism. It takes a scandal to hear about all the complaints that were made but did not get anywhere. When the institution's story of complaint is the one that circulates, other stories do not.

1/ Complaints as Coming Out Stories

On 9 November 2017, journalist Sarah Wildman came out with a story of complaint. Her title gave the bare bones of the story, 'I was harassed at the *New Republic*. I spoke up. Nothing happened.'[1] Sarah tells us it was not a story she 'planned to tell'. Plans change. Movements happen. She explains, 'In the weeks since the Harvey Weinstein scandal erupted, I, like many women, have thought back on any number of small and large incidents I've tolerated in my adult life.' The previous month, on 17 October, actress Alyssa Milano had asked other Twitter users to 'write "me too" as a reply to [her] tweet' if they had 'been sexually harassed or assaulted'.

The Guerrilla Girls taught us there is an art to creating new platforms for people to express their complaints. The #MeToo movement created another kind of platform. Reporters Kara Fox and Jan Diehm wrote 'an anatomy of a viral campaign',[2] less than a month later. They summarize: 'To date, there have been more than 2.3 million #MeToo tweets from 85 countries; on Facebook, more than 24 million people participated in the conversation by posting, reacting, and commenting over 77 million times.' Other hashtags followed #MeToo including #TimesUp, #YoTambien,

#BalanceTonPorc, #QuellaVoltaChe, #Nopiwouma, #SendeAnlat, #AnaKaman, #RiceBunny, #Cuentalo, #Sex4Grades and #Uykularinkacsin.

The #MeToo platform was not unproblematic. As Angela Onwuachi-Willig notes, 'Along with millions of affirming responses', there were also 'critiques of [Alyssa Milano's] request, namely from women of color who were upset that – yet again – a white woman was receiving credit for an idea originated by a woman of color.'[3] Tarana Burke, with whom the expression 'me too' originated, understood it was a 'space for supporting and amplifying the voices of survivors of sexual abuse, assault and exploitation'.[4] If #MeToo too was a kind of collective coming out, we also learnt that some voices are more likely to be amplified than others.

#MeToo went viral whilst I was in the middle of my research. Some of the people who shared their stories with me referred to it: sometimes to explain why they were inspired to get in touch; sometimes as it had heightened their sense of vulnerability, a reminder of the trauma and pain of complaint; sometimes as a way of reflecting on the status of their own complaint as a story. Anne, who complained about bullying, asked herself this question: 'Is it just another story? Another #MeToo?' When I spoke to Stephanie, Kate and Tina about the harassment they'd experienced many years ago when they were students, they shared a hope that they could tell their story.[5] Tina said, 'We think there's a real story there, about three women coming together on this issue. How we have gone through this and come out with this. With all that has happened recently, with everything in the media about sexual harassment, we think it would be really powerful.'

#MeToo helped to change the atmosphere, making it more possible for people to feel that coming out with their stories of complaint 'would be really powerful'. The more stories are shared, the more we learn the scale of the problem. But if we need to know the scale of the problem before it can be addressed, knowing it does not mean it has been addressed.

We pose a problem when we keep exposing a problem.

When we are treated as posing a problem, we can end up the ones exposed. Not everyone can handle the exposure. In 2022, journalist Lucy Siegle asked, 'what impact has the #MeToo movement really had' if the *Guardian* had failed to handle a complaint about sexual harassment by one of its own writers.[6] Having more people share stories of being sexually harassed does not necessarily change the culture of organizations (but then: what does?). Not everyone can or will come out with their complaints. Nor should they be obliged to. But when they do, we need to listen carefully, with feminist ears. And we learn very quickly that we do not simply come out *with* a story of complaint. Coming out is *in* the story.

As LGBTQIA+ people, we typically use the language of coming out to describe the process of disclosing a truth about ourselves, our sexuality or gender identity, that we might have kept hidden because of stigma or shame. Coming out can sound like a sharp transition between inside to outside: from being in a closet, a small, dark and suffocating space, to being released into the bright light of open air. Whilst there are transitions involved in coming out, they are not always so sharp. I think of all the times when someone has referred to my partner as 'he'. I might say, 'he' is 'she', risking being heard as complaining by making a correction. Or I might use a more delicate manoeuvre, sliding 'she' into a sentence. Or I might let it pass, so that 'he' lingers, and I end up in a mini closet almost of my own making, which can sometimes feel like giving myself a little room, a break from the light of being seen, and at other times can be painful because of how I have allowed myself to be passed over.

That some of us have to keep coming out is a reminder that being heterosexual or cisgender is still the default position. To be the default is to be freed from the need to explain yourself. As therapist Umang Kochhar describes, coming out is 'not a one-time thing, it usually happens in circles'.[7] Complaints too can involve circling, going round and about rather than inside out. They are often rather messy and bumpy. To listen to stories of complaint with a feminist ear we need to resist smoothing them out. The four sections of this chapter introduce you to Darcy, Serena, Viola and Laura, taking each of their testimonies in turn. I chose their testimonies because of how they each show that to complain is to be 'in the thick of it', an expression used to refer to 'the most active or dangerous part of a particular situation or activity'.[8] The difficulties and dangers described in their testimonies take place at different times during a complaint process from *before* you make a complaint to *after* you have become a complainer.

LETTING IT IN

When people talked to me about their complaints, they would often describe the experience as an internal struggle or even as an existential crisis. The struggle or crisis was not simply about the need to decide whether to complain. It went much deeper, relating to people's sense of who they were, their core commitments and values.

So much of the dilemma of complaint relates to this simple fact: when you complain about a difficult work situation, you have to give it more of your attention. Although focusing our attention on what is hard can make it seem harder, that focus is useful. It is how we acquire insight into not just the organization in which we are making the complaint, the situation we are complaining about, but also ourselves. The insights that come with complaints are often missed because of how quickly complaints are judged in terms of their veracity: did it happen that way? Is the person making the complaint trustworthy? Can I trust myself?

Let's return to Sarah Wildman's story. Sarah begins by telling us what happened at her workplace, the magazine *New Republic*: 'As the night progressed, Leon Wieseltier, the magazine's intellectual luminary and literary editor, cornered me, alone by the bathroom, and put his mouth on mine. I clapped my hand over my mouth in surprise. "I've always known you'd do that," I recall he said.' A few days later, Sarah told the editor of the magazine what happened. She noted, 'In disclosing this incident to my superiors, the outcome was, in many ways, far worse than the act itself.' She realized why people do not disclose: 'In the days following my disclosure, I felt entirely alone. No one knocked on my door, though I know now that at least one other editor had some idea of what had happened.'

Sarah was quite clear when she was sexually harassed that 'that' was what happened. It was only later, after telling the editor of the magazine, that she became unsure. She was told to talk to Wieseltier. 'In my recollection, he told me that I was acting like a child. In the moment, I felt like one. I had spoken, I said feebly, because I had felt uncomfortable.' She was then called to a meeting. And she heard his version of what had happened: 'He said we had merely "shared" a kiss. I remember that word. It was so breezy. It was so easy. It was so *nothing*.' She began to doubt herself, 'in that room, in that moment', and the doubt 'stayed with [her] for years'. She questioned not just how she had responded but what was real: 'What could I do? What was real, after all?'[9] When Sarah witnessed how easily the harassment was passed over, how she too was passed over, even reality itself became unclear.

If you can lose clarity because of what happened when you complained, clarity can sometimes be what you need before you can complain. I spoke to Darcy, a queer woman of colour from a working-class background. Darcy was the first person from her family to go to university. She fought hard to get where she was. She was where she wanted to be. But there was a problem: she was being harassed by her supervisor. So much of Darcy's story was about explaining why it was so hard to see what was happening. She said, 'It's odd to think back. In this moment, this seems absolutely insane to me, but at the time it was part of the culture of the department we had.' When what you experience 'at the time' is part of the culture, you don't identify it at the time you experience it.

Darcy gave more and more examples: 'A professor I had met with earlier in the programme said that he had to keep a big wooden table between him and his female students so he would remember not to touch them, and then another of our long-time male faculty is notorious for marrying student after student after student. And that was within all this rhetoric of critical race studies, and pedagogy of the oppressed. As I am recounting it to you, I just wanted to say that it is so jarring to look back on it, because it looks so very clear, from this hindsight perspective.' The harassment, the misconduct, expressed in the idea that senior men would need a big wooden table in order to remember not to touch women students, is happening at the same time that all the critical work is happening, or that the rhetoric of critical work is used to describe what is happening; critical race studies, pedagogy of the oppressed, education promised as a site of liberation.

Darcy has to see *through it*, how the institution presents itself, to recognize the violence directed towards her and other women. Clarity can be jarring because to see it is not only to see what you did not see before. It is to see yourself not seeing it.

The longer it takes to see something, the harder it is to see it.

It took Darcy a long time to see it because it took a long time for her supervisor to reveal himself. She explains, 'He positioned himself as a feminist, critical scholar, someone who was kind of holding that space for women, and then over time, and I am sure you are quite familiar with this narrative, over time, I think it was almost a kind of grooming process for him.' Grooming is a process with an end in sight. Until you reach the end, it is hard to notice the process. Darcy goes back over it from the vantage point of the present: 'Over time, with our academic meetings, he wanted to have them more and more in non-academic spaces. So, it moved from, "Oh you know, I don't want to go to campus today, parking's terrible, why don't we meet at this coffee shop that's near campus," and then a while after that it would be, "Why don't you just come over to the house, and we'll meet there."' The pushing back of boundaries – from his office to a coffee-shop to his house – is gradual. She is not expecting that pushing back to be anything other than what he says it is (the parking is bad; it is easier to meet off campus). It takes time for her to realize that she needs the boundaries he pushes back to protect herself.

You can't see harassment all at once when it does not happen all at once. Darcy told me they would have a good supervision, 'And then literally, a few minutes after I would leave the office, he would text me something, "I can't get you off my mind," those kinds of texts, and I just wouldn't reply to him.' When I was listening to her, I could hear that she had had some hope that it would stop or that he would.

Hope is an investment that the paths we follow will get us somewhere.

The longer it takes to give up hope, the more time we invest. The more time we invest, the harder it is to give up hope. That's why losing hope can be clarifying. You see through your own investments.

In telling me the story from the vantage point of having seen through her investments, Darcy described the internal battle she had with herself. She said, 'There was some way in which I encoded, took on his abuse and silenced it myself because all my earlier attempts to have it understood were completely negated and it felt like, that I must have made it happen somehow, that something I did was creating the context for this to happen.' When your previous attempts to 'have it understood', to try to stop it, to say no to it, are negated, you can end up feeling more rather than less implicated. In other words, if he doesn't stop, you can feel you failed to stop him. Sexism is a script as well as a structure: how a woman is made responsible for the violence directed against her (that she *caused* the conduct by what she was wearing or saying or doing). I think Darcy, as a feminist, *knew* she was not responsible. But it can still be hard when you are being harassed not to feel implicated ('creating the context for it to happen'). We call that feeling of implication *shame*. There is shame in a name.

One way people handle harassment is by not naming it.

To complain can then be experienced as something you do to yourself. Darcy explained, 'I felt like, I don't know, it is hard to explain, I felt like I would take myself down by admitting to the kind of violence he was enacting.' For Darcy, admitting the truth about her supervisor would mean she would lose access to what he was providing. Not admitting the truth of the situation, 'the kind of violence he was enacting', was an effort not to lose something. If you have to admit a loss for it to be real, loss has an odd temporality; there is a reversal of sequence. For the person who has lost something, the admission of a loss comes *before* the loss.[10] It is not surprising, then, that to admit a loss can feel like causing yourself to lose something.

Let the truth of this sink in: to admit you are being harassed is experienced as *taking yourself down*. That is how a complaint can feel like killing your own joy, hurting yourself, your own career, your own prospects. **Killjoy truths** are difficult to admit. They can be what we have to labour to reveal. Darcy also said, 'I tried very hard to keep all of the meetings on campus, and to keep the door open.' She keeps the door open, an actual door, at the same time as she closes another kind of door, which I call *the door of consciousness*.

Doors can hold a contradiction. That she keeps the office door open is an admission of the truth of the situation that she handles by not letting it in.

The expression 'door of consciousness' shows how internal and external processes are related. Consider filing systems. A filing cabinet is a familiar piece of office furniture for storing papers in folders. The point of storing papers is that they can be retrieved. When complaints end up in filing cabinets, the point seems to be less about retrieval and more about putting them where they are harder to find. We often talk about our minds as filing systems. Sarah Wildman described how she 'tucked [her complaint] away marked under S for shame and cross-referenced into Y for youth'. To file a complaint can be to cross-reference it as a shameful lesson from our past that we do not want nor intend to revisit. We might file our unmade complaints away or put them in a file called 'Don't Go There', to borrow the term from a colleague. The file 'Don't Go There' tells us where we have been.

Sometimes we try to handle what is hard by putting it out of our minds. Handles can stops working. Darcy realized she could not handle it any more: 'I was sitting with another colleague at another lunch another day and he started texting me these naked photos of himself and I think I just hit a critical mass of, like, I just can't handle it any more. And then, it suddenly started to seep into me, into her, in this shared conversation about, how horrible and violent that I am having to receive these things, right, and so that basically put a process in motion.'

When the handle stops working, the violence seeps not

only into Darcy but into her colleague, into a conversation, into the space in which they are having that conversation.

When violence gets in, it gets everywhere.

We can understand, then, why sometimes we close the door of our own consciousness to stop the violence from getting everywhere, so that we can focus or function.

If a complaint can begin with letting the violence in, you still have to find a way to get the complaint out. Darcy went to the office dedicated to handling complaints: 'They were like, "You can file a complaint." But then they said, "Not much is going to happen: he's really well loved by the university; he has a strong publication record; you are going to go through all of this emotional torment." It was even proposed that he could counter-sue me for defamation of character. The line was, essentially, you can do this, but why would you?' You can be given permission to complain, whilst being warned against it, at the same time. The implication is that to complain would be to hurtle towards a miserable fate, to bring misery upon yourself. Darcy's harasser was from a super-wealthy background. 'I was fearful,' she explained: 'this is a really wealthy man of the world. He comes from a very wealthy, entitled background. I guess that is what gave him such a strong sense of entitlement.'

Darcy used the language of coming out to describe her own fears: 'I think I started to believe that if I came out with this in a public way, that my own career would suffer.' She feared that the further the complaint went, the less far she would. In the end, Darcy did not file a formal complaint, in part because she knew what she was being told: that she wouldn't get anywhere, it wouldn't get anywhere, because he was going somewhere. In my preface to this book, I suggested that approaching complaints biographically allows us to show how complaining and not complaining can have knock-on effects. Darcy's decision not to complain was affected by witnessing what happened to another student who had complained earlier: 'I watched her going through the process of reporting it and the way it effectively silenced her,' she explained. 'Once she made a formal complaint, she could no longer speak about it.'

Darcy's decision not to proceed with a formal complaint was about not having to make her story be about him. She said, 'I got removed from my own story as it became his story or their story about him.' For her, not centring on the harm was a way of not centring on him. It did not follow that she was not concerned with stopping him from acting in this way: she just wanted to find another way through: 'In not filing a complaint, I ended up feeling like I had more voice in what happened.' She felt freer to tell the story in her own way, freer also *not* to keep telling the story.

HITTING THE DOORS

Once you have let the violence in, it can be hard to shut it out. And it is not just violence that gets everywhere. Gina, a professor who made a complaint about bullying by her head of department, said, 'I didn't want to open my emails. I didn't like it when things came through the door. When I saw the university logo on it, I would go into a right panic about it.' To complain can mean being left feeling that anything that comes at you, any letters posted through your door, might come from the institution.

A complaint can make it harder to shut the door on the institution. And yet to complain formally is often to be pulled into another room. And the door is often shut. The expression 'behind closed doors' can refer to the actual doors that are shut so someone can tell their story in confidence. It can also refer to the process of keeping something secret from a wider public. I noticed early on in the research how often doors kept coming up in stories of complaint, actual doors as well as metaphorical doors, the latter used to convey the closing or opening of opportunities.

I spoke to Viola, an early-career lecturer who is neurodivergent and from a working-class background. She made a complaint about the failure of her institution to make reasonable adjustments to her workload after she returned from long-term sick leave. Doors had an integral role in how Viola's complaint came out. She described how she was 'just frightened' and allowed herself 'to go through it very privately' and 'hit all those doors along the way and just came out very guarded by it'. When I read through my transcription of her testimony, I thought I might have misheard and that she had most likely used the conventional expression 'hit all those walls'. I checked the recording again and she said 'doors', not 'walls'. Perhaps walls are sometimes disguised as doors, as if they can be opened to allow an entry but cannot. The doors became part of her story, even told her story, how she 'became very guarded'. That's why I think of becoming a feminist ear as not just listening through the doors but to them.

Viola wasn't aware at first that a complaint was what she was making. 'Being off sick opened a can of worms,' she explained. 'It was only actually through getting in touch with the union that I realized what I was doing was making a complaint.' Even though she found it politicizing to talk to the union, she quickly discovered that talking was exhausting. 'There were so many people involved, and none of those people were in the room at the same time. Making a complaint one hundred times doesn't make it any louder. I could have said it once to one hundred people at the same time, and I would have felt that it had more impact.' Your voice ends up quieter when you have to make that complaint so many more times, hundreds of times even, because each time it is made just to one person.

If the door is shut when you express a complaint, nobody else hears it other than the person in the room with you. Confidentiality can be necessary if people are to share sensitive information. For Viola, confidentiality 'makes you really vulnerable because nobody else knows what is going on'. She suggested that 'closed-door complaint procedures' make the complaint seem 'small'. That is why she had to keep coming out: 'There are like four channels of complaint going on at the same time. But interestingly none of these people seem to be crossing over. You duplicate the complaint at different times, emails, phone calls, occupational health, the union. It is generating all this material and all this paperwork but actually nothing seems to shift. It's just a file, actually.' Viola has to keep coming out because those who hear her don't hear each other. Complaints generate all these materials not because you have got somewhere but because you haven't ('It's just a file, actually').

It is not just that the doors stop each conversation from being overheard by others. The doors stop Viola's complaint from being heard by those who are receiving it. The doors she hits are also the doors of other people's consciousness. When they do not hear her, nothing shifts, or at least that is what it feels like.

We have to keep saying it when they are not hearing it.

One time, Viola spoke to a physician from occupational health: 'I think his sense was that if I was well enough to stamp my foot and complain, then I was well enough to work. So, there was this equation between being well enough to articulate and being active in terms of making sure I was getting the right support. If you are really good at making complaints, you must be well enough to go to work.' Stamp your foot and complain: we can hear how she is being heard. Her complaint is treated as a tantrum, as if she is just being spoiled. Being articulate can be used against a complainer *as evidence you do not really suffer.*

A complaint about an oppressive situation is used as evidence that a person is not really oppressed by a situation.

Viola had to push against how he expressed her complaint back to her. She described how she refused to sign a report: 'He was shocked, I think, that I complained to him in the room face-to-face. He was dictating the letter to the computer, which was automatically typing it, and I think he was astonished that I said I am not going to sign it.' Viola's refusal was another kind of complaint, not allowing him to make the complaint for her, to let the words he read out loud, automatically typed by the computer, his words, be hers. She said, 'You start to disappear in the process even though the process is about giving you a voice.'

A complaint can require saying *no* to those who use their authority to retell your story. A *no* can be harder to keep saying if you don't feel you have a right to keep saying it. Even though Viola kept coming out with the complaint, she did not herself feel confident about her right to do so: 'There is something else which is something to do with being a young female academic from a working-class background: part of me felt that I wasn't entitled to make the complaint – that this is how hard it is for everybody, and this is how hard it should be, and if it isn't hard then it is not work.' To question one's entitlement to complain can be to question whether one has the right to expect anything other than more of the same. Those who have a strong sense of entitlement probably do not question their entitlement to complain. Perhaps it is those with a strong sense of entitlement who dismiss other people's complaints *as* expressions of entitlement.

Viola had to fight all the more because she did not feel entitled to complain. She had to fight against herself, even, her own history, that classed and gendered history, just as she had to fight to complain in her own way, using her own terms. She describes how it feels to have to do this work: 'It was like a little bird scratching away at something and it wasn't really having any effect. It was just really small, small, small; and behind closed doors. I think people maybe feel that because of the nature of the complaint, and you are off work, so they have to be polite and not talk about it and so much of their politeness is because they don't want to say something. And maybe [it is] to do with being in an institution and the way they are built; long corridors, doors with locks on them, windows with blinds that come down, it seems to sort of imbue every part of it with a cloistered feeling, there is no air, it feels suffocating.'

A complaint as something that you are doing can acquire exteriority, that little bird, scratching away, all your energy going into an activity that matters so much to what you can do, who you can be, but barely seems to leave a trace. The harder you try, the smaller you feel. When Viola talked about a little bird, my feminist ears pricked up. You will understand why as I share more stories throughout the book; the little birds will turn up again.

Notice how much Viola notices: the building; the long

corridors; the locked doors; the windows with blinds that come down. This is her own workplace so, of course, she has seen it before. What we have seen before can easily be overlooked. To complain might be to see what we have seen before with a different lens, a magnifying glass, even. We might see that building differently by *seeing significance*; what the lock on the door can do, what the blinds can do; the corridors, too, what you have to go through. And perhaps the building becomes even more suffocating when it is filled with complaint. When you complain about not being given the time or room you need, you become conscious of the little time or room you have. A complaint by entering a room can make the room feel smaller.

What you disclose is treated as a secret, a source of shame. When a complaint is how we come out of a closet, we can end up in another one. What do we come *into* when we come *out of* a closet? Philosopher Judith Butler asks this very question: 'so we are out of the closet and into what? What new unbounded spatiality, the room, the den, the basement, the attic, the house, the bar, the university . . .' Butler then evokes another enclosure with a door, Kafka's door, a door that seems to promise what remains undelivered, the 'light of illumination that never arrives'. They ask the question: 'Is the subject who is out free of subjection and finally in the clear?'[11] They give an answer in how they ask the question: we are not 'in the clear'.

However much a complaint clarifies, to complain is often to become more conscious of what you cannot see; the doors that remain shut. Viola was conscious herself that the secrets were not just kept by the institution with its 'closed-door type procedures', but by other people. When her colleagues didn't speak of the complaint out of politeness, she felt like she had been erased. She said, 'I just faded out.' Viola ended up leaving her post because she could not get what she needed to continue. She used the same word for how it felt to leave: 'I just faded away.'

I felt it too, leaving my post as fading away. This might surprise you since I shared my resignation in public, albeit on my blog rather than on mainstream media platforms. There was something in that word *faded* that spoke to me: if my resignation was public, so much of the work of complaint was not. In a report on the findings of a project on sexual harassment conducted at my former institution, the only reference to any of the work I had done was that I had resigned.[12] When you resign because of what has not been done by the institution, that resignation can be used to remove what else you did. I felt rather like I was watching that work disappear; myself, also. It was hard not to notice when I stopped being invited to certain events. Or that when I spoke at other events they were written up as if I had not said anything. Or that my work was no longer referenced in certain publications on topics I had written extensively about. It was hard not to feel paranoid.[13] When I read an article by an early-career scholar of colour in which my own words and terms were attributed to another, I wondered and worried: had she been told not to cite me because of *that*? I have had to work on myself not to wonder or worry about *that*.

I think that is why becoming a feminist ear, listening to other people's complaints, meant so much to me. It gave me my voice back. I found the confidence and strength to share more of my own story in company with others. When Viola resigned, she found another way to share her story. 'I wrote a two-page letter,' she explained, 'and it was really important to me to put everything in there that I felt so that it was down on paper. And then I asked for a meeting with the dean. I kind of read the letter out in a performative kind of way just to have some kind of event.' Viola told the story, her story, putting everything she could in there, to stop herself from disappearing. That way more of her own self came out with her complaint. That way her complaint filled the room she left.

UNINTENTIONAL COMPLAINTS

We might assume complaints are an intentional action: what you decide to do before you do it. We have already learnt from Viola that you might only realize you are complaining after you began doing it.

Complaints can sometimes come out *despite* our intentions. I spoke to Serena, an early-career researcher who had to leave her job after being sexually harassed by a professor. The harassment mainly took the form of verbal communications – for example, he emailed her about wanting to suck her toes. She experienced the behaviour as annoying but not serious. She did not feel able to ask him to stop – she was junior to him, he was 'a big thing' at the university. So, Serena handled the situation by asking her line manager to ask him to stop. She explained why she took this route: 'I just want someone to have a chat with him and say, please don't continue with this. And [the line manager] assured me that she would do that.' When Serena came out with her complaint, she was not asking her line manager simply to listen. She was asking her line manager to do something, to intervene in the situation.

Despite her assurance, Serena's line manager did not say or do anything. Serena speculated as to why: 'Much later I learnt that because she did not want to complain, nothing happened.' She added, 'It is hard to have those conversations, because you are the problem and the spoilsport; it is easier not to, I suppose. I never spoke to her about why she hadn't, and it clearly wasn't that she forgot.' For the line manager to take the complaint forward by asking the professor to stop behaving in that way would be for her to become *implicated* in the complaint. Perhaps the fear is that by passing on a complaint you would catch the negativity, as if complaints are contagious.

And so, when the complaint was not passed on, the harassment went on. Serena tells us what happened next: 'And then I was in a meeting with my line manager and her line manager and we were in this little office space, like a glass fishbowl-type meeting room adjacent to the main office where all the staff desks were. He emailed me and I made a sound, eehhhhh, there's no way to articulate it, someone's just dragging your insides like a meat grinder, oh god this is not going to stop, and I made that sound out loud, and my line manager's line manager said, what's happened. And I turned my computer around and showed him and he said, "For fuck's sake, how stupid do you have to be to put that in an email." You could see a look of panic on [my line manager's] face. Like, crap, this has not magically gone away.'

When the complaint is made to go away as if by magic, puff, puff, the harassment does not. Her insides felt like they'd been through a meatgrinder; all crushed up. That sound *eehhhhh* is saying: enough! It pierces the meeting, that little glass room, a fishbowl, where they can be seen. Something can become visible and audible despite yourself. A complaint might come out when you realize it is 'not going to stop', and when you just can't take it anymore.

A complaint can be a snap, that moment with a history.

A complaint can be how you are *outed* as someone who is being or has been harassed. What makes a sound a complaint is a *transition* between private and public domains. Even if the transition is not always sharp, we can hear it. How that complaint came out involves *happenstance:* Serena happened to receive the email during the meeting. It can involve a relay of actions: receiving another message, making that sound, being asked "what happened?" when she turned the computer around. And note how the problem once heard is implied to be not so much the harassment itself but the fact that there was evidence of it ('For fuck's sake, how stupid do you have to be to put that in an email'). A sound becomes a complaint because it brings to the surface a violence that is in the room but otherwise would not have to be faced.

The line manager's line manager, now alerted and, importantly, having been witnessed being alerted, initiated a formal process. When a complaint involves non-intentional action, it can be someone else's action. Serena uses the word *imploded* to describe what happened next. She attended another meeting, which 'dragged on and on'. She said, 'It became clear at this point that something is going on beyond what I am involved in. That was the first time I realized the level of mess that is accompanying this.' And then, 'The professor disappeared; he was suddenly not there anymore.' She did not find out what had happened to him, 'whether he had been suspended or whether he quit'. Even though he had left, he got to tell the story: 'The story he had told to my colleagues was that he had been forced out by me. You've heard all of this a thousand times.' The familiarity of a story is its own story; we have heard it so many times before because of how many times it happened before.

There was no way for Serena to challenge the story because it was not made official, circulating only as rumour. And so, his story became the one that other people told. Her colleagues began to refer to her as the woman who forced a man of out his job because he said he wanted to suck her toes. The confidentiality, justified as protecting those who complain, in practice means that those with more connections have more control of the story. The complaint came to feel like somebody else was in control of the story. Serena commented, 'It is like being trapped in some kind of weird dream where, you know, you jump from one section to another because you never know the narrative. I think that's the power that institutional abuse has on you.'

You can know what is happening is not what is supposed to be happening without knowing what is happening. Making a complaint can feel like becoming a character in somebody else's story. Decisions are made without your knowledge or consent. It can feel like being harassed all over again, subjected, yet again, to another person's will.

The university conducted an inquiry into what had happened. An inquiry means more meetings; more times you have to come out with it. This can happen even when the complaint was not one that you made. Serena gave an account of what happened after one 'big meeting', when she was walked out of the meeting and 'taken for a cup of tea' by an administrator because she was so upset: 'We went and sat in this empty big university cafeteria, and I was crying, and I remember being frightened about how much it was going to cost me to move house – I was only renting, but to break my rental contract, if the landlord wouldn't let me out – and the sheer cost of having to move again. As I was crying, the first conversation about money happened. It was very gently done: "It is funny you should say that, and maybe there is something we could do to help you with those costs; we'll write to you about that, we'll find some way to sort of help you." I said, "I never want to come back into this university again," and the administrator said, "You don't have to, you can walk out today, you've got your stuff, you don't have to come back into any other meetings."'

When you tell the story of a complaint, you watch yourself, you go back. She watched herself being walked into a conversation, faithfully being told 'this will happen', 'that will happen', being walked out of the meeting, walked out with her stuff, walked out of her job, gently. In telling me this story, she was watching herself be walked not only out of her job but out of her life. The 'mess accompanying this' is your life.

Serena told me that she realized that she had become a complainer even though she did not initiate the complaint. She likened being the complainer to being a problem child: 'in getting to that point, the complainer, you never shed it, it is like the problem child: having done it, you cannot go back.' Becoming a complainer, for Serena, was about acquiring the tools to name the problem. She explained, 'The feeling of being able to name what is happening to you is very powerful.' Listening to Serena, I realized complaining can be coming out in another way. To complain can be to come out as a complainer.

AFTER COMPLAINT

What if you have already become a complainer before you experience something that might warrant making a complaint? To become a complainer is to know that you will, most likely, be made the problem. You might decide not to complain not because you have shut the door of consciousness but because you have opened it.

I talked to Laura, a Black woman, about her first experience of a complaint process at a university. She had been a trade union representative for a local authority, 'an advocate for people making complaints, Black people making complaints'. Laura knew that to complain would be to become the problem. She still ended up complaining despite what she knew. A senior colleague, a white feminist, had wanted to hire a white woman, her friend. Laura shared her view that another candidate, a man of colour, was more suitable and qualified for the post. The senior colleague responded by asking why her department had to 'bear the brunt of employing Black people'. Laura said it was 'a really terrible thing to have said in front of me, I am a brunt, so another Black person would be an even bigger brunt.' But she didn't do anything: 'I kind of sat there and I didn't do anything about it at all, just thinking about it, thinking I can't continue to work with this woman. I didn't complain internally even, I was thinking about what would happen if I did because, you know, as a Black person you are always precariously positioned, aren't you, in organizations.' She had to sit there not only with the racism, hearing herself positioned as a 'brunt' or as a burden, but with the realization that she couldn't complain, 'internally even' without compromising her already precarious position as a Black person within the organization.

Racism can stop you complaining about racism.

We have already heard how complaints might be withdrawn because of whom they are delivered to, a human resources department or a complaints office. We will hear more in the next chapter about the kind of comments typically made by those tasked with receiving complaints (baby clue: Darcy's experience of being warned is common). You might decide not to complain because of who is on the receiving end. You might not want to complain to 'Sally in HR'. Author and director Kelechi Okafor introduced us to Sally, in an animated video that went viral.[14] Kelechi explained her motivation: 'I created the character "Sally in HR" as a way to address the micro and macro aggressions faced by marginalized communities at work. I was surprised to see just how many people my sketches resonated with.' In one video, 'Sally in HR' is speaking to Morenike (whose name she mispronounces) about a complaint she has received from 'Cathy in Finance', about Morenike's different haircuts and how it makes it difficult to be sure she is giving the payslip to the right person (even though Morenike is the only Black person in the office). Were Morenike to complain about racism, she too would be complaining *to* 'Sally in HR'.

When you complain about a racist organization you complain to one.

If Laura decided not to complain to a racist institution, why did she end up making a complaint? She did so because the man of colour the university did not hire took the university to an employment tribunal: 'The reason he'd done that, the reason he had taken that complaint was because they asked questions at the interview which he felt they'd asked because he was an Asian man, that had nothing to do with the job at all, for example, how would you work with a group of white women. That's a clear giveaway, isn't it. So, he decided to make a complaint. I was contacted as part of this official process. I had to declare if I knew anything material in relation to this case, so I did, I said what it was, I went to tribunal on his behalf as his witness. I didn't have anybody representing me from the university at all; she had a solicitor or a barrister there for the university and, you know, the university was found against.'

Laura's complaint came out because another person's complaint *brought it out*. When she became a witness for him, she said 'what it was', sharing what her colleague had said to her. That's how his complaint became her complaint, too: 'My complaint then became me being vilified internally. I became the woman who told a lie, that's me, told a lie, because that couldn't have possibly happened because this wonderful white woman is such a nice person; she's completely non-racist, she would never say such a thing;

and she kind of walked around crying all the time, looking very upset . . . I was put in a room, then, by myself, with no windows or anything, to protect me from further victimization, so she maintained her position as the head of this course.'[15]

Laura ends up vilified because of what she discloses. She is treated as disloyal to the institution itself but also to her colleague who performs white tears, using them to extract sympathy from others. Racism is often treated as an injury to whiteness, performed, as it is often performed, with tears.

It can be hard to tell the difference between being protected from consequences and the consequences themselves. Even if you are removed to be protected, or that is how your removal is justified, you end up the one who is further away, in that airless, windowless room. Laura explained: 'What I learnt from the complaint process was that white organizations always seem to protect white people because, in protecting the one white person, they are protecting the whole institution from any claim that there is any racism happening at all. There is always this massive PR exercise.' The response to a complaint about racism is to treat it as potential damage to the reputation of the institution. Public relations, the creation of a polished and happy image of the institution, is another way the complaint ends up hidden from view.

Laura could see the 'white institution' because she could see through that PR exercise. Seeing the institution was not a one-time event. Laura explained, 'In order to survive in a hostile environment, you have to do this work of institutional analysis all the time. They are going to do this, and

I have to do that, and then I do this, and they do that: you know what I mean? It's constant, this watchfulness that you have to have in order to protect yourself from being really knocked.' To protect yourself is not to protect yourself *from* what you know. To protect yourself is to protect yourself *because* of what you know.

When Laura left her job, she did not leave her complaint behind her. It travelled with her as a state of constant alert. She said, 'You have a lot of strain and mental anguish which comes out in different ways, and the way that mine came out was in my back. That was when I started having this really bad back problem.' When our bodies express our complaints, they also bear the weight of them.

The body of a complainer is testimony to the work of complaint.

A body can be another way complaints come out, another story of complaint. That story is shared and not just when we tell it. Laura, when reflecting back on her act of supporting another person's complaint, said, 'It was something I had to do because of my politics; a wrong had been done. I had to make sure it had been put right even at my own personal expense, it turned out. I'd still do that again. I'd do it for another person, not for me.'

Approaching complaints as 'coming out stories' teaches us how complaints, even when they are lonely and isolating, involve other people, sometimes in rather unexpected ways. A complaint might come out because you see someone else's reaction to what you are receiving (Darcy), or because you only realize you are making a complaint by talking to the union (Viola), or because someone else hears your reaction (Serena), or because somebody else's complaint brings yours out with it (Laura). And I think, too, of how my own complaints came out with theirs and how, as a reader, your complaints might come out, too. Once out, where do complaints go? On which paths do they travel? It is to the institutional lives of complaints that we now turn.

2/ A Complainer as an Institutional Plumber

In 2021, Ashley Kosak shared a story about why she left SpaceX, a company that designs, manufactures and launches advanced rockets and spacecraft. She began as follows: 'At SpaceX, we're told we can change the world. I couldn't, however, stop getting sexually harassed.' Her account of what she was not able to stop, being sexually harassed, was a story of what did not happen when she complained. 'I told my supervisors what he had done, then met with HR and reported the inappropriate behaviour, but no one followed up,' she said, adding, 'I reported each incident of sexual harassment I experienced to HR, and nothing was done.' There were more meetings, and, 'In the end, nothing happened – except I was given a warning that recording the meeting was in violation of SpaceX policy and Florida law. Each and every man who harassed me was tolerated despite the company's so-called no-tolerance and no-asshole policy.'[1] I want to pause here and consider how 'nothing happened'. It takes so much to get to the point of reporting. So, when nothing happens, that *nothing is everything*. So many complaints lead to 'nothing happening', even if the routes to get there (or nowhere) are different. Whether nothing is inaction or the result of many different actions, nothing is always an achievement.

When I read Ashley's account of doing all of this work only for nothing to happen, I was reminded of an experience shared with me by Helen, a diversity practitioner, back in 2014. She was trying to get a new policy for appointment panels adopted. She went through the proper or formal mechanisms: the policy was agreed by the diversity committee. It was then sent to the council to be ratified. But the head of Human Resources removed the decision about the policy from the minutes. Somebody at the council who had been at the diversity committee noticed the decision had been removed. So, the minutes were sent back to be corrected. The policy was eventually agreed and adopted. But then other people in the organization acted as if it did not exist. When Helen pointed to the policy, 'they looked [at her] as if she was saying something really stupid.'

In this particular example, different actions could have stopped the new policy from being used. It *could have been* the removal of the policy from the minutes; it *could have been* the failure of anyone to notice this removal; it *could have been* the failure to amend the policy and return it to the committee. It was none of these things. It was the way that people acted as if the policy had not been agreed. If the first attempt to stop the policy had worked, these other methods would not have been necessary. The more methods fail, the more other methods are used, the longer the sequence.

What stops movement moves.

It is exhausting when you have to keep moving to stop yourself being stopped. In the end, Helen was so exhausted she left for another job at another institution. And when she left, she took the knowledge of the new policy (and perhaps even the policy itself) with her. That is why I began to think of diversity practitioners as institutional plumbers: they acquire knowledge of blockages in the system; how change can even be stopped by being agreed.

To make a complaint involves a similar knowledge and expertise. You have to use different methods to get your complaints through the system because of how you are blocked by it. That's how you learn about the system. Later in this chapter, you will hear from one student, Anna, who participated in a collective complaint about sexual harassment. Anna described her complaint as an 'energy zapper'. I rather imagined the drumming bunny in the old advertisement for Duracell batteries.[2] When the battery lasts longer, the bunny spends more time drumming, going round and round.

This metaphor of the complainer as an institutional plumber has its limits. After all, we hire plumbers to unblock the system, not just diagnose the cause of the blockage. By using the descriptor 'institutional plumber' I am not suggesting that to complain is to fix a problem (although, as I will show later, some organizations ask those who complain about racism to fix it). Rather, I want to show how to complain is to learn about the nature of the problem: complaints get stuck *in* or *by* the very systems that are designed to handle them.

FROM INFORMALITY TO FORMALITY

The lives of complaints are messy in part because of how complaints collide with other complaints. Leia, who talked to me about her experience of administering as well as making complaints, said, 'It's messy and it's cyclical: you file the complaint, this process happens, which can cause another complaint.' So many people shared stories of how they had to make another complaint about how their complaint was handled. The second complaint might even take the place of the first.[3]

Complaints enter that ecosystem we sometimes call *administration*. Although most of the stories shared in this book are told from a complainer's point of view, I spoke to some administrators. Sam, who is now an independent consultant but previously worked in university management, got in touch with me and asked to be interviewed for my study. She wrote in her initial email, 'Many are working very hard to change their processes and reporting structures and are thinking about the more challenging task of changing their culture.' Sam wanted to convey that managers and administrators were participating in the project of building less hostile institutions.

Sam became less optimistic about institutional change the more she talked about complaint. She said at first that complaints should be viewed as 'the best form of feedback'. She expanded, 'Students will complain if they're annoyed, frustrated or something has gone horribly wrong and that gives you data with which to try and reverse engineer that and try and fix what has gone wrong in the first place.' But then she gave a powerful account of how complaints end up stuck in the system: 'So, your first stage would require the complainant to try and resolve it informally, which is really difficult in some situations and which is where it might get stuck in a department . . . And so, it takes a really tenacious complaining student to say, no, I am being blocked. It takes a lot of energy and a lot of confidence. If something bad has happened, and you are not feeling that way inclined, you can understand why a student would not have the tenacity to make sure that happens, and to advocate for themselves. They might go to the student union, and the student union is really bogged down.'

Sam takes us through the stages of a complaint process. As I noted earlier, procedures are often represented as flow-charts, with clear lines and arrows telling the would-be complainer where to go, whom to speak to. Blockages can occur through conversations; if those you speak to are 'really bogged down', you can get bogged down. So, if the institutional story of complaint is the flow-chart, the complainer's story would look rather more like a mess of lines: once you get in, it can be hard to work out how to get out.

Sam evokes the figure of the complainer in her account of the complaint process. You would have to become a complainer, a 'really tenacious complaining student', to say, 'No, I am being blocked.' What you need to make the complaint

A complaint.

(confidence and tenacity) might be what is taken away by the experiences that led to a complaint ('something bad has happened', 'not feeling that way inclined'). The very experiences you need to complain about make it difficult for you to do so.

Sam's suggestion that the first stage would be for the complainer 'to try and resolve it informally', is both a common recommendation and common practice. The Advisory, Conciliation and Arbitration Service (ACAS) gives the following advice: 'Many problems at work can be resolved informally, for example through an informal chat. An employee could raise a problem informally by telling their line manager or someone else at work, for example, another manager or someone in HR. It does not have to be in writing at this stage.' Indeed, ACAS instructs managers in organizations to take a disclosure of a problem 'seriously', otherwise 'it could become a formal grievance' later, which 'can affect your organization's reputation, take time and be difficult for everyone involved'.[4] That the complaint procedure is not supposed to start with a formal complaint procedure might seem right and obvious. Surely, we should try to avoid what would be a time-consuming and difficult process?

Some problems are not only hard to resolve informally but are a result of informality. I spoke to Hana, who made an informal complaint about professional misconduct and bullying by her supervisor. She was asked to attend a meeting by her head of department. She went on her own. She wanted to record the meeting, but he said, 'No, this is informal.' She realized afterwards she 'should have insisted on it'. She described how the head of department had 'framed it as an informal chat', but that 'it wasn't at all. It was an interrogation. It felt like a scene from a Mafia film.' The head of department used the informal meeting to try to intimidate Hana into not complaining. Because the meeting was called 'an informal chat', it was not witnessed or recorded. In fact, the head of department's conduct was 'so extreme', Hana felt other people would not believe her if she told them what had happened; that they would hear her as 'being extreme and therefore irrational and a drama queen'.

When organizations resolve complaints before they are formalized, they do not need to record that a complaint was made. I talked to Kate and Tina, who made an informal complaint to the human resources department of their former university. This was a historic complaint about sexual harassment and sexual assault they had experienced as students twenty years previously. They were invited to a meeting with two members of Human Resources: 'They didn't record it or take any notes,' remarked Kate, 'I think there were one or two lines written.' Tina commented, 'It was very odd.' Kate agreed, 'You did feel it was a kind of cosy chat. Very odd.' Tina added, 'They were sort of wrapping the conversation up, because it had gone on,' so 'I said, "This is us making a formal complaint", and there was a shift in the atmosphere. And I said again, "We do want to follow it up as a complaint."'

In sharing reflections on the 'oddness' of the meeting, Kate and Tina worked towards a shared understanding of what was going on. They understood that informality was a way of both setting a tone and wrapping up the conversation. You can wrap up a casual conversation more easily or more quickly. When they made it clear in the meeting that they *were* making a formal complaint there was a 'shift in the atmosphere'. I am reminded of being a feminist killjoy at the table. So many dinners ruined. So many atmospheres.

So many meetings too! Ellen Pao, in her account of filing a complaint at a Silicon Valley venture capital firm, describes formality as a change in atmosphere. Her complaint was first handled informally. The person who listened to her did not even take notes. (I was reminded of one student, who told me about the person who listened to her complaint jotting down the details of what she was saying on the back of an envelope!) Pao uses the term 'puppet theatre' to describe the informal handling of her complaint. Her employer made 'three attempts to have the dispute mediated, to make it disappear quietly'. She explains, 'They wanted to figure out a quick way to appease me and to carry on doing things exactly as they always had,' adding, 'After I sent one formal memo, all the goodwill I'd built up vanished.'[5]

Informality is sometimes offered as a solution to a complaint. I talked to Stephanie about her experience of being assaulted when she was a student by a professor in her department. Stephanie described the assault: 'He pushed me up against the back of a door and tried to kiss me and I pushed him away – it was an instinctive pushing him away – and tried to get out of the room, and it was a horrible moment because I realized I couldn't, actually, it was very difficult to operate the latch.'

Stephanie decided to make a complaint at the time. First, she talked to a friend, and then to a representative from the students' union. Under the guidance of the latter, she submitted a letter. So, where did her letter go? 'It went to the dean, the dean notified the head of department, and there was obviously some discussion going on there.' She added, 'The dean basically told me I should sit down and have a cup of tea with this guy to sort it out.' The people who receive complaints are often in discussion with those whom the complaints are about ('there was obviously some discussion going on in there'). A response to a complaint about an assault is to treat it as what can be sorted out by a cup of tea, that English signifier of reconciliation. The 'solution' to the problem makes light of it. The assault is treated as just a minor squabble between two parties.

That some complaints are not formalized is treated as evidence that some problems have been resolved (there is no complaint made, so there is no problem). That complaints are not formalized can be *how* some problems remain unresolved (there is no complaint because of the nature of the problem). I spoke to Ray about their experience of making a complaint about transphobia as a hostile environment. During their interview, Ray commented, almost in passing, on an earlier experience they had as an undergraduate student. They had been raped on campus by another student: 'The person in question lived in the same stairwell as me at the college where I was studying. I don't know if I was trying to make an actual complaint or not, officially, but I was really strongly discouraged from doing anything, first by a student union officer in the college who was really good friends with the perpetrator, who was like, you should drop it, and then more senior academics in the college as well were saying it was a bad idea to take it any further; all they offered was to move me into a different room in the college, in a random corner, in a faraway block really far away from everyone else. It was the principle of it: that that is what they were prepared to do. At the time it did not seem especially surprising or shocking, but now looking back at it, it was really bad what they did.'

Ray was trying to process a traumatic experience. And at the time, they were told to 'drop it', that it was a 'bad idea', by people who had a vested interest in a complaint not being made. When Ray told me about what had happened, I was struck by how the trauma was passed over, both at the time and in the retrospection. Ray was telling me this story as a background to another story about a later complaint. It was only by 'looking back on it' they realized it was 'really bad what they did'.

It is not uncommon to be discouraged from complaining before you complain. This was Rosie's experience. She was harassed verbally by another student during a lunch break at a conference – he began to target her after she did not laugh along at his sexist jokes. Rosie left the room and was followed out by a member of staff who 'started a conversation'. She said, 'This is when, probably in hindsight, it started to get difficult. The staff member started to lean on me. Immediately he said to me, "Oh, you know what he's like; he's got a really strange sense of humour, he didn't mean anything by it."' Rosie is pressured not to complain even though she hadn't indicated that she might (perhaps leaving the room was indication enough). The pressure not to complain about harassment can be a continuation of the harassment. That is in fact *how* many complaints are stopped before people have decided whether or not to make them.

Rosie was not dissuaded. But it was still difficult to transition from an informal to formal complaint because of the time it took to find the complaint procedure. She called it a 'mythical gold egg'. And when she did eventually find it, it was 'so big' that it took 'weeks trying to get through the small print, to find out what the complaint process was'.

It can be hard to go through a complaint process if you can't find the procedure or if, once found, it is difficult to decipher. I spoke to Emily, who was considering whether to complain about transphobia and bullying by the director of a project team. She contacted the Human Resources department: 'They did not have any complaint procedures. I wrote to the appropriate contact in Human Resources, "I am resigning because of bullying and transphobia in the project", and her response was "No, we have never had anything like this before."'

To be told there is no procedure to deal with a problem can be how you are told it is not a problem ('we have never had anything like this before'). It is not enough for procedures to exist. They have to be talked about in a meaningful way before they can be used.

FROM WARNINGS TO THREATS

So, let's say your complaint has not been stopped by an informal conversation or by the absence of a meaningful formal procedure. What next? You might then have to prepare that complaint, perhaps by speaking to a member of your Human Resources department, if you have one, or by submitting a written document. Some people are discouraged from complaining *before* they complain, others are discouraged *when* they complain. Lucy Siegle comments on the word *discouraged* in describing her experience of making a complaint about sexual harassment at the *Guardian*. She writes, '"Discouraged" is a soft word for a hard action that leaves the complainant facing double jeopardy; on one hand, you have disclosed something important to someone that you no longer trust, and on the other hand, having played your card, you have nowhere to go. I felt that I was now in a double bind.'[6] Many who begin the complaint process only to be discouraged from proceeding feel that bind; having started it, they are left without a path forward.

Discouragements can take the form of warnings. Warnings are *redirectives*. You might hear the sound of an alarm, beep, beep: danger ahead! The point of a warning is that it is delivered early enough for a person to avoid a situation. Warnings can be delivered too late, after a person has committed to a course of action. I think I was given a belated warning by a journalist. He asked why I was not worried about 'being blackballed', after speaking out about institutional harassment. I had not realized at the time that I was basically making myself unemployable, at least as an academic at a British higher educational institution. I hope that if I had been warned in time, I would *not* have heeded it and would have remained committed to that course of action.

But mostly, warnings tell us what situations to avoid. They can be articulated softly, expressed as concern, or be stern or alarming, even threatening. June, a postgraduate student, was deciding whether to complain about sexual harassment and had a conversation with the chair of her department: 'His response was essentially, "Well, we are just thinking about your career, how this will affect you in the future."' You might be told they are thinking about your career, or that you should be. Stephanie, who was advised to have a cup of tea with the lecturer who assaulted her, was also told that she 'had to think about [her] career'. The implication is that to complain is to think about something else other than your career (such as dealing with an assault or preventing yourself from being assaulted). Thinking about your career seems to mean learning to avoid doing anything that might compromise it, even if that means putting up with being harmed or harassed or discriminated against.

Some people are warned not to complain to avoid becoming a complainer. Tanya, a student of colour, wrote to me about what happened when she complained about racial discrimination. She had been promised one of two teaching fellowships that were subsequently given to white students less qualified than herself. Tanya was advised by her supervisor not to complain because the supervisor 'didn't want other people to think [she] was a troublemaker'. That warnings can be made with reference to 'other people' has much to teach us. It might be that the supervisor used 'other people' as a polite placeholder for herself. Or it might be that the warning was telling Tanya that she needed to manage other people's perceptions, to avoid being perceived as somebody who might cause trouble, now or in the future.

Despite the warning, Tanya complained. She couldn't afford not to: without the promised fellowship, she would not have enough income to stay on the programme. She describes what happened next: 'After I made a complaint against them, I felt all sorts of overt discrimination, as if the complaint made everyone free from the mask they used to put on when they were dealing with me before.' It was not that by complaining, Tanya became a troublemaker. She was already one. The warning, by telling Tanya to manage other people's perceptions, was also telling her to try and distance herself from how she was *already* perceived. Compliance, for some people, might be expected as if in compensation. When Tanya complained rather than complied, she went from being, in her terms, a 'mute diversity trophy' to the person 'damaging their department'. Warnings expressed as concern for another person's career can indeed mask something else. The concern being expressed might have *really* been for 'their department'.

A warning not to complain can be how some people receive a message that the department in which they work is not theirs. Or it can be a message to put other people and 'their department' first. I mentioned earlier Rosie's experience of having a lecturer try to stop her complaining about harassment by another student just after she was harassed. In the end, Rosie complained with the support of three other students. Anna was one of those students. She, too, was warned: 'I was repeatedly told that "rocking the boat" or "making waves" would affect my career in the future and that I would ruin the department for everyone else. I was told if I did put in a complaint, I would never be able to work in the university and that it was likely I wouldn't get a job elsewhere.' She was being informed that the potential damage caused by the complaint would travel; that she would ruin her own career, yes, but also ruin the department or even the whole institution.

Anna was repeatedly told she was 'rocking the boat' and 'making waves'. A rocking motion is more dangerous for those with less stable footing. As a group, she and her fellow students understood that their futures were at stake: 'We started to realize that we could actually get kicked out because of this, we could lose our jobs because of this, and the university was making it quite clear that they are a really big institution, and we are four PhD students with not very much power or resources.' Warnings are used to remind people of the precarity of their situation. 'In just one day,' she reported, '[I was] subjected to eight hours of gruelling meetings and questioning, almost designed to break me and stop me from taking the complaint any further.' Anna was becoming an institutional plumber, aware of how the system for handling complaints was designed (or almost designed) to stop them being made.

You can stop someone from doing something by making it harder for them to do it.

When the system does not work, when complaints are not stopped, warnings are quickly turned into threats. There might be no turning involved; a warning could be a threat-in-waiting. Anna explained that in the same meeting, the head of department referred to her source of funding: 'And then she said, "Have you looked at your agreement with the [funding body] because there is an agreement that says that if you appear to be slanderous against the university that's a reason to have your funding withdrawn." So, it was explicit: she said we can take away your funding, we can discredit you as researchers for being unethical for talking about this complaint.' Threats are not always made explicitly. No one has to say, 'We will take your funding away.' They just have to mention the source of funding. A threat can be a reminder of what can be taken away. Perhaps you are being told that to complain would be to appear ungrateful for what you have been given.

FROM BRIBES TO BLANKS

Warnings and threats are negative methods of stopping complaints; they say, 'Don't go there, don't do that.' Complaints can also be stopped by lighter or more positive methods. In the same meeting in which Anna and Rosie were warned by their head of department, they were given an incentive not to complain. Anna again: 'Then the next thing came, and [the head of department] said, "I have still got some money, so how would you like to organize a massive international conference, and we can give you money; who would you want for your dream list of academics to come and do this conference? [. . .] That way you can educate everyone about women."' Anna and Rosie began talking excitedly about how they could use the money, who they could invite to the conference, before what was going on dawned upon them. In becoming excited about the offer, they had been distracted from the complaint. Note also how the solution being offered was presented as a more positive route ('That way you can educate everyone about women'). They realized they were being offered something akin to a bribe; they would be given a feminist conference, given resources to use for their own purposes, in return for not proceeding with that complaint.

Silence is incentivized. Anne, a senior researcher, was considering whether to take her complaint to an ombudsman. She received a letter from the head of the organization in which she had made the complaint. The letter was an invitation to collaborate on future research grant applications:

'When I talked to other researchers, that's when I found out, this offer of working and collaborating with them, with them knowing how passionate I was about my work, was conditional on me not going to the ombudsman.' She understood what was being implied: the condition of the offer was not taking her complaint any further.

Non-Disclosure Agreements can function unofficially as a form of bribery because they give somebody something in return for silence. I say unofficially because NDAs are legal agreements and bribery, a gift that is intended to influence action corruptly, is unlawful. In part as a result of the #MeToo movement, there is now more consciousness of how NDAs are used to silence those who complain about sexual harassment in the workplace. There are many reasons people sign NDAs. You can have your reasons without having much choice. Nadia, a woman of colour academic, wrote to me about why she signed one despite her own desire to write about what had happened when she made a complaint about racial discrimination. She signed the NDA because she was offered a sabbatical in return. She needed that sabbatical. A complaint can sometimes mean you end up even more under the influence of the organization because what you need to survive the very process that they put you through is what they can provide.

Positive methods are not simply about rewarding people for not complaining; they are also how complaints are stopped by being encouraged. In chapter 1, I shared Viola's experience of having to keep making the same complaint to many different people. She noticed that one of the senior managers kept saying *yes*: 'I would say he's a yes man. So, whenever I'd talk to him, he would say yes, but I knew the yes was definitely not a yes; it was a "we'll see".' A *yes* can be more easily said when there is nothing behind it. Viola described 'Yes-saying' as a management technique, 'this weird almost magical thing that happens when you speak to people in management'. She explained: 'You are really fired up and you kind of put your complaint, your case, your story to the person, and then you sort of leave as if a spell has been cast, leave feeling, like, okay something might happen, and then that kind of wears off a few hours later and you think, oh my gosh. It is like a sleight of hands, almost like a trick, you feel tricked.' The feeling that something might happen can be what is being achieved by that yes. Being left with a sense you are getting somewhere is how you end up not getting anywhere. *A yes* can stop a complaint from progressing by diffusing the energy of the one who complains, like a fire being dampened.

A *yes* can sometimes take the form of a nod. At her first meeting with him, Rosie's head of department 'seemed to take it on board, he was listening; he was nodding'. But then, she reported, 'Ten days later I still had not heard anything and a space of limbo opened up.' To be in limbo is to be left waiting. Nodding is how the head of department is communicating that he is listening, taking it 'on board'. Maybe that is why there is so much nodding around a complaint: it is how people *appear* to hear.

A hearing can be about appearing to hear.

I pointed out in my introduction that hearing a complaint requires more than just receiving it. But that is how many organizations use hearings – as if once a complaint is heard nothing else needs to be done. Patricia, a professor, made an informal complaint to her dean about the misogyny she had experienced at an away day. The dean was sympathetic. 'I had a hearing,' Patricia acknowledged, only to qualify this quickly: 'But I think it was just to placate me.'

Shazia told me about a complaint made by students in her department. The students had stopped coming to research seminars because of the conduct of the professors. When they were sent a reminder that attendance was compulsory, they made an informal complaint about the conduct of the professors. At a departmental meeting, the professors decided to offer the students an 'open meeting'. Shazia said the point of that meeting 'was just about calming [the students] down'. I call this mechanism *institutional venting*. Once people have vented their frustrations, got the complaint out of *their* system, the complaint is treated as out of *the* system. Venting is used as a technique for preventing something more explosive happening. The mechanism is rather like a pressure relief valve, which lets off enough pressure so it does not build up and cause an explosion. In being let out, a complaint disappears, becoming air. A hearing as a disappearing, that magic trick; puff, puff.

The management of complaints can thus be about

controlling *where* and *when* they are expressed rather than simply stopping them from being expressed. Another tactic is to turn the complainer into an informant. Mia made a complaint about bullying from her head of department. During the inquiry, he was required not to contact her. She described how her management team told her to report any instances where he breached the conditions. 'So, of course, I reported these things, and they did nothing.' Being told to report gave her the feeling she was doing something. When she told me this, I recognized something from my own experience. Early on during the inquiries into the students' complaints, I had been told by a senior administrator to report any further instances of professional misconduct to him. And I did report further instances because there were further instances. When HR instructed me to pass the information to them, they could ensure it would be deposited in a safe space, somewhere nobody else would find it. I rather suspect they were just trying to stop me from doing something more explosive (like sharing information on my blog). I guess that strategy worked until it didn't.

There is another way of not saying *no* we can call *blanking*. Organizations (and individuals) can avoid saying *no* by not saying anything at all. Helen, the diversity officer who introduced a new policy, was most certainly blanked. Her colleagues had to blank her to keep following the old policy precisely because she had evidence of a new one. Rohina, a woman of colour researcher, told me what happened during a meeting about her complaint about racial discrimination: 'From the very beginning I get into the room the provost doesn't look at me during the entire meeting. It was like this weird thing: she is actually going to pretend I am not in the room.' It is weird but it works: when they don't acknowledge you, you might as well not be there.

To be blanked is to be busy; when you don't get a response, you have to work to get one. I spoke to Samia, a woman of colour academic who made a complaint about plagiarism. She described her experience thus: 'I was told it was now a formal process. I had to look at all the policies. I found there was this fog. It was constant. Every time I found clarity – isn't it supposed to happen in accordance with policy blah-blah-blah, which has been around ten years, isn't this supposed to happen, and they would be like, no.' We already heard how organizations can blank a new policy. In this instance, an old policy is blanked. Samia knew those policies and procedures not only existed on paper but had been around a long time. And she knew these policies could come into force at any time: 'I had to push them because, according to their policy, there were so many days you had after submitting the complaint for it to be investigated . . . A month and a half went by since my complaint went in and nothing happened. So, I had to keep pushing.'

The harder it is to get through, the more you have to do.

You have to push to get an organization to follow its own procedures, otherwise your complaint will be dropped in accordance with its procedures.

Blanking can come quite late in a series of actions, only necessary because someone has persisted with a complaint. I think of a conversation I had with Mary, who had been trying to put forward a grievance about the sabotage of her tenure case by a senior white male academic. Despite numerous attempts to initiate an inquiry, she was not getting anywhere: 'I had to send an email to [the head of Human Resources] with the subject line in all capital letters with an exclamation point, my final email to her after seven months. THIS IS A GRIEVANCE! THIS IS A GRIEVANCE! And her obligation under the university rules and the process is that she had to put it forward. She did not. She did not put it forward.' That capitalized subject heading has much to teach us about hearing. Sometimes you have to shout because you are not heard.

When you have to shout to be heard, you are heard as shouting.

The effect of not being heard makes it even less likely you will be. You become worn out by the struggle to get a complaint through.

ADMINISTRATIVE VIOLENCE

Those who complain often end up worn down by the very system they are complaining about. I use the term *administrative violence* for the methods used to stop not just complaints being made but the people making them. Why call these processes *violent*? Violence is understood primarily as an interpersonal phenomenon involving deliberate acts of harm. But systems can also be violent, causing harm to populations, sometimes, but not always, as a direct result of policies.

I opened my introduction to this book with reference to the fire that destroyed Grenfell Tower, citing Peter Apps's powerful critique of how Grenfell was 'let happen'. On 4 September 2024, the 1,700-word final report of the inquiry into Grenfell was published. It pointed to the systematic failure of government to restrict the use of combustible cladding products despite mountains of evidence warning of the risks. Some warnings are not heeded. Peter Apps commented on the findings: 'at every stage, government advisers and officials – those who should have been acting in the interests of the citizens they represented – hummed and hawed and did nothing. For years, the bereaved and survivors have thrown a two-word accusation at those they see as responsible: they knew. This report confirms that.'[7]

'Hummed and hawed and did nothing' – these are not just inactions but actions. Sociologists Vickie Cooper and David Whyte analyse the Grenfell fire as a form of 'institutional violence'. They begin with a question: 'Have we witnessed a more devastating and extreme public act of violence than the Grenfell Tower fire in living memory in this country?' They use the term *institutional violence* not only to describe this extreme public act but what led to it; the policies of austerity, the positioning of people in social housing as 'scroungers' on the state; the 'bonfire of red tape', the brutality of bureaucracy. Cooper and Whyte show how the 'series of events that led to the fire were routine and mundane – the driving down of costs, undercutting health and safety measures and the systematic refusal to listen to tenants when they warned of the deadly risks they faced'.[8] Grenfell, they affirm, brought the 'violence of contemporary capitalism into view'.

Violence can be *slow* until it becomes extreme; people are worn down or out by what they have to do to survive.[9] Administrative violence points to how people's vulnerability to violence is magnified *because* they have to go through an administrative process to get what they need. Administration is more than paperwork: it means entering different offices, dealing with a number of different people appointed to assess your claims (to assess you, too), sometimes having them enter your home. Researcher China Mills describes how accessing disability benefits means having to deal with 'the violent bureaucracy, assessments, waiting, being made to feel like you're undeserving, being told the problem is you and not the system'. This kind of state violence 'passes under the radar for apprehending violence. But not for everyone. Not for those who experience it firsthand, full-on, every day, stitched onto skin and bone.'[10] Violent bureaucracy, or *suspicious bureaucracy*, surrounds people who need access to welfare like an atmosphere, getting under their skin, making them feel they are the problem. This violence is unseen for those who don't experience it, passing 'under the radar'.

Even when the effects of a complaint process are extreme,

the process remains unseen. I talked to a woman of colour, Mira, whose internal complaint ended up in the courts. She spoke of a situation of sustained racial and sexual harassment, some of which led her to complain and some of which followed complaining. The stress of the situation was so severe that Mira had 'a terrible accident and nearly died'. She told me this story in tears: 'I was so stressed . . . I hit my head. I was distracted for a fraction of a second, and walked into a steel girder, which hit me on the head, and fell back directly on my head, and I fell back onto concrete and sustained a minor traumatic head injury – a brain bleed. I lost speech; I lost my ability to walk down the stairs. I could have died, basically. I was very lucky in some respects that I wasn't worse.'

Mira became disabled as an effect of the immense stress she was put under. She said that, in the settlement, they tried to 'scrub out the disability', to erase the effects of the violence. And so, she received compensation but not justice. The terms of the settlement meant Mira was stopped from being able to tell her story for at least six years. And, as she said to me at the end of her testimony, 'This is quite a story, isn't it.'

Administrative violence does not just refer to the effects of a complaint process. It can be a deliberate strategy to make complaints unaffordable or unsustainable. In simple terms, *the effects are techniques*. Alice, a Black single mother and a precarious worker, complained about bullying from her line manager even though she could ill afford to: 'They are hoping each time they will get me to stop. So, there is a risk they will bankrupt me. They are trying to bankrupt me, a single mother on a low income. They know I don't have any money, and they are using that to try and stop me.' By force, we are talking about the deliberate effort to deprive someone of what they need to make do or get by. You make it harder to complain 'each time' by making it more costly to complain. Note how Alice keeps referring to 'they'. Her complaint leads her into contact with multiple actors working on behalf of the institution. These processes, however institutional, are not impersonal. There are still people making and communicating decisions.

Nevertheless, administrative violence can help us to explain how complaints are stopped by processes *without the need for deliberate action*. I spoke to Drew, a student with a chronic illness. She talked to me about the additional work she had to do in order to secure reasonable adjustments: 'It's just like a mess of documents and this back-and-forth and all this paperwork and me writing these seventeen-page letters itemizing the failures of the university and them just writing the same letter back in response.' Her description teaches us how the creation of standards by an organization can allow the lessening of effort ('writing the same letter back') but also how administrative failure can mean more effort is required by those who make complaints ('itemizing the failures of the university').

There is a correlation between the decrease in energy used by the organization and the increase of energy exerted by the complainer. Drew had to complain because she was not given the time she needed. But then she was not given the time she needed to make the complaint. She commented wryly, 'Yes, I was interrupted but if I stop being a student I don't stop being disabled.' Drew described her complaint as a kind of detective work: 'I uncovered all these failed processes. You register with disabled services, disabled services get your docs, and then they send a memo to your department and then something else happens with it. And what was supposed to happen was that it was supposed to go from Disability Services to the Disability Liaison Administrator who was just the head secretary who would then cascade it around relevant staff but who never did that.'

Drew's complaint uncovered 'failed processes'. Her complaint then became another 'failed process'. I call these processes 'strategic inefficiency', to point to what they achieve. Strategic inefficiency was the name that came to mind for what I kept hearing in stories of complaint: documents disappearing, missing policies; confidential folders going astray, sometimes because they were posted with incomplete addresses; whole complaint files going missing; meetings that were not properly minuted or that were assembled haphazardly in contradiction with procedure. I began to wonder if inefficiency was not just about the failure of the system to work but about how it worked. Why? Because what was lost always seemed to be in the interests of the organization that had received the complaint.

Strategic inefficiency is the institutional version of 'weaponized incompetence', when some individuals demonstrate an inability to perform certain tasks to avoid being given them. One example from my own experience: a senior man was never given any marking of course work. I had assumed it was because he was considered too important, as marking is sometimes judged to be a mundane task. I found out later that administrators did not give him marking not because they thought he was important but because he mostly failed to do it on time, and they did not want the students to suffer. One administrator told me she found the scripts for a whole course behind his desk. The reason incompetence is a 'weapon' is because it is beneficial: that person is given less work or less of the less-valued work. Strategic inefficiency points to how failed processes are beneficial for institutions. Strategic inefficiency is rather efficient because organizations don't have to do very much to stop the complaint; they can just keep failing to do what they usually fail to do. A bumbling person who keeps losing his scripts becomes a bumbling organization that keeps losing its files.

You can stop a complaint by losing it.

Organizations might lose files or miss deadlines. Andrea described how her university took seven months to respond to her complaint. It then took them another seven months to respond to her response to their response to her complaint. If the organization had followed its own procedures, it would have taken no more than three months. Andrea had her own explanation for what was going on: 'It is my theory they have been putting it on the long finger and pulling this out, dragging this out over unacceptable periods of time, to try and tire me out so that I will just give up.'

You tire people out so they are too tired to address what makes them too tired.

Some people experienced long delays as attempts to catch them out. Stephanie said there were 'long periods of time' when there was 'no response', from the university to which she had submitted a formal complaint. But 'then they would give you a week to get back to them. And you know these are arbitrary deadlines.' An arbitrary deadline is one that is pulled out of the air. And, of course, if the deadline is not only tight but unexpected, you might not be able to make it or you might have to rush to make it. Alice's university gave her 'a tiny timescale' to respond to a report that had taken a very long time to produce. She commented: 'That's not part of the procedure. They are just making it up as they go along.' Making it up as you go along, bumbling along, can be a technique for catching people out. It is hard to meet the requirements when you do not know what they are.

Organizations that fail to meet their own timelines can and do enforce them for those who complain. I think of a conversation I had with Sonia, who submitted a complaint about bullying from her head of department. 'I basically did it when I was able to, because I was just really unwell for a significant period of time,' she recalled. 'And I put in the complaint and the response that I got was from the deputy vice-chancellor. He said that he couldn't process my complaint because I had taken too long to lodge it.' Some experiences are so devastating that it takes time to process them. The length of time taken to make complaints can sometimes be used to disqualify them. The requirement to follow the procedure, to fill in a certain form, in a certain way, at a certain time, is how many problems are not recorded. When organizations avoid triggering a complaint process on technicalities, they save time and money.

What organizations save, complainers expend. I referred earlier to a conversation I had with Hana, who described an informal meeting as a 'scene from a Mafia film'. Despite that attempt to intimidate her into not making a complaint, she went on to make one. She experienced multiple delays: 'Months went by. Nothing. They really botched my complaints procedure just by virtue of missing their own deadlines.' First the organization missed its deadlines. And then her whole complaint file went missing.

It was an excruciating wait. Hana, as an international student, was waiting for her complaint to be processed at the same time as her visa was running out: 'Ten days before my visa was about to run out, I applied for a new visa. And they were like, how can we give her a visa if she is on probation? You have to have good standing to get a visa, and they were like, this complaint thing is open.' Hana describes her life during this time: 'I had no money, I couldn't work. Every week, they were like, we will give you an outcome next week, then the next. I couldn't renew the lease where I was renting. I really couldn't continue with my work as I wasn't sure I could stay. Everything depended on the outcome of the complaint. I was, like, homeless, staying with a friend on a couch.'

Although long and arduous complaints processes are

difficult for everyone, they are potentially devastating for those who are more precarious because of their residential or financial status. When you are living on the edge, a delay could mean everything topples over; you can be left homeless, even more dependent upon the good will of others. I suggested earlier that this picture can be how a complaint looks (or feels) like from the complainer's point of view. That mess can be a picture of your life.

A complaint can be how a life unravels, thread by thread. The complaint is not the starting point of that mess; it might even be the last thread.

For some people, administrative failure *is* administrative violence. Philosopher Abigail Thorn created a powerful video documenting how the administrative failures of the National Health Service impacted the lives and wellbeing of trans people.[11] She made dramatic use of her own story: Abigail was reliant on her GP to refer her to a Gender Identity Clinic in order to get the hormones she needed. For

A life.

over a month, the GP said they would not refer her. She eventually received a letter saying that they would. But then nothing happened. After waiting much longer than she should have in accordance with the NHS's own timelines, Abigail decided 'to start sending some emails'. She found out which Trust runs the Gender Identity clinic she'd been referred to and wrote to their Head of Compliance. After numerous emails, he eventually replied, stating: 'They don't always meet the targets' (even though, as Abigail points out, a timeline is not a target). Abigail finally was given a meeting with the person who runs the Gender Identity clinic. But he did not turn up. That meeting had to be rescheduled: more emails. When the meeting did take place, Abigail realized it had been arranged 'not to solve the problem but to try and get rid of [her]'. She commented, 'He took my complaints about the failure of the system as an attack on his character and made the conversation about his feelings.' She was then told she could make another complaint, 'to the parliamentary and health service ombudsman'. When she finally made that complaint, she was received more sympathetically. But then, several months later she was told the complaint was being dropped.

Legal scholar and activist Dean Spade uses the term *administrative violence* to denote how some people become more subject to surveillance and control. He explains: 'Rather than understanding administrative systems merely as responsible for sorting and managing what "naturally" exists, I argue that administrative systems that classify people actually invent and produce meaning for the categories they administer, and that those categories manage both the population and the distribution of security and vulnerability.'[12] If accessing healthcare for trans people is an administrative process, it is also a system. After all, Abigail's complaint biography began with her need for a referral by a GP to a Gender Identity Clinic in order to get hormones. Cis women do not need any such referral to get hormones. You will not get blocked by a system if you don't need to access it. Abigail's complaints (about the system) follow in the pathway of the other materials she had already sent (through the system), the many letters and phone calls from the requests for referral on. And it went on. Abigail entitled her video, 'I emailed my doctor 133 times'. A number can tell a story, or at least some of it.

Strategic inefficiency means that some people have to do so much more work to get what they need. They might even end up administering their own complaints. Zenab, who made a complaint about transphobic harassment from their supervisor, reported, 'I am the one who has to arrange all this information and send it to different people because they are just not talking to each other. I had to file the forms in order to get the Human Resources records; I had to do all the Freedom of Information requests. It was on me to do all of this work, which raises the question of why have Human Resources officers at all, because I am literally doing their job. And I am the one who made the complaint, and I have all the emotional damage around that to deal with.' The person who makes the complaint, who is already experiencing the trauma or stress of the situation they are complaining about, has to become the *conduit*, holding the information so it can be passed to the right people.

The experiences that lead to a complaint can make it hard to hold yourself together, let alone direct an unwieldy process. Zenab remarked, 'When I was sitting down with Human Resources, doing a Human Resources investigation, it was very clear that the person presiding over the case, and the Human Resources officer who was assigned to it, simply didn't know how to handle a case that involves transphobia. They never really asked for my pronouns, they never really asked for my name, like my chosen name.'

When you complain about what you come up against, you come up against what you complain about.

Zenab added, 'No individual person in the complaints process is going to see the whole of it, as it affects you.' The process reminded Zenab of other dehumanizing experiences: 'The ways these complaint procedures are done ends up triggering these other experiences of abuse and hardship. Because you feel surrounded, and you feel like no one is listening to you and it feels endless.'

So many people who complain feel as Zenab did that 'no one is listening'. To become a feminist ear is not just to hear *who* is not heard. It is to hear *how* some people are not heard. When complaints go round and round in our heads, they also go round and round institutions: more movement not to get very far. That is why it is not just the voices of complainers we hear. We hear the sound of the system: the clunk, clunk, of how institutions are working; the gurgle, gurgle, of pipes being blocked; the bang, bang, of doors being slammed; the beep, beep, of warnings being delivered; the puff, puff, of complaints being lost. To become a feminist ear is to do more than listen. We have to find a way to get complaints out of the system so they can reach the people and the places where they can do something. That is, we need to dismantle institutional barriers, the walls and the doors that render so much of what is said, and what is done, inaudible. So many complaints will not get anywhere unless institutions change.

Part Two

Changing Institutions

Even to indicate you might complain within an institution is to receive many messages from it that tell you about it. Remember Darcy's experience: she decided not to complain because she was told by the institution, or at least those responsible for administering complaints, that the professor who was harassing her would be protected (and she would not). She met a set of beliefs I call *institutional fatalism*, assertions that what institutions *are* is what they *will be* (institutions will be institutions!). She was told there was no point in complaining given the person she was complaining about was 'well loved'. To be told 'institutions will be institutions' is to be told who they will and will not love, who they will and will not protect. Institutional fatalism sometimes combines with gender fatalism, 'boys will be boys'. Darcy also said she didn't complain formally about her supervisor because it would most likely become 'a note in his file'. Were he to be freed from any consequences of the complaint, she thought she would be the one to suffer them.

I suspect it is not so much that senior managers or administrators believe institutions cannot change but that they want other people to believe it, or at least to act as if they do. And the people they want to believe it are the very people who act as if they don't. That is why the people who are more likely to complain are also more likely to know about institutional fatalism. Emma, a woman of colour, shared her knowledge of institutions with me. Explaining why she didn't complain about the sexism and racism she experienced in her department, she said, 'There's an agreement between people not to rock the boat. People would talk about the institution as a kind of legacy project and would imply that you just didn't understand how the institution was formed. The implication was that you have to be respectful of how this place was organized and what its traditions were, essentially.' This expression 'rocking the boat' came up earlier in warnings not to complain. That phrase is used here to imply agreement among members of an institution to treat it as a legacy project.

The institutional culture is that you do not complain about the institutional culture.

To become part of the institution is to take up the task of protecting it *from* complaint and sometimes *by* complaint. There are, of course, many different kinds of institutions. At one level, the term is used simply to denote scale: an institution can refer to a large and important organization (so, if you work for a bank, you are part of a financial institution).[1] Institutions are how we preserve the past, not only in a story we tell of 'how the institution was formed' but by our conduct, being 'respectful of how this place was organized'. When we use the term *institutions,* we are not just pointing to traditions but to the act of incorporating them, how we learn to fit in or to do things in the right way. Many of the rules that govern behaviour are not written down in instruction manuals but shared by word of mouth or through imitation or suggestion. Becoming part of an institution can reference the time it takes to say *yes* to its demands, until it becomes almost automatic to do so. That's why, when complaints teach us about the nature of institutions, they are teaching us how social forms persist over time: those who say *yes* are more likely to progress.

That *yes* has a history, even when it is automatic, or especially when it is. Historian Timothy Snyder opens his important book *On Tyranny* with an instruction, 'Do not obey in advance'. He suggests that citizens who obey in advance of an order, a phenomenon he calls 'anticipatory obedience', are 'teaching power what it can do'. Disobedience is indeed what we need in the face of the rapid rise of authoritarianism, the hard-to-check abuses of power by oligarchs and patriarchs, the increasing hostility towards, and scapegoating of, minorities.

Snyder's second instruction is to 'Defend institutions'.[2] Snyder is pointing to how institutions should function to prevent power from being concentrated in one person or party; when tyrants get into power through democratic institutions, they seek to destroy those institutions as quickly as possible. In this part of the book, I show how many institutions function to teach people to obey, to say *yes* in advance of an order, not least because of how they reward compliance. Using Snyder's logic, institutions would then be sowing the seeds of their own destruction, creating citizens ill-equipped to fight for them by fighting back against those who seize power by illegitimate means. Institutions that reward compliance themselves become more compliant, less willing or able to stand up to tyranny.

The word *obedience* derives from ear, to obey is to give your ear to the law or to the tyrant who suspends the law by replacing it with his own will. A feminist ear might be how we hear the instructions by refusing to follow them; hearing with defiance, not compliance. The data of complaint is generated because people can and do defy the instructions, saying *no* to institutions, despite being told that there is no point in doing so. This data is also a series of snapshots of institutional resistance to change. If the title of this part of the book gives the impression that I am going to share some rather more positive stories about complaints, how they succeed in changing institutions, that is not what I am doing. There is nevertheless something positive in these stories. Even when complaints do not succeed in a simple or straightforward way, they teach us that institutions can and do change. And so, most importantly, they help reveal that institutional fatalism is a lie.

3/ Complaint as Feminist Pedagogy

In the UK, the Sex Discrimination Act (SDA) (1975) made it unlawful to treat a woman 'less favourably' than a man 'on the ground of her sex'. The Act did not reference sexual harassment. It took a political movement, the women's movement, for sexual harassment to be recognized as discriminatory. It also took a complaint. Historian Louise Jackson writes: 'In 1986, a complaint brought by Jean Porcelli finally resulted in the "first definitive ruling by a British court" that sexual harassment constituted discrimination within the terms of the SDA.'[1]

Jean Porcelli had made her initial complaint two years earlier, in 1984. She was working as a lab technician when two new technicians were hired. A campaign of harassment followed:

> It started with low-level stuff – they would move my papers around and mix up my chemicals. They would slam doors in my face when I was carrying apparatus. But quite quickly it took on a sexual connotation. It wasn't because they fancied me – they were using the sexual stuff to make me frightened and intimidate me. They would do things like brushing up

against me and standing close to me, trapping me between them, laughing when I got distressed.[2]

There were more instances: 'Once, when I asked one to get something for me from a shelf, he said: "If you can't climb a fucking ladder, you shouldn't be in a job, so get back home to your family."' Sexual harassment can be how you are given a message: go away or go home.

Jean complained because she did not want to go away or to go home. She explains, 'I didn't see why I should leave my job. My reputation was at stake. I had 15 years' service to defend. I had to fight it – for my children and my family.' But the more Jean complained, the more she was harassed. She received many threats from a widening circle of people, including rape threats.

When you complain because you are harassed, you are harassed because you complain.

So, what did she do? Jean contacted her employment union, but they did not respond to her letters. Yes, to be blanked can mean to be busy. Jean could not afford a lawyer. So, she represented herself at an employment tribunal. The judgment went against her, concluding that sexual harassment didn't come under the terms of the Sex Discrimination Act. Jean appealed with support from the Equal Opportunity Commission. A year later the decision was overturned. The Law Lords said the abuse of Jean amounted to a 'sexual sword – unsheathed and used because the victim was a woman'. Jean Porcelli's complaint about sexual harassment was how it came to be recognized as a form of discrimination.

A complaint can make it possible for others to complain.

I suspect that many people living and working in the UK do not know about Jean Porcelli. Even when complaints lead to lasting change, they are not always remembered.

We can inherit the effects of complaints without knowing about them.

If Jean Porcelli's complaint changed policies, it came at an enormous cost to her. She suffered from severe stress that led to health conditions, which meant she was unable to return to her job. In a recent interview marking the anniversary of the complaint, she also spoke about the experiences of her daughter: 'My daughter suffered a similar problem a few years ago. She was really trapped because she knew she would find it hard to find any other work if she kicked up a fuss.' That Jean's complaint led to a change of policy did not make it any easier for her daughter to complain. We have to keep complaining, collectively, because of what has not stopped.

Feminism itself can be a complaint or many complaints – *a no* that is passed around or passed down. We can inherit the effects of complaint not just in changes to policies but in a fighting spirit. In my preface, I spoke of some of my early experiences as a wilful child who was taught, at home and at school, that authority meant the right to be wrong. I have always been interested in theorizing from how I have been judged; that is, after all, how I ended up making the feminist killjoy my assignment. So, having been called a wilful child, I began researching that figure. By following her around, I found a story, 'A Wilful Child', by the brothers Grimm. It is their shortest story, and it is rather grim:

> *Once upon a time there was a child who was wilful and would not do as her mother wished. For this reason, God had no pleasure in her, and let her become ill, and no doctor could do her any good, and in a short time she lay on her deathbed. When she had been lowered into her grave, and the earth was spread over her, all at once her arm came out again, and stretched upwards, and when they had put it in and spread fresh earth over it, it was all to no purpose, for the arm always came out again. Then the mother herself was obliged to go to the grave, and strike the arm with a rod, and when she had done that, it was drawn in, and then at last the child had rest beneath the ground.*[3]

The wilful child has a story to tell, short and snappy. She is disobedient; she will not do as her mother wishes. Wilfulness is a diagnosis of the failure to comply with those whose authority is given. The costs of such a diagnosis are high: through a chain of command (the mother, God, the doctors) the child's fate is sealed. It is ill-will that responds to wilfulness; the child is allowed to become ill in such a way that no one can 'do her any good'. The rod is an externalization of the mother's wish but also of God's command, which transforms a wish into will, a 'let it be done', thus determining what happens to the child.

The Grimm story is not a feminist story, let alone the story of a feminist complaint. And yet it captured more than my imagination, because of the arm, how it kept coming up before it was struck down. The word *complain* derives from Vulgar Latin *complangere*, originally meaning, 'to beat the breast', and shares a root with the word *plague*.[4] The arm, a rather striking image, is evocative of that plague. The arm inherits wilfulness from the child. Or perhaps the arm embodies her will, making a complaint on her behalf.

I first read the Grimm story whilst supporting the students who made a collective complaint about sexual harassment where I worked. I heard something of our struggles in the story, as have other people who shared their complaints with me.[5] Anne, who made a complaint about bullying, told me how reading about the wilful girl and her arm helped her to understand what happened to her: 'Reading of it was upsetting but at the same time it makes sense. They are hurting me because I am raising my arm.' One student, Poppy, wrote to me about her experience of publicly naming her harassers. She was forced to remove the posts. She said: 'I feel like the wilful child, the one in the Grimm fairy tale . . . the rod beating her down, beating her arm down, the arm still fighting to live, while the body is dead.

And then she rests. That wilful child is me. I had to get into a settlement. I had to remove the posts.'

We know about power from what follows raising our voices or arms. To share our complaints is to share lessons about power.

INSTITUTIONAL POWER

To say *no* to a person with institutional power can mean loss of access to institutional resources. Feminist scholars Leila Whitley and Tiffany Page point out that 'it is difficult to say no to a person who wields institutional power over you'.[6] We need complaint procedures precisely because of this difficulty. But when institutions give some people more power, they also give them the means to mobilize institutional resources – and that includes complaints procedures. The system designed to stop some people from abusing power can be used by them to abuse their power.

> **Power works by making it hard to challenge how power works.**

But what do we mean by power? It can be dramatic, like the rod that comes down on the wayward arm in the Grimm story. Power can also be full of drudgery; the long, slow time of becoming worn out or worn down; like the arm that ends up 'at rest beneath the ground', an image that associates rest with the end of resistance and even death. The Grimm story is part of a tradition that psychologist Alice Miller called 'poisonous pedagogy', methods for instructing children that assume they are stained by sin.[7] Remember that old saying, 'Spare the rod, spoil the child'.

Alice Miller's book is entitled *For Your Own Good*. The Grimm story is a reminder of how force was justified as an aid to the development of moral character. This is why the story remains relevant to contemporary institutions. Complainers are often treated as wilful children judged not only as obstinate but morally immature. We heard this judgement in Viola's testimony; her complaint was treated as her 'stamping her feet', as if by complaining she was losing her temper; her grievance a mere grudge. A trans student, Ray, said their complaint about transphobia in their department was received as if they were having 'some kind of tantrum for not getting [their] way' rather than 'being a fundamental issue about existence'. Anna and Rosie, in describing the very long meeting with their head of department, both said they felt like they were positioned as naughty children. Anna said, 'The line I really remember was "We are not going to leave until we get this sorted," because we were treated like five unruly girls who needing disciplining.' Rosie observed, 'I always felt they were treating us like siblings who were having an argument.'

The Grimm story is not just the story *of* a child, it is addressed *to* children or to any people assumed to be subordinate, to be lesser or lower, to come after or later, those who are supposed to receive and carry out instructions.

When the child in the story is punished, that punishment is a warning to others not to become her. Warnings are not just made to people who threaten to complain. They circulate 'out there' in public culture in the form of tragic stories of the disobedient and the morally wayward. They circulate within institutions in the form of sorry stories of complainers. One student, June, was in the middle of giving me her complaint biography, when she shared a story about another woman who had filed a complaint earlier only to become 'an outcast'. 'No one goes near her,' June said, adding, 'People told me the story. It is so difficult to get my head around because at the time I was so willing to go along with it. And now there I am, recognizing that if I were to move forward, I would likely be experiencing some of the same things she did.' A complainer can be a warning sign, embodying the danger of lost connections or a lost career. To complain can be to enter an unwilled proximity to those who have been cast out.

The Grimm story can thus be read as an institutional parable. If you disobey an instruction by complaining, the institution will do what it can to stop you or to cast you out (that relay of authority from colleagues to administrators, to managers, those who are willing to use the rods or to become them). An institutional parable is also a story of how power is distributed within an organization. Political theorists often contrast *power over* with *power to*.[8] *Power over* references how some people have power over others to the extent they can force them to do something against their will.[9] In contrast, *power to* is about one's capacity for action or being able to actualize one's own will. In the case of institutional power, *power over* is *power to*. In other words, some people have power because they control the resources necessary for other people to actualize their will. This is why doors matter. It is not just that to complain is to end up behind a door. Institutional power is about who 'holds the door' to the institution, in other words, who gets to determine for whom the door is opened or not.

To complain is to risk being locked out of a profession or programme. I talked to Andrea about her experience of complaining whilst studying for her master's degree. She had hoped to do a PhD. But after she complained, she said, 'that door was closed'. Andrea had entered the MA programme only to find the syllabus was not what she hoped for. The core course was taught by the most senior professor in the department. He 'left anyone who wasn't a white man essentially until the end of the course'. When she 'brought this up', he said, 'Well, last year there were no women on the syllabus, so be happy with what you get.' It turned out that he had only added women to the end of the course after students in previous years had complained.

Andrea became a complainer. During a tutorial with the professor about her essay, she told him she wanted to write it on gender and race. He replied, 'If you write on those fucking topics, you are going to fucking fail my course; you haven't fucking understood anything I have been talking about if you think those are the correct questions for this course.' If you ask the wrong questions, you hear the violence of correction. And then, he added, 'Wait, you know what, you're so fucking old, your grades don't really matter, you're not going to have a career in academia, so write whatever essay you wanted to write. You are going to fail, but it doesn't matter.' She heard herself be written off. A prediction can be a threat: he had the power to make sure she was 'not going to have a career in academia'.

Andrea went to the course convenor, a relatively junior lecturer, and told her what had happened. She received a warning: 'Be careful, he is an important man.' If warnings are how some people are told they are not important, they can also tell you who is important. Andrea went ahead with the complaint. By complaining, she 'sacrificed the references'. And that is when she said, regarding the prospect of doing a PhD, 'That door is closed.' References can function as doors, what you need to progress, how some people are stopped from progressing.

The one who says *no* ends up with nowhere to go.

Andrea understood that closed door as retaliation by the professor. Retaliation is against the law but hard to evidence. It can be about unopened doors, opportunities missed. It is hard to provide evidence of what is missing.

It is rather striking that Andrea used the language of sacrifice to describe her missing references. Complaints can be about what you are willing to give up, almost as if to complain is to shut the door on your own career. One of the main reasons people have given me for not complaining is, in fact, that they need the references. I introduced you earlier to Tanya, a student of colour who made a complaint about racism only to fulfil the expectation that she was a troublemaker. She was finding it hard to get into another programme, so she asked to see her references. She was shown one. The professor had written that she was 'good at transcribing data'. The reference did not mention Tanya's research, the awards she had received, or the classes she had taught. 'It was a very short and weak letter,' she concluded. Power can operate through a very light touch. You don't have to refuse to write a reference, just make it 'short and weak'.

Power can be enacted in a positive register as the power not only to say *yes* but to make that *yes* stronger or weaker. This is why powerful people often represent themselves as being benevolent and generous. They might stress what they can do for more junior people, as if they hold the keys, can open door after door. They don't necessarily need to hold the keys to convince other people they do. I had an informal conversation with Lou, who was harassed by her supervisor. She said that whenever she achieved something (such as getting a good mark on an essay or funding for her project), her supervisor implied 'It had something to do with him.' People can become more influential by the mere *implication* they already are, as if any or every opening is another debt. When an open door is a debt, or at least implied to be one, it can be used as a threat: that the door will be shut if you do not do what they want you to do.

To have institutional power means you don't need to

issue any such threats yourself but can rely on other people to make them on your behalf. So, in Andrea's case, it was not the 'important man' himself who warned her not to complain. It was a relatively new and junior lecturer. She might already be indebted to him for giving his support to her appointment or she might anticipate being indebted to him in the future, to give her a positive reference so she can be promoted. The warning she issued to Andrea, 'be careful; he is an important man,' might be one she had received herself.

A door can be a deal: the lecturer might have closed the door on Andrea's complaint to keep that door open for herself. And not just herself: she was also keeping the door open for the 'important man', so he could keep doing what he had been doing, where he had been doing it, behind closed doors. Behind many an institutional door, you will find such a deal.

It is not surprising, then, that the effort to stop someone complaining about those given importance can involve so many different people. Andrea herself watched her whole department fall into line 'to protect the professor'. She said she received 'solidarity' from one tutor, when they happened to meet 'on the stairs'. But the next day this tutor asked to speak on the phone so Andrea 'wouldn't have a record of it in writing' and basically told her she had no grounds for complaint. Andrea said she 'sounded scared' and concluded someone had 'got to her'. Andrea felt sympathy for the tutor; she understood she was just 'trying to protect her precarious position', and that she had been 'set up to throw students under the bus'. Even when protection is achieved through coordinated actions, it does not mean they are all performed voluntarily.

Protection can sometimes be about what people don't know. I spoke to Lily, a student, who had been sexually harassed by a senior man in her department, another 'important man'. She sought advice from a lecturer who said she could not 'do anything' because 'she did not know enough'. The lecturer did not take any time to find out more from Lily about what was going on: Lily said she was hurried out of her office. She was probably shutting more than her office door. I suggested earlier that when you complain and nothing happens, nothing is an achievement. 'Not knowing enough' can also be an achievement. It is not just that some people don't do anything because they don't know enough. It is that they don't listen *because they don't want to know any more*.

The doors that keep so much in the shadows are used by institutions, and some people in them, to obscure what is being done and by whom. There is a profound investment in things remaining unclear. But this lack of clarity can be superficial. When workplace abuses come out, it is common for people to say it was 'an open secret'. An open secret is information that people know without it ever being officially disclosed. Some people manage to protect abusers by keeping that abuse as secret from themselves as they possibly can, doing their best not to know the full extent of it. That's how people can be shocked by a Weinstein whilst participating in the very culture that created him.

When 'important men' are brought down, it becomes clear *that power does not reside in just one person, magically, as a possession*. It becomes clear that every Weinstein has an army of assistants, giving that person access to other people whose careers are made dependent on saying *yes*. We learn that those who said *no*, who refused or complained, were likely silenced by another army, including of lawyers, through secret deals, sealed by NDAs. The more other people *invest* in a person, the more power that person acquires, but a power that can appear distributed or even diffused.

To be important is to be protected on other people's behalf. Some people stop themselves from going down because of many other people would go down with them. Institutions might justify protecting that person as a form of *damage control*. That's a term typically used in emergency situations. A ship might be at risk of sinking perhaps as a result of a rupture of a pipe or hull below the waterline. You stop the ship from going down by locking off the damaged area from the ship's other compartments. That's where the data of complaint ends up, in the locked-off area. Actor and activist Amber Heard offers an illuminating description of a powerful man as a ship, 'like the *Titanic*'. She explains, 'That ship is a huge enterprise. When it strikes an iceberg, there are a lot of people on board desperate to patch up holes – not because they believe in or even care about the ship, but because their own fates depend on the enterprise.'[10] An institution can be that ship, sometimes easily confused with a person. Some people keep themselves afloat, doing what they are asked to do, patching up this hole or that, to stop themselves from sinking, the whole thing from sinking, issuing the same warnings they've received.

LOYALTIES AND LEGACIES

Institutional culture is also about creating the right kind of people, those who are willing to protect the institution when called upon to do so. My action of disclosing information about the inquiries into sexual harassment (not patching up a hole but using it to release information) was perceived as not just damaging but disloyal. In other words, it wasn't just the disclosure that was the problem; it was my attitude.

One time, I was milling about in the hallway of the college's main administrative building with students from the Feminist Postgraduate Forum. A senior administrator came up to me. She said something like, 'Sara, there is another side to the story.' She was not referring to the complaints about sexual harassment. She was referring to the case of Bahar Mustafa, who had been targeted by the press mainly for daring to organize an event for Black and brown students.[11] The college's PR team had responded as if members of the press and public were making legitimate criticisms, failing to back up Bahar and other students of colour. The administrator knew I was angry about the college's response; just as she knew I was angry about how they were handling the sexual harassment cases by keeping a lid on the inquiries.

I knew what she meant by 'another side of the story'. She was going to be justifying the college's actions by making the students the problem, again. I turned away. She then grabbed my shoulder, her fingers pulling my sleeve. I did not say anything but pulled away firmly, even forcefully. When I think back to that moment, I still feel emotional. It was a turning point, even if I did not realize it at the time. I was not going to be pulled into discourse with the administration any more. I was not going to be pulled away from the students. Instead, I turned towards them. That's been my direction ever since.

What is being set by this scene? Loyalty can be how we are pulled in by an institution so that we see things from its point of view, feel its ups and downs as our own. It can begin with a directive: come this way. It might be a slow process, one that is hard to notice, of gradually being encouraged to express loyalty to the institution by the direction we take, especially in emergency situations, when there is a risk to institutional legacy.

Let's return to Emma, who did not complain because of how the institution was treated as a legacy project. She implied that to complain would be to confirm your status as a *newbie*. In other words, if you are not loyal to legacy, it was 'because you had not been there for ten years'. The complainers would be those who had not yet internalized the norms of the institution, those for whom the project of the institution has not yet become their own. Emma didn't complain even though she hadn't internalized the project of the institution. She didn't complain because she did not want to stand out any more than she already did as one of only two brown people in a mainly white department.

Not complaining about problems does not make them go away, although complaining about them does not always make them go away either. And, because the problems did not go away, Emma decided to leave for another post. Her colleague of colour left at the same time. She submitted a resignation letter, in which she made her complaint about how racism and sexism were part of the institution: 'After we resigned, they said we were the wrong kind of people. This is the two brown people in the department of around fifty people.' Being the wrong kind of people is used to explain and deflect that complaint. When some complaints are dismissed as coming from people who are too new to abide by, or respect, an institutional legacy, other people will be dismissed as complainers no matter how long they have been in an institution.

When institutions are treated as legacy projects, we are being told they belong to some people, those assumed to come first or who assume they come first. A legacy can be what is passed on to those who come after or later, those who are willing to receive it or deemed capable of doing so.

I spoke to Samia, a woman of colour academic, who filed a complaint about academic misconduct against a postgraduate student who had plagiarized her work. Samia received a four-page letter from 'the interrogation committee' (yes, that is what it was called), asking her questions about her work. She asked a friend, a legal expert, to read the letter. Her friend came back to her and said, 'You basically have to defend why you should not have had this happen to you, despite all the evidence.' Samia had complained about plagiarism, but she ended up 'the person to be investigated'. Why? The student who plagiarized Samia's work was supervised by a senior white man in her department, another 'important man', no doubt. Ideas are assumed to be passed down a line from a professor to his student. When Samia, a relatively junior woman of colour, claimed misconduct against a white man professor's student, she crossed that line.

When Samia complained about plagiarism, she was given a lesson in legacy, questioned whether her ideas were worth taking. I am reminded of that scene in *A Question of Silence*, which first inspired the idea of feminist ears, when a secretary sits in silence as a man is congratulated by other men for saying what she said. Silence can be thick with unspoken complaints. Plagiarism is an old *feminist complaint* because of how women have had to voice our complaints to stop having our ideas be attributed to others. It might also be an old feminist-of-colour complaint, given how women of colour are often treated as secretaries, 'good at transcribing data' (to borrow terms from Tanya's reference letter), rather than having ideas of our own.

When Andrea was warned not to complain about 'an important man', she too was being taught a lesson in legacy. An 'important man' has a legacy. Or perhaps he is one. But Andrea complained anyway, because she 'did not want other students to go through the same practice'. She recognized that, unless someone said *no*, other students would have to go through what she went through.

It can take a complaint not to reproduce a legacy.

In being warned not to complain, Andrea received another instruction, to be more positive about that professor, less critical, to complain less. Remember: to hear the sound of sexism is to hear with a feminist ear. Andrea was being told *not* to be a feminist ear. Sexism is received wisdom. It is not that the patriarch is wise, but you must receive his instruction as if he is so, taking whatever he says in. The warning given to Andrea used the word 'careful'. Being careful means becoming more conscious of the doors that could close if we do not smile in agreement. When the door is closed on Andrea's complaint, it is closed on Andrea. She will not be there, bringing to that institution what she might have brought to it, a critical questioning of how powerful people are acting, a refusal to benefit from an open door.

When those who try to stop a culture from being reproduced are stopped, a culture is reproduced.

This is what we can call a reproductive mechanism: those who are *more* likely to complain are *less* likely to progress within organizations. Warnings not to complain are part of a wider genre we typically call *career advice*, a set of positive instructions about how to go further in any given profession. I have talked to many people who were advised not to complain, not to be too critical of an institution, until later, when they had forged a path, become more established. The problem with later is that it usually comes too late.

> **What you are told you need to do to progress further or faster in a system reproduces the system.**

If you learn to speak the institutional language, you might end up speaking it too fluently. And so, by the time you have permission to be critical of the institution, you might have lost the capacity or will to be so. Maybe that's the institutional hope. And when you speak the institution's language to maximize your chances of getting more resources from the institution, you might have to keep using that language to protect those resources.

Power can be offered in a promise, say yes and receive more. The Grimm story, with its brutal warning, might also contain a promise, *be willing and you will be spared*. To be willing is to experience a reduction of force. That's why power goes *with* the will and not just *against* it. When you are willing, your route through the institution is made easier. You do not need to be issued any further instructions. You might even be the person who issues them. Another way of describing this process is *professionalization*. Edward Said's description of professionalism remains ever pertinent: 'not rocking the boat, not straying outside the accepted paradigms or limits, making yourself marketable and above all presentable'.[12] Not rocking the boat is about much more than not complaining; it is about increasing your value to the institution by accepting its paradigms and limits.

We often learn what it means to be professional when we fail to accept these paradigms and limits. When I shared information in public that there had been inquiries into sexual harassment where I worked, a feminist colleague wrote me a strongly worded email. She said my actions were 'rash' and 'unprofessional', and that they would cause 'a fall-out which damages us all now and in the future'. I have been calling myself an unprofessional feminist ever since!

My colleague also suggested that, rather than sharing information in public, I 'should have called a meeting with women professors'. I had already called many meetings about the problem of sexual harassment, although I did not restrict invitations to women professors. The recommendation was really about dealing with the problem 'in house', by doing the same things we were already doing in our professional lives (meetings and more meetings). Perhaps in being told I should have called 'a meeting with other women professors' I was also being told that *as* a woman professor my loyalty should have been to other women professors. Maybe that is another way my arm was being pulled.

We might assume speaking out about sexual harassment is part of the job description for feminists. I have learnt to give up that assumption. Feminists who distance themselves from *feminist complaints*, or at least those that implicate their own institutions in wrongdoing, are more likely to be resourced by institutions. Silence might be how some women achieve or preserve seniority. I am probably describing how liberal feminism functions, institutionally.

When dealing with problems internally protects the institution, it also protects colleagues or at least some of them. I don't think the recommendation that we deal with problems 'in house' is intended to protect colleagues who have had complaints made against them *specifically*. But *that* is the consequence. Sometimes we are asked, nay expected, to make that our intent, to protect colleagues when complaints are made against them. We might be requested to write them character references to support their defence against a complaint without even being told what it was about. I have read many such letters by good colleagues or about them. Just one example. On 4 February 2022, an article appeared in the *Harvard Crimson* stating that thirty-eight professors at Harvard University had signed a letter in support of the anthropologist John Comaroff after he was sanctioned for violating the university's policies on professional and sexual conduct.[13] He is described in the letter as an 'excellent colleague, advisor and committed university citizen', as if being an excellent colleague or citizen is evidence that a person has not abused their power.

In time, we learn what it means to be a good colleague or how to be one. Good colleagues perform actions that demonstrate their allegiance to a shared project. Good colleagues would not complain about their colleagues. The actions that protect those who abuse power derive from what are commonly understood as institutional virtues or even moral character. In other words, you would write these letters *because* you are loyal, collegial, part of the team, committed to a shared project, and so on.

Institutions can operate rather like families, with ties that bind. Beatrice, a lecturer, was considering whether to make a complaint after a colleague shouted abuse at her in the school office: 'So I went to the head of school and I said this happened, and she said, "You know, [he] is like the naughty uncle of the school. That's just how he is, you just have to let it go."' There is a kind of familial fatalism in operation here: as if every institution, like every family, has their version of a 'naughty uncle', and you have to accept that behaviour because that is what families are like and that is what families do. To be loyal is show that you are willing to accept the abuse or to excuse it.

I talked to Mia, a senior lecturer, who had been bullied by her head of department. She had been to her union, who had advised her to leave any meeting in which he displayed this behaviour. During one meeting, he began shouting at her. She tried to leave. 'So, then he started to yell, and I stood up . . . You go out of the office and then to the left is a little passageway to the door. So, I went up to the front door and it has two locks that you have to turn in two different directions, and I had all my bags on me, and then up behind me came a pair of hands, and they pulled my hands off the lock . . . He sort of wrapped his arm around me and so I was constrained with my arms by my sides. I thought, I don't know what to do . . . I thought, if I try to go to the front door he may grab me again.' The lock turns in two different directions; it is hard to know which way it turns, which way to turn. And then, the hands come up, pulling her hands off the lock. The lock becomes a hand, or a hand a lock, stopping her from getting out.

Mia did get out, but it was hard. She decided to make a formal complaint. The head of department was suspended during an inquiry. But then he was cleared of wrongdoing and kept his position as head of department. Mia was asked to move to a different department (and eventually did). She was called 'uncollegial'. While she was called uncollegial for complaining about a physical assault, the assault itself was not called uncollegial. Collegiality only protects *some* colleagues. In fact, collegiality might even be how harm to other colleagues is overlooked or even justified; other colleagues become bad colleagues or noncolleagues. You don't have to be moved to another department to become a noncolleague, though it helps.

How was the head of department cleared? There are clues in the report written by the head of the inquiry. The head of department is described as having 'a direct style of management', as if being physically violent is like blunt speech, being rough a way of expressing himself. When harassment is treated as speech, it can be protected as free speech. What about the assault itself? It was described in the report as 'on par with a handshake'. On par with a handshake, on par equals equal. A physical assault is turned into a friendly greeting.

When I listened to Mia, I remembered Viola's reference to 'windows with blinds that come down'. Description can be a blind. The violence of an action is removed by how it is described. It is not that the violence is not seen because the blinds are down. The blinds come down because the violence is seen. To complain can be to see the blind come down, how what is seen is unseen. Maybe that is why there is such clarity in complaint, and why clarity can be so jarring, to allude back to Darcy's testimony.

Consider again the drama of the Grimm story. Sometimes the drama disappears, and the rod with it, through the drudgery. That is why the banality of administration matters. We can extend the range of actions that fall under the heading *administrative violence*. It can reference not only the violence directed against those who complain, but how evidence of that violence is removed from the paperwork or by it. Legacies are protected, the paper kept shiny, by removing complaints from the official records. Papering over is how people don't have to see what they are doing by doing it.

POLICING THE CRITIC

We might have to be disloyal to institutions, to have the wrong attitude, to peel off that paper, showing what lies underneath, the violence that has not been dealt with. Earlier I referred to Amber Heard's image of a powerful person as being like a big ship, whose career is patched up by many different people, keen to keep their own careers afloat. She offered this image in an op-ed with the title, 'I spoke up against sexual violence – and faced our culture's wrath: That has to change'.[14] Heard observes that when she became 'a public figure representing domestic abuse', she felt 'the force of our culture's wrath for women who speak out.' Heard did not name Johnny Depp in her piece, but he famously filed a defamation case against her for it. His defamation case succeeded. The whole episode seemed to demonstrate the truth of Heard's point about the 'force of our culture's wrath' directed against women who speak out.

Killjoy truths can be confirmed by the consequences of articulating them. You speak *of* the wrath that follows speaking out and wrath follows. Reporter Bryce Court suggests that #MeToo led to 'a quiet but effective legal backlash': 'The accused have turned around and sued their accusers, effectively silencing them.'[15] Another reporter, Ali Medina, describes how survivors are silenced by 'bringing or threatening to bring defamation suits'.[16] If #MeToo changed the atmosphere, making speaking out about sexual harassment more possible and more powerful, it brought with it ever more public demonstrations of retaliation. Retaliation for speaking truth to power is not new. As I pointed out earlier, retaliation is common but hard to evidence. Retaliation can sometimes be *purposefully evidenced*, made spectacular or turned into theatre.

You can police the critics by making examples of at least some of them, punishments issued as warnings to others. That policing can happen in public, but it can also be achieved through the complaint apparatus itself, which, as a communication and technical network, extends beyond a specific organization. To make a complaint is to *call in*, you send an alert by speaking to such-and-such person or persons, perhaps located in HR, about such-and-such person or persons. Many different materials go through the apparatus along with complaints themselves, including the kinds of letters I referred to earlier, written in support of people who have had complaints made against them. These letters might follow on from phone conversations: it just takes one person to indicate they might complain about 'an important man' to hear phone lines becoming busy, loans called in; buzz, buzz.

The more we speak out about sexual and institutional violence, the more the complaint apparatus will be used against us. After feminist barrister Charlotte Proudman complained about 'the boys' club attitude' in the legal profession, over one hundred complaints were made against her to the regulatory body, the Bar Standards Board (BSB). She describes not just the number of complaints but how they were incited: 'Following some barristers' calls for complaints about me, an incel wearing a frightening mask produced a video last year with a step-by-step guide of how to complain about me to my regulatory body, chambers and the university where I teach. In a matter of minutes, people fired off dozens of sickening complaints, accusing me of misandry and radical extremist views.'[17] The communication network was indeed busy; people were told not only to complain but how to do so quickly. You don't need to have seen that 'incel in a frightening mask', to know that these complaints were intended to intimidate Charlotte into silence. Although the complaints did not succeed, she has had to live with them, and not just while they were being investigated.

Harassment can be the incitement to complain about those who complain about harassment.

Whether we send complaints into the system, or make complaints about the system, complaints come back at us. Complaints made in response to complaints are typically called *counter-complaints*. I communicated informally with a lecturer, Holly, who made a complaint against a colleague for academic misconduct and bullying. 'He systematically undermined me at work,' Holly reported, 'including removing me and my academic ownership from a research council project we had won together.' She decided to make a formal complaint when she found out that a number of students were putting in complaints against him for sexual misconduct and bullying. He submitted a counter-complaint against Holly, stating she 'had bullied him'. And it was his countercomplaint that got uptake.

'I think what's interesting in my case is the way that the Equalities Act was leveraged against me (e.g. he claimed I was the bully),' she observed. 'The fluffy terminology of university policies (if they feel upset, it is bullying) was used to his favour here: e.g. being made responsible or called out on your behaviour obviously is upsetting (like a gender equivalent of white fragility) and it makes it so easy to flip victim and offender. He went off work sick with depression and anxiety, which was used as 'proof' of how my bullying affected him (rather than the fact that he was depressed and anxious about having multiple women file complaints about him – the emotional impact of which for him doesn't make the complaints wrong). It was like his distress was worth so much more than mine, because mine were cheap female emotions. The whole thing felt so misogynistic.'

Although multiple complaints were made against him, each complaint was treated as an individual unit of expression. So, the pattern was not seen. And his own individual complaint was upheld. Power is also the ability to influence how we are received. When some people matter more, their feelings matter more ('his distress was worth so much more than mine'). The means available to us to challenge abuses of power from complaint procedures to anti-discrimination policies, to equality policies, to the very language of harm and oppression, can be used to extend that abuse.

A bully with a complaint procedure is a bully with another weapon.

An institution can be that bully, making a weapon out of a complaint procedure. On 11 January 2025, law professor Katherine Franke announced in a public statement that her employment at Columbia University had been terminated.[18] Franke had supported the rights of students to protest 'the Israeli government's genocidal assault on Palestinians after the October 2023 attacks'. She explained she 'truly believed that student engagement with the rights and dignity of Palestinians continued a celebrated tradition of student protest at Columbia University', but that 'instead, the university has allowed its own disciplinary process to be weaponized'.

In her statement, Franke shows how internal disciplinary processes were used alongside techniques of surveillance: 'Colleagues in the law school have videotaped me without my consent and then shared it with right-wing organizations outside the law school. I have had students enrol in my classes with the primary purpose of creating situations in which they can provoke discussions that they can record, post online and then use to file complaints against me with the university.' She claims her own institution failed to correct a Congresswoman who had misrepresented her comments in a hearing in April 2024, even though, in her view, they knew these comments were 'grossly inaccurate and misleading'.

I suggested earlier that when people disobey an instruction by complaining, the institution will do what it can to stop them, with a relay of authority from colleagues to administrators, to managers, who are willing to use rods or to become them. When institutions try to render certain viewpoints illegitimate (such as anti-Zionism or criticism of Israel or 'critical race theory'), complaints can be how they stop those views from being expressed, with that relay of authority extended from colleagues, administrators and managers to media and government, who are willing to use rods or to become them.[19]

When complaints are sometimes stopped to protect an institution, they can also be made to protect it. The complaint apparatus can operate rather like Neighbourhood Watch programmes, in which neighbours are invited to become 'the eyes and the ears' of the police by reporting suspicious activity. After 11 September 2001, Neighbourhood Watch was turned into a national programme: members of the public were encouraged to report anything or anybody 'suspicious' to the police to counter the threat of terrorism.[20]

Some people are more likely to be seen as suspicious. Samia, the woman of colour who complained about plagiarism only to end up 'the person to be investigated', described the complaint apparatus as a 'tripwire'. Your complaint sounds an alarm or alert, a beep, beep, as if announcing an intruder.

When people of colour complain, the eyes and ears of the police often end up on us. That's true even for people of colour who are the police. On Wednesday, 15 April 1998, DS Gurpal Singh Virdi was arrested 'on the spot' for 'sending racist messages to ethnic minority colleagues at Ealing Police Station'. The police then raided his house for over seven hours. 'It all seemed so surreal,' he said. 'Are they really expecting to find racist hate mail in a bag of lentils?'[21] The previous year, Virdi, along with eleven other Black and minority ethnic colleagues, had received a letter in their pigeonholes with an image of a Black man accompanied by the message, 'Not wanted. Keep the police force white or else.' The initials NF (National Front) were printed in the corner. So, Virdi was accused of sending fascist and racist messages to himself as well as to his colleagues.

How did this happen? The raid itself was authorized by Deputy Commissioner John Stevens. A few weeks beforehand, Virdi had raised concerns about Stevens's investigation of a near-fatal stabbing of two boys of colour by five white men. As journalist Paul Foot describes, 'Mr Virdi complained to his superiors that the attack had not initially been classified as racist (as it eventually was).'[22] Virdi's complaint that the attack was not classified as racist was itself a complaint about racism in the police handling of the case. It is worth noting that the very concept of 'institutional racism' had come out of the investigation of the police handling of the murder of Black teenager Stephen Lawrence five years earlier. Virdi went from complaining about racism to being accused of racism not much later. He had his own explanation for why: 'As soon as you raise your head above the parapet, your career is finished, and everyone in the police service knows that.'

By complaining, Virdi ended up under interrogation for what he had complained about. So 'the eyes and the ears' of the police landed on him; the police certainly policed their critic. In 2002, Virdi was successful in bringing a racial discrimination case against the London Metropolitan Police. And then in 2007, he won a victimization claim after repeatedly being passed over for promotion.[23] But although Virdi returned to his post, and received an apology from the Deputy Commissioner, his career was over and he retired early. It was not only his own complaint that was decisive in determining this outcome. The letter sent to Black and brown officers could itself be called a racist complaint, one that came with a clear instruction, to protect an institution by keeping it white. The act of retaliation against a brown officer who complained about racism *fulfilled that instruction*.

Institutions protect themselves not only by blocking some complaints, or removing those who make them, but by the speed with which other complaints travel. Complaints by valued donors, for instance, are much more likely to bypass the slow administrative processes I called institutional plumbing, going straight to heads of organizations or to the tops of piles. Take the decision by Oriel College, Oxford, in 2016 not to remove the statue of slave-trader Cecil Rhodes despite the many successes of the Rhodes Must Fall Campaign. At the time, they offered a weak rationale for the decision. It was later reported that donors had threatened to withdraw gifts and bequests worth more than £100 million.[24]

The speed with which some complaints travel is not simply or only about how institutions protect their investments. We can return to 'Sally in HR', introduced by Kelechi Okafor. Sally is the one who receives complaints. Sally might be called by 'Karen', whom you are probably familiar with, a name given to a white woman who complains. As American scholar André Brock notes, the Karen meme comes especially from Black Twitter (now X) sharing videos of different Karens becoming a way of communicating feelings about 'the injustice of the situation'.[25] Brock points out that the Karen meme speaks to how whiteness became a project 'in need of defense or protection'. When Karen calls Sally in HR (or the police), complaining about Black or brown people, that complaint is more likely to get uptake because of how it participates in a belief system. We call that belief system *racism*. A belief system involves not just the content but the relaying of messages, a person calling *on* somebody with authority to protect them *from* someone else.

Journalist Pamela Paul wrote an article telling us not to 'call her Karen'. She was referring to the case of Sarah Patricia Comrie, named 'Citi Bike Karen' after she was videoed by a group of young Black men whilst she was shouting at them, claiming they were taking her bike. When I watched this video, it was obvious to me that Comrie was calling upon passers-by, using tears effectively and deliberately, to position herself as being harmed or potentially harmed by Black men who were 'taking her bike'. In entitling her article 'Don't call her Karen', Paul's redemptive purpose is clear. She presents Sarah sympathetically – giving her a name, a biography (her status as a healthcare professional), and a body (referencing her pregnancy). Paul does not give any such care or concern to the young Black men, who remain nameless and faceless. She talks about how being called Karen hurt Sarah. Of course, that is exactly why she is called Karen; she knows her hurt will be received sympathetically. Paul's conclusion: 'The choice for a white woman is stark: either not to have any complaints or to shut up about those that you do.'

White feminists have complained that they cannot complain about being called Karen without being called Karen. Helen Lewis writes, 'What is more Karen than complaining about being called "Karen"?'[26] Victoria Smith notes that, 'complaining about the use of Karen makes you a Karen.'[27] By making Karen into another complaint, white feminists avoid focusing on the reasons why Karen was called Karen in the first place: that she was making *a racist complaint*, a complaint that is so old and familiar that it tends not even to be heard as a complaint but as a statement or a report made by a responsible citizen, that Black people or people of colour have taken their bikes, their parks, their culture, are 'too loud' or 'too much'.[28] The same complaint apparatus designed to receive racist complaints quickly, as an alert of a danger *to* a complainer, treats complaints about racism as an alert of the danger posed *by* a complainer.

Some complaints travel further not just because of who makes and receives them, but because of whom they are made against. Take, for example the controversy surrounding the work of children's author Kate Clanchy. A quick summary: Clanchy made a complaint on social media about a review of her book *Some Kids I Taught and What They Taught Me* by a reader, posted on Goodreads. The review of the book was itself a complaint about its racist and ableist descriptions of children. Clanchy's tweet basically claimed the sentences quoted were not in her book. But they were. Clanchy was, in effect, encouraging other people to complain about a complaint, even though it was supported by the evidence of her own words. When other people also read that book and found the sentences quoted, she admitted that they were in the book and apologized. The book itself was pulled by one publisher but later republished by another.

Three women of colour, Sunny Singh, Chimene Suleyman and Monisha Rajesh, took the complaint further, showing how Clanchy's response to the original complaint first denied racism and then deflected it by treating it as a personal insult or injury. Clanchy's response to their complaints was to call them a campaign of harassment. Other people rushed to give her support, including writer Philip Pullman, who at the time was director of the Society of Authors. He described the complaints about Clanchy's work as 'policing the imagination', even evoking the Taliban, connecting the complaints and the women of colour who made them to terrorism as well as fundamentalism. Even though he later apologized, these associations stuck. As Rajesh observes, 'It's a familiar pattern: pointing out racist language is labelled "aggressive" and "instigating a pile-on".'

Numerous articles have since been published that present Clanchy as the victim of targeted harassment and cancel culture. 'No one is safe from the woke mob,' declared *Spiked* columnist Joanna Williams.[29] It was Clanchy who repeatedly got to tell the story, not just to make a complaint but to frame it; the person supposedly cancelled whose voice was amplified. I showed earlier that some harassment is defended as freedom by being treated as speech. The reverse is also true. Some speech is critiqued as censorship by being treated as harassment. Racism can be the sum of *that* difference. When we protest or complain about racism we are heard as restricting other people's speech rather than speaking for ourselves. I return to this conflation of some complaints with censorship, and how 'woke' functions as counter-complaint, in the next chapter.

A WILL TO POWER

Some people become the problem because they draw attention to the machinery of power whether by complaining internally or by speaking out publicly. When we critique power, we are often understood as having a 'will to power'.

Let's return to complaints about sexual harassment. Broadcaster and academic Aoibhinn Ní Shúilleabháin was told that if she reported her harasser she would 'damage his career'.[30] When some people complain, they are warned they will hurt not just their own career prospects but other people's. Researchers have shown that many women do not make formal complaints about sexual harassment even though they want the harassment to stop, because they do not want harassers to be 'punished' by losing posts or positions.[31] Those who abuse the power given to them by virtue of position are protected from consequences because of how complaints are treated as, or presumed to be, punitive.

Mariame Kaba, in her brilliant book *We Do This 'Til We Free Us*, differentiates punishment from consequences. For Kaba, punishment means 'inflicting cruelty and suffering on people'. In contrast, 'Powerful people stepping down from their jobs are consequences, not punishment. Why? Because we should have boundaries. And because shit that you did was wrong and you having power is a privilege. That means we can take that away from you. You don't have power anymore.'[32]

As we have been hearing, it is hard to take power away

from someone once they have it. I talked to Patricia, a professor, about her experience of supporting a collective of students who had made a complaint about the conduct of a lecturer in her department. 'A student, a young student, came and said to me that this guy had seduced her, basically,' she reported. 'And then, in conversation with another woman, she found out he had done the same to her. And then it snowballed, and then we found out there were ten women, he was just going through one woman after another after another after another.' The lecturer defended himself: 'He came up to me and said, "It's a perk of the job." I couldn't believe it. He actually said it to me. It was not hearsay; this is a perk of the job. I can't remember my response, but I was flabbergasted.' He was defending his abuse as an entitlement. Patricia added, 'The women: they were set up as a witch-hunt, hysterical, you can hear it, can't you, and as if they were out to get this guy.'

Being deprived of power is experienced by those with power as punishment.

The complainers are treated as being punitive simply because of how they could deprive other people of power. That is why those who abuse power often present themselves as being in a precarious position, as potentially losing their power. Power operates defensively, experienced not just as what some people *have* but as what could be *taken away*. Some people might *feel like an arm, act like a rod*.

The phrase 'a perk of the job' implies that having sex with your students is rather like having a company car, what you are entitled to because of who you are or what you do. In other words, students are treated as property, objects to be consumed. Objects are not supposed to speak, let alone complain. When students complain about abuse or call a conduct *abuse*, refusing to be somebody else's entitlement, they are quickly judged as being entitled or over-entitled themselves. So, when Andrea complained about the abusive behaviour of a professor, she was told she was 'being a very neoliberal person'. 'Maybe I am just a perfect neoliberal subject,' she commented. 'Or maybe I am a person who doesn't want to be abused.'

A number of students have told me they have been called neoliberal for complaining about sexual harassment and sexual misconduct by lecturers. It is worth pausing here and asking why. Political theorist Wendy Brown shows how neoliberalism operates as more than a set of economic policies on privatization and the deregulation of markets but as a 'governing rationality in which everything is economized', and which casts people as 'human capital who must constantly tend to their own present and future value'.[33] When students who complain about sexual harassment are called 'neoliberal', their complaints are treated as motivated by private concerns, the enhancement of 'their own present and future value'. Neoliberalism, turned from a governing rationality into a psychological profile, is easily confused with the person who refuses to accept abuse and who acts accordingly. In refusing to be consumed, students are treated as acting like consumers, their complaints complicit with the transformation of education into a marketplace.

I suspect calling complaints neoliberal is an effective technique for dismissing them simply because neoliberalism is generally viewed by those committed to education as a bad thing, undermining models of education as a public good. So many abuses of power, in which other human beings are treated as private possessions, disappear under the sign of the public good. I spoke to Jane, who made a complaint about a professor on her programme. The other students on the cohort agreed his conduct was abusive. But they still positioned her as selfish for complaining because 'their education was now being disrupted'. Complaints can be treated as causing disruption not only to the person who acted abusively but to those *who accepted the abuse as a condition of access*. When those who complain are set apart (or are understood to be setting themselves apart), collectivity is confused with compliance. Complainers are treated as individualistic as well as punitive: as if they are trying to hurt not just one person but many.

That 'many' can extend beyond colleagues or peers. When Asana, a lecturer, tried to complain about a colleague who had plagiarized her work (yes, that old *feminist complaint*), she said that her head of department kept reminding her, a lesbian, that '[he] had a wife and child.' It is assumed that if she were to complain she would be hurting not just him but his family. When women are discouraged from complaining, they are also encouraged to put 'the family' first, and not just their own. We might be encouraged to make some complaints, what cultural critic Lauren Berlant called *female complaints*,[34] moaning about love and loss, rather than *feminist complaints* that challenge authority or the ownership of ideas. Or it might be that *feminist complaints* are dismissed as *female complaints*, as if some of us only challenge authority or critique power because we are lonely or lost.

And yet, as we have already learnt, some feminists distance themselves from *feminist complaints*. They might do so by accepting the very framing of complaints as punitive. It is not just those who are deprived of institutional power (or potentially deprived of that power) who conflate consequences with punishment. A student, Millicent, told me about a complaint she made with other students about sexual harassment and sexual misconduct by a professor. After a long period of being blocked, the complaint finally got uptake, and a disciplinary procedure began. She was told by a feminist academic, 'They should have used restorative justice.' Millicent was disturbed by the lecturer's assumption that all the students would have had to do is talk to the professor for him to change his behaviour. The professor had, in fact, repeatedly refused to listen to students' complaints over many years. The suggestion that they 'should have used restorative justice' was how those who complained about the abuse were made responsible for it, as if the complaint was necessary because of what they had not done, rather than what he did.

My own view is that recommendations made by some feminists not to make formal complaints to deal with abuses of power are not far off from how organizations themselves offer informal solutions. It is a way of making light of the abuse. Hence 'restorative justice' is indexed rather weakly, rather like that 'cup of tea', a light and loose signifier of reconciliation. Philosopher Mary Peterson describes the problem very well: 'The trouble with restorative justice is that, short of profound cultural transformations, restoration too often looks like restoring the perpetrator back to the position that enabled the violence to occur in the first place.'[35]

In part because of how 'restorative justice' is used by the state and the criminal courts, feminists tend to use the language of 'transformative justice' to describe non-retribution models of justice centring on reducing harm and addressing the relationships that produce it. When I listened to a panel on transformative justice, one survivor said the language of transformative justice was 'misused' as 'a network of support' for her abuser. I understood exactly how that would happen. Journalist Moira Donegan describes how the 'tendency to condemn all forms of consequence or punishment for sexual violence' is often accompanied by a concern to avoid negative emotions such as anger.[36] There is an implicit instruction to survivors to forgive and repair rather than complain. But complaints are often made *because* those who act abusively refuse to recognize what they are doing. To appeal to transformative justice before perpetrators have recognized the harm they have caused, or without that recognition, would be a way of avoiding rather than demanding accountability, as well as recentring on the feelings of those who have caused harm.

We can return to Mariame Kaba's important distinction between punishment and consequences. Even though depriving people of institutional power is not punishment, it generally requires a commitment to an institutional process. And herein lies a difficulty. One of the main reasons people don't complain is because they don't trust institutions. They are concerned their complaints could be used by hostile management to justify decisions they themselves would not make. Damn it, I share this concern!

Those with power have a concerted interest in making institutions untrustworthy.

You can make a complaint without trusting the institution.[37] But then, when you make that complaint, it can be used as evidence that you not only trust the institution but are willing to give it more power. The students I worked with told me that they had been dissuaded from lodging complaints about sexual harassment by lecturers in their department because of how those complaints would be repurposed by senior management to close their department. The implication was that the university was trying to close the department because it was 'too radical' and that complaints would give them the means to do so. Many students dropped their complaints even though they objected to the conduct of their professors because they shared an allegiance to that radical project. Institutional loyalty is often not to an institution in an abstract sense but to a project that is hard to disentangle from that institution. For those who believe in a project, it is hard to do something that could threaten it.

One way some people abuse the power given to them by institutions is by entangling their projects with their institutions. They might still identify themselves as *against* the institution even when they are resourced by it. They might present themselves as mavericks, outlaws, transgressors of social and moral norms. They might also justify their own conduct – professors having sex with students, bosses with secretaries – as a refusal to comply with moral mandates. I have even heard of sexual misconduct justified as a commitment to equality as if it stems from a disbelief in hierarchies rather than being enabled by them. Yes, 'I will fuck anyone' can be expressed as if it is an equal opportunity policy.

I recognize the profile of radical sexual harassers from many stories shared with me. The film *Ginger and Rosa* (2012, dir. Sally Potter) explores this profile very well. Ginger's father is a radical. He wrote a book entitled *The Idea of Freedom*, speaks of autonomous thought and opposes marriage and convention. He ends up sexually exploiting young women, his students and Ginger's own best friend, Rosa. He fulfils a sexual and social norm under the guise of transgressing it. In the end, when his behaviour is exposed as harming others, including his daughter and his wife, he retains his self-identification as radical. He recalls his own history of disobedience, how he went to prison as a conscientious objector. Someone has to say 'no', he says. He says 'no' as if it describes, explains, even condones, his behaviour.

The transgression of the norm is how that norm is freely expressed. That 'no', then, is not really a no, but a *yes*.

A 'no' can sometimes be used as a screen. Another example: multiple complaints were made against a lecturer for sexual assault, domestic violence and sexual harassment. Despite the number and severity of the allegations, he was able to convince many of his colleagues that he was being unfairly targeted. I spoke informally to some of the women who made these complaints. A professor, Jules, said, 'His narrative was apparently that he was being accused of making sexist comments and the "feminazis" were out to get him.' Terms such as 'feminazis' will be familiar to feminists. We only need to consider how quickly #MeToo was framed in this way, as a persecution of innocent men by a feminist mob wielding power through accusation.

What was striking about this case was how his colleagues, including feminist colleagues, were convinced by his claim. 'Many colleagues,' Jules reported, 'about sixty-eight to seventy, came forward on his behalf to suggest that really, he was a "good guy", just a regular "northern cheeky chappie", maybe a bit of a rough diamond. They had no idea of what he was being accused of, other than what he offered up to them as his own narrative.' Sexual harassment is again treated as a manner or style of expression (we are back to that blunt speech). These descriptions, 'rough diamond', a 'northern cheeky chappie', seem to suggest that the complaints derived from a failure to appreciate how he was expressing himself, that they were perhaps a form of class prejudice. Marnie, a student from a working-class background described how enraging it was to be positioned as middle class, as if working-class women never complained, as if working-class women did not have their own militant feminist history and were not themselves instrumental in the battle to recognize sexual harassment as a hostile environment in the workplace in the first place.

We might assume feminists wrote letters on his behalf because that is what good colleagues do. But I think there is more going on. His explanation that complaints were used to discipline him for minor transgressions (such as how he was speaking) could easily be turned into a story of being disciplined by the institution itself (and not just the 'feminazis'). Feminist colleagues who had 'no idea of what he was accused of', might have found *that* story of an institution 'out to get him' rather more convincing because of their own experience of being targeted for speaking out or because of what they know about institutions.

Those who complain are treated as disciplinarians, trying to stop some people from expressing themselves freely. The Grimm story, as a story of discipline, created a rather clear and dramatic distinction between the arm and the rod. Within institutions, it can be hard to tell who is being disciplined by whom, in other words, who are the arms, and who are the rods. This is not just because, as I suggested earlier, some people might *feel like an arm but act like a rod,* experiencing power as what could be taken away by complaint, but because the arms and rods can switch places, reversing not just power but position. Those who abuse the power given to them by institutions pass themselves off as the arms, as the one's being beaten by a disciplinary regime.

I use the word *pass* deliberately here. To pass is to approximate something real. We have already heard how complaints can, indeed, be used as disciplinary techniques. It can be hard to tell the difference between those who are disciplined by institutions for dissidence and those who pass themselves off as being so. One article included a list of people who had been disciplined for 'not fitting' with institutional mandates because of their 'after-hours recreations' as well as 'political convictions'. In this list, a person who kept her job despite having a complaint about sexual harassment upheld against her is casually positioned next to a Palestinian academic left unemployed after a university used complaints about his criticisms of Israel to justify a withdrawal of a job offer.[38] Sexual harassers are positioned (or position themselves) as if they are critics of the institution, threatened with the loss of posts and positions because of their 'political convictions'.

When those who abuse the power given to them by institutions pass themselves off as the arms, the complainers become the rods, the managers, the police and the prison guards. This helps to explain why some people who complain formally about sexual harassment are called *carceral feminists* even though complaining within organizations does not involve calling the police or sending people to prison.[39] That the complainer is called a carceral feminist can be a measure of how passing succeeds; the arm and rod have switched places. I suggested earlier that the violence brought out by a complaint is often papered over. That violence then reappears *as if it originates with the complaint itself.* That's how raising your arm to protest violence comes to be seen as enacting violence. That's how those who challenge abuses of power come to be judged as abusers of power.

It can be rather clear who has power within institutions, who can open and close doors, controlling access to resources. But when those who abuse the power given to them by institutions pass themselves off as being disciplined by institutions, power is obscured.

Power works by making it unclear who has it.

To change that system, we have to learn to see it. That's a complaint: the feminist pedagogy we need.

4/ Complaint as Diversity Work

Margaret Price begins her book on how institutions fail to be accessible with a powerful statement about what disabled people know. She calls it a litany. Also, a rant. We could call it a complaint.

> We know what kind of handle the door has. If the door is unlocked, we know how heavy it will be. We know what the room where we're going looks like, and we know how to ask – with charm and deference – if we need the furniture rearranged, the fluorescent lights turned off, the microphone turned on. We know how much pain it will cost to remain sitting upright for the allotted time. We know how to keep track of the growing pain, or fatigue, or urge to urinate (there's no accessible bathroom), and plan our exit with something resembling dignity. We know what no one else will ever know.[1]

Price shows how disabled people's knowledge of institutions covers so many details, from the heaviness of a door handle to the length of a meeting. When complaints are necessary, so too is knowledge: disabled people need to know these details to do their work, to get in or get by and, if necessary, to get out. That knowledge is practical: you might also need to know whom to ask (and how to ask) to make changes – for the furniture to be rearranged or the lights turned off or the windows opened to let in more air. That knowledge can be exhausting: you constantly need to monitor the situation, including your own body.

That some people have to work harder to be accommodated by institutions teaches us whom they are built for. You come to know whom institutions are *for* when you are *not* whom they are for. Consider the signs that indicate accessible doors. Tanya Titchkosky explains that if you have to use a sign to indicate access, 'there must be an assumption of a general lack of access.'[2] You can look at a building and likely see some of the modifications made to render it more accessible. Jay Timothy Dolmage describes these modifications as 'retrofitting', for instance, having new ramps placed alongside old stairs.[3] Retrofitting teaches us not only that institutions need to change to become accessible but that they can.

In my book *What's the Use? On the Uses of Use*, I used an image of a postbox that has become a nest as an example of what I call *queer use*; how things can be used in ways that were not intended or by those for whom they were not intended.[4]

The birds turn the postbox into a nest. The postbox can only become a nest if it stops being used as a postbox; hence the sign 'Please do not use the box' addressed to would-be posters of letters. This image is a rather happy and hopeful one. Mostly, to enter spaces that are not intended for us, we need to do more than just turn up. By 'need to do more', I

Queer use.

am referring to diversity work. Diversity work is the work some people have to do in order to be accommodated by institutions. It can also be the work we do to change institutions so they can accommodate more people.

DIVERSITY WORKERS

A common way of referring to diversity work today is through acronyms, typically EDI (equality, diversity and inclusion) in the UK and DEI (diversity, equality and inclusion) in the US. Both terms are used to describe policies that promote the representation and participation of people of different ages, races, ethnicities, abilities, disabilities, genders, religions, cultures and sexual orientations within organizations.[5]

These acronyms have acquired a life of their own and are increasingly used in stigmatizing ways. In the US, it is almost impossible to talk about DEI without hearing how it has become associated with danger, even death. Especially since Donald Trump began his second term as US president in January 2025, DEI has been blamed for anything and everything, from the weakening of the economy, to the loss of rights and freedoms, to plane crashes and fatal fires. Pronouncements of 'death by DEI' are about more than speech. Institutions have been threatened with the loss of funding, or with being disbanded, unless they complied by removing evidence of DEI commitments. Journalist Judith Levine called DEI a 'capacious euphemism', which in the 'Right parlance' does not stand 'for the policy or the program' but the people it is assumed are being served, 'people of colour, queer people, people with disabilities'.[6] Removing commitments to DEI has even meant the erasure of evidence that such groups of people lived and fought and died.[7]

The attacks on the very principles of diversity, equality and inclusion did not come out of nowhere. And nor are they specific to the US. In 2024, Esther McVey, who had the unofficial portfolio of 'minister of Common-Sense', in the previous Conservative government in the

UK, announced a 'ban' on jobs in EDI in the civil service, describing them as 'woke hobby horses'.[8] Since 2024, many powerful multinational companies (including tech companies Meta and Google) have announced cuts to their EDI/DEI programmes, thereby handing us evidence that their previously stated commitments to equality were at best superficial. I am not sure we needed this evidence. Nor do I think we should start with it. As diversity workers, we gather our own evidence about the nature or extent of commitments to equality. That way we can ask whether there is any relationship between commitments to change and actual change, rather than assuming there is one.

I undertook a study of diversity, based on interviewing practitioners in the early 2000s, well before EDI became the main framework.[9] I began the research at a time when more diversity practitioners were being appointed within public sector organizations in the UK as a result of changes in legislation that redefined equality as a positive duty. Organizations had to do more than prevent discrimination. They had to promote equality – and evidence how they were doing so. This change required the development of new equality policies and action plans.

Many of the practitioners I interviewed were appointed to write these new policies. And many offered strong critiques of, even complaints about, the term *diversity* itself. One practitioner, Ella, was so suspicious of the term that she refused to use it on her business card, even though it was officially in her job title. She explained, 'So now we'll talk about diversity and that means everybody's different but equal and it's all nice and cuddly and we can feel good about it and feel like we've solved it, when actually we're nowhere near solving it.'

Diversity can be how institutions feel good by appearing to have solved a problem without solving it. Ella understood the use of diversity as *how* institutions resisted being changed. Diversity is used more because it does less. And yet, changing institutions was part of Ella's job description as a diversity and equality officer.

When institutions appoint people to change them, it does not mean they are willing to be changed.

Ella described her job as 'a banging-your-head-against-a-brick-wall job'. A job description becomes a wall description. When the wall keeps its place, you end up rather sore. And what would happen to the wall? All you seem to have done is scratch the surface. And that is what diversity work often feels like: you are scratching the surface or 'scratching away at something', to evoke Viola's 'little bird'. For those who are not trying to change institutions, that wall does not appear. The organization might seem as open as its mission statement, as happy as its diversity statement.

It is not just those who are appointed as diversity officers who end up doing diversity work. Anyone from a group that is historically under-represented might be called upon to do so. You might end up on the front of the organization's brochures, allowing organizations to appear more diverse than they actually are. I know of many people who had to complain about being used to brand organizations in this way. Educational scholar Heidi Mirza captures the labour of that complaint about diversity very well. She explains, 'Visual images of "colourful" happy faces are used to show the university has embraced difference. My "happy" face appeared on the front of the university website – even though every week I asked for it to be taken down, it still kept popping up.'[10]

Some of us are assumed to bring diversity with us as if doing diversity just requires being it. But to be diversity, or to embody it, is work. You might be asked to be on the diversity committee. We are often invited to be on diversity committees because of who we are not: not white, not cis, not straight, not able-bodied.

The more nots we are, the more committees we end up on.

Since I was first appointed to a race equality committee back in 2000, and as long as I was employed by a university, I was never not on a diversity committee. It can be frustrating that some of us and not others are asked to be on diversity committees, especially when the work of these committees tends to be less valued than that of other kinds of committees. I rather liked diversity committees because I tended to have more interesting conversations in them with people that I found more interesting. I was less likely to be the only brown person on these committees.

I still understand why doing diversity work can feel like collusion. When diversity is how organizations can appear to be doing something, *we end up implicated in that appearance*. So, what do we do? We might bring our complaints *to* the diversity committee. And what happens, then? I talked to Shazia, a woman of colour, about her experience of being on such a committee. She said, 'I was on the equality and diversity group in the university. And as soon as I started mentioning things to do with race, they changed the portfolio of who could be on the committee, and I was dropped.' Just say the word *race* and you will be heard as complaining, as being negative or destructive or obstructive. When she is dropped, so too is that word, so too is that work.

If we are not supposed to use words like *race* on a diversity committee, it is not surprising that embodying diversity can make it harder to complain. I spoke to another woman of colour, Rohina, a postdoctoral researcher, about her experience of racial discrimination. She was hired as part of a diversity programme. And she knew that the programme was precarious: 'I don't want to do something that is going to threaten a programme that is supposed to diversify the faculty.' She used the term *coercive diversity* for how the university wanted to make use of her body and her research as evidence of its commitments whilst undermining her. Rohina described her own task as 'chipping away at the foundations of white supremacy. I am trying to chip away at it with my fingernails.'

Banging your head against the wall, chipping away at the foundations: these descriptions are clues as to how the work of diversity becomes the work of complaint. In her important article 'Unreasonable Accommodations', Kay Inckle observes: 'Many universities promote themselves as positive environments for equality and diversity, and yet this is not the experience of disabled academics.' She describes what she had to do to be able to work:

> *During my career I have been told that I cannot be scheduled into wheelchair-accessible teaching rooms for a variety of reasons, including: that to do so would involve 'disrupting' someone else and changing their timetable (even though they are not a wheelchair user and therefore do not specifically need that room); that accessibility is not a 'first priority' of timetabling; that I will have to 'make do' with a 'not ideal' room (e.g. one which has no emergency egress); that the university could deem it 'reasonable' to expect me to go downstairs on my bottom in some situations rather than reorganizing my timetable to ensure I have reliably accessible rooms (the last was said by an 'Equality Officer' in defence of timetabling).*[11]

I want you to pause at the idea that it could be even thought to be reasonable to expect that Inckle could 'go downstairs on her bottom'. This is a proposal from an equality officer, someone who not only knows about the organization's equality policies but is responsible for implementing them. Inckle's work helps us to understand ableism not only as a structure that is there (like a building), although ableism is a structure that is there (like a building), but also as what is perpetually justified and reproduced *by* those who are enabled by that structure. You might have to keep complaining that they have booked an inaccessible room because they keep booking such a room.

You have to keep saying it because they keep doing it.

We are back to that *broken record*. It is not just that to complain is to repeat yourself. Access is not complaint. Nor is asking for reasonable accommodations. But when access to work is heard as complaint, eventually it might have to become so, by which I mean, you might have to formalize a complaint *because* you do not have your access needs met.

Some people become complainers *before* they complain. I spoke to Esther, a disabled student, about doing the work of access. She observed: 'The reasonable adjustment duty is really clear that the reasonable adjustment is supposed to bring some kind of parity between disabled people and non-disabled people, but they experienced my need for adjustment as making their lives a complete pain in the ass and they wanted at the very least grovelling gratefulness on a daily basis in order to continue providing it, preferably considerably more than that. I think if I had turned up with some kind of cheerleaders for them, I think then maybe they would have thought it was acceptable.'

Requests for access are treated as being inconvenient. To make those requests requires performing emotional labour; you have to appear positive, 'grovellingly grateful', even a 'cheerleader' for the institution, in order to receive what they have a duty to provide. Emotional labour is a concept introduced by sociologist Arlie Hochschild in 1985, drawing on her research with flight attendants. Hochschild quotes a pilot saying to them, 'Smile girls, your smile is your biggest asset.'[12] Smiling, for service workers, becomes a job description, and for diversity workers, too. When you have to fight for access with a smile, you also have to suppress the negative feelings that having to fight that fight surely entails. You have to grin and bear it.

Even though she performed that labour, Esther did not get what she needed. So, she ended up making a formal complaint. She described her experience thus: 'They dragged the whole thing out and treated me hideously and they would be like, "Oh, we see you have had a friend over last night, maybe you could write more essays if you tried harder?" They were just brutal; they got loads of letters from my doctors and so on, saying, "[Esther] has to have extensive medical procedures, and loads of things take a long time, and she doesn't have the same amount of energy as everyone else and she's got these genetic incurable conditions and the only way to manage them is to have a lower level of activity in daily life", and they wanted pie charts of how long it takes me to go to the toilet, wildly, intrusively bizarre requests.'

Having the eye of the institution land on you is to be subjected to more and more requirements; you have to tell them more about yourself, intimate details about your life, even though they have evidence that explains your needs. Esther told me what she would *not* complain about given what she learnt from the intrusiveness of the complaints process: 'I wouldn't make a complaint about toilets because I feel that being cross-examined about whether I am humiliated by pissing myself in toilets is too much.' When a complaint requires sharing a humiliating experience, you might avoid it to avoid further humiliation.

The work of complaint is work some people would not have to do if institutions were as committed to creating open, inclusive and accessible environments as they claim to be. Those who do not need to complain to access institutions are more likely to be convinced by these claims. Let's return to the figure of an 'important man' introduced in Andrea's testimony. He was evoked in a warning not to complain. Heather, a retired academic, brought up another 'important man'. She told me that her application for promotion to professor was 'put in the bin', after the university decided to award only one professorship. She asked a rhetorical question: 'So who did get put forward?' 'And of course, it was a man far less qualified than any of the women who had applied,' she said. 'The head of department's argument was that he had very important contacts, very important contacts in the community . . . In order to keep this guy, they had to give him the promotion because they didn't want to lose him.' A door was opened to him because of who he brought with him. So, Heather had to complain about not getting promoted, which took more of her time. An 'important man' ends up with more time on his hands. Being freed of the need to complain is how he acquires more velocity, going forward, moving faster.

Privilege is an energy-saving device.

For Heather, sexism and ableism were both implicated in what made it harder to proceed. She tried again for promotion – and this time, she succeeded: 'I got a letter from Human Resources stating that although the professoriate committee had awarded me the professorship, they weren't going to allow it to go through. They said that, because I had a mental health disability, I wasn't in a fit state to carry out the responsibilities of a professor.' Such a letter is an explicit example of disability discrimination. She decided to fight it: 'I thought, fuck you lot. I am going to fight you over this because you are breaking the law.'

Some have to fight for what is theirs by right. Heather told me some of the steps she had to take: 'So I first went to my head of department and I said, look, you are breaking the law. This is blatant, illegal discrimination. And he was like, there is nothing I can do; Human Resources have decided.' When he did nothing, she had to do more. What followed was a long, time-consuming and draining process. In the end, after Heather indicated she would take them to an employment tribunal, Human Resources backed down. But she decided to leave the post as her trust in the organization had gone. Even when you do finally get the promotion, the more you had to fight for it, the more is destroyed by it, your relationships to colleagues, your relationship to a department, to an institution.

Time is room. In chapter 1, I introduced you to Viola

who had to fight to get the time she needed to return to work. That fight just took up more of her time. After Viola left her post, she was diagnosed as autistic. She told me that whilst the diagnosis mattered to her, she should not have needed it in order to be heard: 'A lot of the adjustments I was asking for could have been made in my job, even without the diagnosis, if they had listened.' For Viola, it was the failure of anyone to listen that was cruel. When she used the image of complaint as a 'little bird scratching away at something', she was trying to capture how it felt to keep complaining; how you can feel smaller in the face of something larger. Viola's

'A little bird scratching away at something.'

little bird reminded me of the birds that had turned the postbox into a nest. Complaining can also be the effort to create room in an otherwise hostile environment.

HOSTILE ENVIRONMENTS

To inhabit spaces not intended for us can feel like entering a hostile environment. But how do environments become hostile? Judgments by employment tribunals and employment appeal tribunals in the UK have offered definitions of the 'environmental' aspect of hostile environments with reference to time and duration. One judge argued, 'Dignity is not necessarily violated by things said or done which are trivial or transitory, particularly if it should have been clear that any offence was unintended.' The judge stressed that it is 'important not to encourage a culture of hypersensitivity or the imposition of legal liability in respect of every unfortunate phrase'.[13] Another judge concluded, 'Although we would entirely accept that a single act or a single passage of actions may be so significant that its effect is to create the proscribed environment, we also must recognize that it does not follow in every case that a single act is in itself necessarily sufficient and requires such a finding.' He added, 'An environment is a state of affairs. It may be created by an incident, but the effects are of longer duration. Words spoken must be seen in context; that context includes other words spoken and the general run of affairs within the office or staffroom concerned.'[14]

For something to be part of an environment or a 'state of affairs', we need to show that it is lasting or endures, otherwise we would 'catch' every 'unfortunate phrase', creating 'a culture of hypersensitivity'. There is an acknowledgement that a single act or 'single passage of actions', can create a hostile environment, but that the act is not 'in itself necessarily sufficient'. I understand the need for a concept of harassment that does not catch 'every unfortunate phrase'. But the environment itself might end up being of 'longer duration' because of how we are taught to receive 'unfortunate phrases' as 'trivial and transitory'.

Consider Rosie's experience. She was away from her department for some time. But then she went to an away day, and she found the culture to be very different to how it was before: 'There was a lot of touching going on, shoulder rubs and knee pats. It was the dialogue. They were talking about milking bitches. They were making jokes, jokes that were horrific. They were doing it in a very small space in front of [academic] staff, and nobody was saying anything. And it felt like my reaction to it was out of kilter with everyone else.' She couldn't 'quite get to the bottom of where the jokes were coming from' but noted that 'people were just laughing along.' And then, she said, 'You start to stand out in that way; you are just not playing along.' One student in particular seemed to be behind the jokes. 'He specifically went for me, verbally,' she reported, 'at a table where everyone was eating lunch. It was a large table with numerous amounts of people around it . . . I was having quite a personal conversation with someone [on a topic related to her PhD] and he literally leant across the table or physically came forward, he was slightly ajar to me, he was really close, and he said, "Oh my god, I can see you ovulating."'

The hostility that was in the room ended up focused on Rosie, probably because she found the jokes 'horrific' rather than funny. If she became a target because she did not laugh, other people, by laughing, avoided becoming one. That's how hostility recruits more people. To participate in hostility is how you are spared from becoming its object.

There is a clue in Rosie's story about time and the environment. Even though Rosie 'could not get to the bottom of where the jokes were coming from', she knew how they kept going; the laughter gave them momentum. So yes, it would take a complaint to stop the hostility from becoming just how things were. But Rosie was told by a lecturer seated at the table that she was being 'a bit oversensitive' and that she 'couldn't take a joke'. We can think more about the singularity of the sexist expression 'milking bitches'. It might be rather easy to hear it as an 'unfortunate phrase', a minor matter. But it was not. It was a running joke, sustained in or by conversations. Behind the judgement that it is oversensitive to complain lurks an expectation that people need to learn to filter sentences such as these out, perhaps by treating them as unfortunate – exceptions to, rather than examples of, the culture of the workplace. A hostile environment can function as a sieve; a tool used to filter out smaller-sized materials.

That some sentences stand out might be telling us something about how most hostility remains in the background.

The word *harass* comes from the old French, 'to vex, or tire out'. It can refer to the repetition of trying experiences. Scholar Annika M. Konrad introduces the concept of access fatigue as 'the everyday pattern of constantly needing to help others participate in access, a demand so taxing and so relentless that, at times, it makes access simply not worth the effort'.[15] Konrad is drawing on her study of how blind and visually impaired workers navigate their access needs. She cites one participant, Nadine, who 'heard a peer refer to her as "the blind girl".' Nadine said, 'It hit me so hard, like a ton of bricks.' That comment brought home to her how she was objectified, talked about as a genre not an individual, a problem not a person.

Comments hit harder when they bring out a hostility that is already there. Stephanie started a new job as head of a department. She describes the culture of her department as misogynist as well as homophobic. She said, 'They know enough not to express it openly – though sometimes it comes out – because they realize it is not OK.' That hostility mostly came out in jokey or pointed comments. She gave one example of being 'all around a big table', and then, during an icebreaker, someone said, 'This is Larry, and Larry used to be a woman', followed by laughter. In another instance, during a discussion about a colleague's son who had someone over to stay, 'it was a joke about whether it was a girl or a boy.' Stephanie said, 'A colleague turned to look at me in recognition that I would find that difficult.' Hostility might be directed to those who cannot participate in the norms that are casually sustained in conversations people have about their lives. Another time, when Stephanie was introduced as a lesbian head of department by a student, 'there was some discussion of that with colleagues, like I had some banner to fly, pushing students to get involved with this.'

Even identifying yourself as a member of a minority can be heard as raising a flag. Maybe you are being told that if you are lesbian, it is better not to say you are. If to be different is to stand out, a consequence of hostility is that some people do what they can not to stand out. I sometimes call this work 'institutional passing', how we minimize the signs of our difference. I first used this term for how many Black and brown people described 'softening' their appearances to counter perceptions they might be a problem in the workplace, perhaps by wearing or not wearing certain clothes. One woman of colour manager said that to wear a sari to work would be to 'rock the boat' (rather like making a complaint, then). I know of many gender non-conforming people, cis and trans, who use dress as a deliberate strategy to try and fit in with the culture of their workplace, not because they do not want to be themselves but to lessen the likelihood of confrontation. Diversity work can thus include the work of trying to avoid hostilities by appearing less different.

Institutional passing is not always possible or successful. Philosopher Amy Marvin observes, 'Non-normative gender expressions run counter to good feelings; such gender self-cultivation distracts from proving one's worth as an employee, and workplace cohesion is disrupted when coworkers feel aggrieved by their proximity with gender alterity.'[16] Marvin draws on the work of political scientist Dan Irving on how neoliberal service work can involve emotional labour, cultivating 'an outwardly pleasant appearance and embodiment that appeals to customers, clientele, co-workers, and employers'.[17] Irving shows how for trans people, who can cause trouble just by being seen as trans, it is harder, as it were, to do that appealing job. He quotes from a trans woman: 'Everywhere I go there's people looking and you have to build up a wall against that.'

Trans people might have to do what they can to protect themselves from the hostility that surrounds them, the pressure of being under scrutiny. That is how 'not complaining' itself becomes a form of emotional labour. Journalist Sarah Jaffe shows how many different jobs today come with 'affirmative traps', where 'you must show up with a smile on your face or be tossed out.'[18] Many workers will know what it is like to suppress negative feelings that come with doing the job. For some workers, not complaining can be about distancing themselves from the negativity *coming at them* not only as workers but because of who they are perceived to be.

It is hard to complain about a hostile environment when you are in one.

Hostilities in workplace environments are usually picked up from elsewhere. In the UK, there has been an endless barrage of media reports that present trans people as endangering other people, especially 'women and children'. One headline reads: 'Transphobic? No, we are just worried about the children.'[19] The headline demonstrates how transphobia is enacted by how it is denied – presenting trans people as threats to children. Transphobia does not always mean people feel fear or animosity towards trans people; it is how ideas about trans people circulate, so that trans people are treated with suspicion, as people to be feared.

The word *hostility* in fact denotes strangers, coming directly from Latin *hostilis* 'of an enemy, belonging to or characteristic of the enemy', and from *hostis*, in earlier use 'a stranger, foreigner.'[20] A stranger might seem suspicious, loitering, up to something. I suggested in the previous chapter that some people are more likely to be seen as suspicious. Some people see themselves seen as suspicious when they are questioned or made questionable: who are you, where are you from, what are you doing here; even, what are you? A trans student of colour, Zenab, made a complaint about sexual harassment and transphobic harassment from their supervisor, who had kept asking them deeply intrusive questions about their gender and genitals. Zenab commented: 'People were just trying to evaluate whether [the supervisor] was right to believe there would be some sort of physical danger to me because of my gender identity . . . as if to say he was right to be concerned.' The same questions that led Zenab to complain are asked when they complain. These questions make the concern right or even into a right; a right to be concerned. So much harassment today is expressed as a right to be concerned.

People might not hear the hostility of such questions because they are thinly masked by concern. They might not hear how the questions and concerns are repeated. Take the statement, 'Sex is real', endlessly repeated by those involved in the 'gender critical' or 'sex realist' movement.[21] Statements such as these are not hostile when taken in isolation. But they are not made in isolation. They slide quickly into other statements about how trans people are *not* real; that they are 'deluded' or 'disassociated' from reality, to employ terms regularly used. The subtitle of just one article is typical: 'How to Defeat a Mass Delusion'.[22]

Statements that trans people are 'deluded' are (or should be) understood as self-evidently hostile to trans people, suggesting they are mentally ill or living inauthentically. It could be argued that it is *possible* to make statements such as 'sex is real', without creating an association between trans people and danger or delusion. This very possibility is turned into *an instruction* to treat such statements *as if they can be detached from the contexts in which they are made*. Those of us who refuse that instruction, who show how such individual statements participate in a wider discourse we call *transphobia*, are quickly judged as creating a hostile environment for the people making these statements.

Sociologist Jo Phoenix argued that 'vexatious complaints' and 'protest about transphobia' should be treated as 'harassment, full stop'.[23] This slide between 'vexatious complaints' and 'protests about transphobia' implies that to protest *transphobia* or even to use the word *transphobia* is itself harassment. For many of us, this suggestion translates as follows: some people will be free to express views we consider transphobic, but we will not be free to express our views that they are transphobic. When examples of transphobia are filtered out as too light to matter, the word *transphobia* is filtered out, too.

A hostile environment stops us from talking about a hostile environment.

The judgement that some statements are *not* hostile can also function as a filtering mechanism. So much racism is dismissed as *just banter* at the very moment it is identified as racism. Take the experience of Somalian-born cleaner Faisal Abdi, who eventually won his case by taking it to the employment tribunal. His line manager had used racist language against him calling him 'Gollywog' and 'cheeky monkey'.[24] When Abdi made a complaint to his bosses, they suggested to him that these terms had been used as 'terms of endearment'. He was told he needed to appreciate 'cultural differences in language'. When racism is disguised as being friendly (no one needs to be convinced by this disguise for it to work), to call racism out is treated as causing hostility by imposing that interpretation on others.

Those who point to hostile environments might end up leaving because of them. Journalists April Glaser and Char Adams reported on complaints made about sexism and racism against Google in 2024. They quote from a Black woman who stated to a manager that Black, Asian and Latina women had different experiences to white women only to be told 'brusquely' that her point was 'not relevant'. When she complained, she was told she could 'coach the manager about her problematic response', or 'take medical leave to tend to her own mental health'. A diversity worker who identifies a problem is either asked to solve it or is made the problem. The article was published a year after two prominent Black women, Timnit Gebru and April Curley had been pushed out.[25] It quotes Timnit Gebru, who described what happened whenever she raised 'concerns' about workplace culture: 'They're like, "Well, if there's something wrong with you, here are all these therapy resources . . . And I would respond that no amount of support system is going to get rid of Google's hostile work environment.' We are learning what it means to be the location of a problem: a complaint about racism is treated as being about your mental health rather than a hostile work environment.

Hostile environments endure because those who point *to them*, refusing to function as sieves, are removed *by them*. Let us return to Shazia, who was dropped from the diversity committee for mentioning things to do with race. It is worth asking why she kept mentioning those things. Racism, that's why. Shazia had set up a writing group in her department because she wanted to create a more collaborative research culture. But the meetings became dominated by senior men: 'What I found in each of the meetings were senior men who were bullying everyone in the room.' The bullying took the form of the constant belittling of the work of more junior academics as well as postgraduate students: 'The first session someone was being just really abusive about someone's PhD, saying it was rubbish.' Racist comments were made: 'I'm from London and London is just ripe for ethnic cleansing.' She described how people laughed, how the laughter filled the room.

What to do? Shazia did not want to be a sieve, that is, to treat each sentence as immaterial. She decided to complain because she 'wanted it recorded', and because 'the culture was being reproduced for new PhD students'. A complaint becomes a recording device. We have to record what we do not want to reproduce. She gathered statements from around twenty people in her department. The complaint created was a collective complaint, although, as the person who gathered the statements, it was she who was named. A meeting was set up in response to her complaint. The head of Human Resources described her as having 'a chip on her shoulder'. Shazia observed, 'They treated the submission as an act of arrogance on my part.' Even a collective complaint can be heard as a personal grudge. It is as if she put a complaint forward as a way of putting herself forward. Her complaint was treated as self-promotional: 'It was all swept under the carpet and exactly the same things continued.'

When Shazia was dropped from the diversity table for mentioning things to do with race, her colleagues *were given permission to make racist comments at that same table*. Under the banner of diversity, you are allowed to say something racist but not say it is *racist*, just like you can say something transphobic but not say it *is transphobic*. To remove these words is to remove the people who use them. Shazia said, 'Whenever you raise something, the response is you are not one of them.' Of course, as a woman of colour, she was already 'not one of them'. By complaining, she does more than reconfirm the judgement; she is stopped from participating. She said her department was a 'revolving door,' because when 'women and minorities' entered, they exited soon after; whoosh, whoosh.

Remember that postbox that became a nest? There could have been another sign on the box: Birds welcome!

Diversity is *that* sign. And when diversity is *that* sign, it obscures the hostility of the environment. I suggested earlier that a hostile environment functions as a sieve; all the smaller-sized materials pile up. A hostile environment is what is *under the sieve*: those materials become the letters in the box, taking up all the space, until there is no room left, to breathe, to nest, to be. That is how those comments, those racist comments, function. They are how some people occupy institutions, claiming them as their own. All that needs to happen is what usually happens for other people to be displaced.

CHANGING POLICIES

For institutions to change, we need new policies. Behind many a new policy, you will find a complaint. We heard in the previous chapter that it took a complaint for sexual harassment to be recognized as a form of workplace discrimination. When I worked with the students to address sexual harassment as an institutional problem, we tried to

Diversity obscures the hostility of the environment.

get the 'conflict of interest' policy amended. One student in particular invested a huge amount of her time and energy in getting this policy changed. She emailed the rest of our group in frustration:

'I've just checked the college website and discovered that the "conflict of interest" policy remains unchanged, a full two years after I first began advocating for it to be removed and rewritten. It still contains this line: "The College does not wish to prevent, or even necessarily be aware of, liaisons between staff and students and it relies upon the integrity of both parties to ensure that abuses of power do not occur."

I've lost track now of the number of meetings with management in which I've tried to get this policy taken down and changed. Two years! Has anyone heard about or been shown any new versions of this policy lately?'

I only learnt about the policy myself after I attended that initial meeting with the students to talk about their collective complaint. Leila Whitley, Tiffany Page, Alice Corble, Chryssa Sdrolia and Heidi Hasbrouck explained what the policy told them as students: 'We had looked up their process and found that as a matter of policy the university considered faculty–student relationships a private matter. For us, this meant that, *by policy*, the institution actively did not want to know about abuses of power.'[26] It is hard to complain about a form of conduct when institutions state they endorse it or do not want to know about it.

We needed a policy to state that the conduct was not permitted. The policy was eventually changed after the intervention of the equality officer on our behalf. But because all of this activity was kept confidential, there was no conversation among staff about the old policy, and why it needed to be changed, which meant that the new policy (rather like sexual harassment itself) was kept secret. It was not just that the new policy was not sufficient to change the culture but that how it was agreed was evidence it had not changed.

As diversity workers, we learn how hard it is to change institutions by policy. Let me return to my earlier experience of writing a race equality policy. In that policy, we used a critical vocabulary, naming whiteness as an institutional problem. We included the definition of 'institutional racism' from the Macpherson Report on racism in the police force, although we fell short of calling the university 'institutionally racist'.[27] To explain the need for an equality policy in a policy is to turn the policy into a complaint.

I learnt so much from what happened to that policy. We had a new vice-chancellor that year who used celebration to bring members of the university together. Our policy had been ranked 'excellent' by the Equality Challenge Unit, which at the time had responsibility for overseeing race equality in higher education. The vice-chancellor, in an address to the university, waved the letter around, congratulating us all on being good at race equality. A document that documented race inequalities was used as evidence of race equality. It was a feel-good moment, but those of us who wrote the policy did not feel so good. You can write a policy as a complaint but that does not mean it will be received as one.

It was a complaint about racism that had led me to become a member of the group responsible for writing the policy in the first place. This trajectory from complaining to writing new policies was not unusual. I talked to Eric, a trans lecturer who made use of the Equality Act to challenge his failure to be promoted on the grounds that transitioning should be understood as a career interruption. Eric ended up drafting a new policy on equality for trans people at his organization. It was only by complaining that he found out they did not have one: 'Now I am developing guidelines for a trans equality policy. I hope to take this new path.'

Complaints sometimes reveal the absence of policies. Ellen Pao realized her employer did not have any policies on sexual harassment when she filed a complaint: 'There was no sexual harassment training, no handbook, no rules, no HR person.' Eventually, her complaint led to the adoption of a new policy. 'My filing also resulted in a sexual harassment policy for the company, though it had a curious clause. It forbade us from telling one another about any discrimination or harassment. A partner said, "You have to tell people in authority, but you can't talk to one another about it." '[28] The problem is not just that a new policy can be introduced without conversation. A new policy can be used to avoid any further conversation.

Complaints can lead to conversations about the limitations of old policies. Take, for example, the complaint made by Ms Permila Tirkey against Mr and Mrs Chandok in 2014 for caste discrimination. The respondents had tried to have the case struck out on the ground that 'caste' did not fall within the definition of 'race' in the Equality Act. When Permila's complaint was successful, caste was judged to share 'many characteristics' with ethnic origin. She explained why she complained: 'I want the public to know what happened to me as it must not happen to anyone else. The stress and anxiety that this sort of thing creates for a person can destroy them. I have not been able to smile because my life had been destroyed. Now I am able to smile again. Now I am free.'[29] Permila's complaint led to a public consultation on caste discrimination and a consideration of whether to insert caste as an aspect of race in the Equality

Act. In the end, they decided not to add caste to the Equality Act but to rely 'on emerging case-law as developed by courts and tribunals'.

Many decisions by employment tribunals in the UK reference the fact that even when organizations have equality policies, people do not seem to know about them. Take, for example, Rose Taylor's case against Jaguar in 2017 for discrimination in relation to the protected characteristic of gender reassignment. Rose is non-binary. She had raised a complaint with HR after two of her colleagues referred to her as 'it'. They responded, 'Well, what else would you want them to call you?' The company had argued that her identity as non-binary did not fall under the Equality Act protected characteristic of gender reassignment. As part of the ruling, the tribunal stated:

> It was very clear [Parliament] intended gender reassignment to be a spectrum moving away from birth sex, and that a person could be at any point on that spectrum ... it was beyond any doubt that somebody in the situation of the Claimant was (and is) protected by the legislation because they are on that spectrum and they are on a journey which will not be the same in any two cases.[30]

Lawyers Adam Cooke and Oscar Davies noted that Jaguar had pre-existing Equal Opportunities and Dignity at Work policies, but that no one in HR or management 'knew they existed'. They concluded that the case was consequently 'a prime example of how having a policy in place cannot, in and of itself, absolve an employer of liability when related grievances arise'.[31]

The implication of Cooke and Davies' observation is that some employers could use policies to absolve themselves of liability when 'related grievances arise' and respond to grievances (especially those that are made public) by writing new policies. Perhaps they can then point to the policy as evidence they are doing something.

Creating evidence of doing something is not the same thing as doing it.

Some such policies function as statements of commitment. After the murder of George Floyd by a white policeman in 2020 led to a global outcry, many organizations made statements of commitment to Black Lives Matter. Some people call these statements 'performatives', by which they probably mean they are theatrical rather than substantive.[32] I call them 'non-performatives'. I came to this term via a reading of the work of feminist philosopher Judith Butler and how they engage with speech-act theory, in particular J. L. Austin's *How to Do Things with Words*.[33] Judith Butler argues that performatives, 'bring about the effects that they name'.[34] I define non-performatives as speech acts that do *not* bring about what they name.

Crucially, non-performatives are treated *as if they are* performatives, as if they bring something about. Returning to statements of commitment to Black Lives Matter, the problem is not just that these statements do not do anything. The problem is that they do not do anything *by appearing to do it*. Ella, the diversity practitioner who refused to use diversity on her business card, observed, 'Well I think in terms of the policies, people's views are "we've got them now so that's done, it's finished."' In Ella's view, this was 'even worse than having nothing, that idea in people's heads that we've done race, when we very clearly haven't done race'.

You can change a policy without changing the culture.

Policies that don't change the culture can still be used as evidence of change. That's what makes (non-performative) policies and commitments so useful and that's why you will find them so frequently referenced in how organizations respond to complaints. For example, an official spokesperson for one university answered a complaint about the whiteness of its campus by claiming, 'We do a lot here to promote diversity . . . we have just celebrated One World Week, which we tied in with Black History Month.'[35] I know of multiple instances when those who complained have been told that what they said happened could not have happened because the organization had a policy against it.

Having a policy against something is used as evidence it does not exist.

Many of the examples discussed in this book can be illuminated with the concept of the non-performative to hand. In chapter 2, I mentioned Helen's experience of trying to get a new policy on diversity training agreed. In the end, the policy was agreed but people acted as if it had not been.

Agreeing to something can be how you stop it from happening.

A *yes* might be said when there is not enough behind it to bring something about. That's a non-performative. Note that the policy still existed on paper. So even if the policy did not come into use, it could still be used as evidence of how the organization had changed. If you complain (perhaps with evidence of how the organization has not changed) and you receive a nod, the energy that brought you to complain, to say *no* to something, is dissipated. A yes, *however empty*, can diffuse a no, *however forceful*. Agreeing to something is an effective way of not bringing it about because it avoids the costs of disagreement.

Diversity too can be offered as a *yes*, a 'let's do this', or a nod – another non-performative. I spoke to Beatrice, an early-career lecturer, about her experience of appointment panels. Her university had introduced a numerical system for evaluating the performance of job candidates in an effort to ensure equality of treatment. She described what actually happened during the appointment process: 'Someone would say, that woman's presentation was outstanding, but, really, he's the guy you'd want to have a pint with, so let's make the figures fit.' The figures are made to fit when a person is deemed to fit. Fitting can also be about *fitting in*. The person most likely to be appointed is still the one who can participate in a shared culture; 'the guy you'd want to have a pint with'. That policies are non-performatives helps explain why the same people keep being appointed in the same old way, despite equal opportunities policies, those taglines that say: minorities welcome, come in, come in!

Just because they welcome you, it does not mean they expect you to turn up.

We can think again of the sign, 'birds welcome.' There would be no point welcoming the birds if the postbox was still in use as they would just be displaced by the dropping of the letters into the box. The point of a diversity policy might be to create the appearance of being welcoming without having to do anything else at all.

Those who complain formally often become conscious of the politics of the non-performative; how organizations *do not do things with words*. I think of a conversation I had with Mia, whose testimony about being bullied and assaulted by her head of department I shared in chapter 3.

A diversity policy.

Mia made a formal complaint in part because her university had invested a great deal of time and money in developing new policies on harassment. She wrote to me, 'I thought, great. The policy has just been implemented. I have a means to complain.' One effect of introducing new policies is that people are more likely to use them. But when new policies lead some people to complain, they do not necessarily change what happens when they do. If Mia thought the new policies 'meant what they stated', she learnt they did not. She told her senior manager responsible for the changes,

'This policy means absolutely nothing.' Policies can be how institutions appear on paper ('paper institutions'). They can be that shiny paper, how legacies are protected by what is papered over.

Mia's complaint was about bullying and harassment from her head of department. She later attended a meeting chaired by the deputy head of Human Resources to discuss a new policy on bullying: 'In the meeting I started crying. We were supposed to talk about all this material, and I had just been bullied.' With the support of her union rep, she tried to set up another meeting, 'The director of Human Resources tried to get out of a [further] meeting, [my union rep] said, "Sorry this is really serious, you have to make time and meet with us."' That Mia had been bullied made it harder for her to be in the room to discuss a new policy on bullying. The administrator who had written the policy did not want to meet with the person who had been bullied. Creating a new policy to deal with a problem becomes another way of avoiding that problem; and by problem, I mean a person.

I spoke to Penny, a Black woman who was a senior manager at her institution. She ended up being dismissed from her post. Her case began as a dispute about how marks were allocated at an examination board. She had evidence that the university had not followed its own policies and procedures. The more evidence she had that they were wrong, the more she was treated as being in the wrong. She observed, 'Whatever you think of the university's procedures, you don't challenge them in that way; you swallow it.' Pointing to how organizations have failed to follow their own procedures is treated as an act of insubordination because it implies that those who govern organizations should be bound by something other than themselves (as, of course, they should be). Penny provides us with a summary of their position: 'Policies are for the others.' The ease with which procedures are bypassed teaches us more about the nature of institutional power.

**Power is the right to suspend what is
binding for others.**

Power means some people do not have to follow the rules, but other people do. Even though Penny was a senior manager, she became one of 'the others'. She has her own explanation as to why: 'Race and gender are always in there. I thought, this has never happened before. The first time it happens is when you have a Black woman dean.' However far some of us get, we can still be demoted to the rank of 'the others'.

FORCED CHANGE

Those of us seen as the others or the strangers, not from here or not *really*, might be welcomed on condition we don't change things too much. We might be asked to 'swallow it', to be compliant. The difference between compliant and complaint is only two letters, but they are worlds apart.

When we don't comply, saying *yes*, accepting things as they are, or at least appearing to, the hostility intensifies.

That hostility is not new, but we notice it when it intensifies. I think back to my experience of being a co-director of the Institute for Women's Studies between 2000 and 2003. We were one of the strongest such institutes in the country, with a vibrant research culture as well as undergraduate, MA and PhD programmes. I remember the dean used to call us 'a jewel in the Crown'. That expression tells us *how* we were valued not just *that* we were: as shiny, a display, as if we belonged *to* the institution rather than belonging *in* it. When we became more successful, we began to experience a gradual withdrawal of support. Maybe we were expected to be small as well as shiny. In a meeting, a senior manager called both me and my co-director a 'two-headed monster'. At a social event, a lecturer from another department remarked jokingly, 'We wondered if you all went to the same hairdresser.' There is homophobia as well as anti-feminism in these comments. At a certain point, when you gather in numbers, as lesbians, as feminists, you come to be seen as monstrous, more of the same, hard to tell apart, 'too much', as well as 'too many'. In the end, being 'too much' and 'too many' meant the end of Women's Studies at the university, at least in that form.

Let's return to Stephanie's testimony about the hostility she experienced as a lesbian head of department. For Stephanie, becoming more senior, acquiring or appearing to acquire more control over institutional resources, led to an increase in hostility: 'I was the first female head of department,' she reported, 'and everything became stuck to me. The fact that there had been fire doors put in all the rooms to replace the solid wood ones, ones with windows in, that was my fault, that was me wanting to spy on people; the fact that faculty was going over to electronic calendars, and I said, what do you think, shall we use these, how shall we use them, that was me wanting to spy on people. It was absolute scapegoating.'

Stephanie refers to the solid doors being replaced by glass ones. She explained that the LGBTQIA+ network on campus knew 'why those solid doors were turned into windows'. The replacement of the doors was the result of decades of complaints about sexual harassment in her discipline. That sexual harassment policy is treated as forcing change, depriving people of a privacy they would otherwise still be able to enjoy. The implication is that she, as the first woman (and lesbian) head of department, has *imposed* these changes because she is an imposter, not only not one of us, but also not who she says she is; a spy, no less (herein lies another reversal, given it is often diversity workers who have the eye of the institution land on them).

I hear an old homophobic trope at work: that queer people are *recruiters*, trying to recruit other people into our lifestyles or lives because we cannot reproduce ourselves. Even the most superficial or small signs of queer inclusion can be treated as evidence that institutions have fallen under a malevolent or sinister influence. Take rainbow flags and Progress Pride flags. They have been described by politicians as monstrous as well as malevolent. Former

Home Secretary Suella Braverman stated, 'The Progress flag says to me, it says to me one monstrous thing: That I was a member of a government that presided over the mutilation of children in our hospitals and from our schools.'[36] The Progress Pride flag, designed by non-binary artist Daniel Quasar, includes 'black, brown, pink, pale blue and white stripes, to represent marginalized people of colour in the LGBTQ+ community, as well as the trans community, and those living with HIV/AIDS.'[37] This is the flag Braverman was describing as monstrous. The flags themselves have been removed from some public institutions on the grounds of 'imposing beliefs' such as 'gender ideology'.[38]

Even superficial gestures that include trans and non-binary people are framed as an imposition of an ideology that such people exist. To call these signs superficial is not to say they do not do anything. Numerous studies have shown that symbols of inclusion matter to LGBTQIA+ people precisely because of hostile environments. One such study quotes a staff member: 'It is the tiny, little gestures such as putting your pronouns in your email signature or wearing a little pin badge with the rainbow flag on it for the start of February. It's those little, tiny gestures that actually make a huge difference, because they make you feel safe.'[39] Small gestures of acceptance can make a difference to those who haven't been accepted.

Of course, it will take much more than pins and pronouns and flags to counter the hostility of an environment. I suggested earlier that diversity is used more because it does less. Even doing less can be doing too much. Rainbow flags and pronouns in signatures are now routinely described as 'woke'. You can also be called woke if you use colour-blind casting on a miniseries, entertain the possibility of a fictional character such as James Bond being played by a Black actor or not being portrayed as a 'womanizer', or include disabled people and same-sex partnerships on a ballroom dancing show on the BBC. In the judgement of 'woke' we hear complaint. Just let Bond be Bond: you can hear that plea in the panic of headlines such as 'If James Bond has gone woke, he might as well be cancelled.'[40]

In 2024, the programme *Strictly Come Dancing* was, in fact, the subject of a number of scandals after complaints were made against two of their professional dancers for 'abusive behaviour'. The scandals had nothing to do with the same-sex partnerships, but that year the programme did not include any for the first time since they'd been introduced. A source from the BBC was quoted as saying the programme was returning to its 'traditional roots'.[41] There was a vague sense that the scandals had something to do with the changes, coming from the diversification of the format and not the format itself.

Another meaning of complaint is 'something that is the cause or subject of a protest or outcry'.[42] You can become a complaint just by embodying a change to a tradition or by being seen as the end of one. You can almost hear the beep, beep of a warning turned into an error message: wrong! Woke is not simply used wherever or whenever there is a change to, or widening of, a social convention, but because it pathologizes the sources of change. Hostility is redirected not only to changes themselves, whether it is new policies on sexual harassment, new words or ways of speaking about our identities, new fields of study (such as Gender Studies and critical race theory) or new formats to programmes, but *to those judged to be the cause of them*. One Conservative politician described 'wokeism' as how activists are given power over institutions by forcing their leaders to 'fight endless fires of grievance, stifling freedom, embittering the workplace and sowing division'.[43] The anti-woke use *woke* as a *counter-complaint*, a complaint about complaints, those mischievous minorities with their minor grievances.[44] To use *woke* as a counter-complaint is also to call for a return to some mythical past, assumed as unchanging, where people could act as they so wished or willed without complaint.

To complain is to encounter other people's investments in an unchanging culture. I referred earlier in this chapter to Shazia's experience of complaining about racism in her department. She left that job. In her next academic post, the most senior people (also all white men) conducted themselves in a similar way, making rude and derogatory comments about the work of more junior scholars and students. The students stopped going to their seminars: a complaint can sometimes be a withdrawal or refusal to participate. When the students were reminded by the department that attendance was compulsory, they wrote a letter, complaining in another way. Shazia explained their action: 'They wrote a letter stating that they actively chose not to go to these seminars because they were designed for a handful of senior white men in the department.' The students were suggesting that the conduct of the senior men was part of the design. So, when the professors conducted the seminars in a certain way, they were claiming that space as theirs, as being *for* them, at the same time as they were enforcing a hierarchy, treating other people as lesser than themselves.

How did the professors respond to the complaint? 'The first thing the director said is that we must defend ourselves,' reported Shazia. 'Perhaps these people didn't attend the sessions because they found them too intellectually challenging.' This confusion of prowess and skill with bullying behaviour is what is being achieved, as if other people object to offensive language because they are not up to being 'intellectually challenged'. 'We must defend ourselves' is a perfect description of what happens when complaints are made about the culture of an institution. Self-defence takes the form of a defence of a cultural norm.

An idea common across many different professions, especially those with long histories of hierarchy, is that to belittle others is to toughen them up, and thus to participate in their growth as future leaders. Conduct is not only about behaviour; it is also a transmission system (just like how electricity is conducted by wire). To stop forms of conduct means you have to stop the transmission of messages about what is acceptable to do or not do. It is not just that to complain is not to be respectful of the content of this or that tradition. It is that traditions often depend on a select few being given the freedom to express themselves *however they wish*, including being demeaning towards others.

Moral and equality frameworks such as 'dignity at work' are thus judged as *weakening* an elite, the guardians of institutions and their legacies.

These critiques of diversity and equality suggest minority groups are trying to take away 'our freedoms' by remaking institutions in their own image. This idea that equality is artificial or even a form of 'social engineering' has a long history in the UK and includes much of the work we would be right to refer to as *eugenics*. Philosopher Herbert Spencer wrote in 1873 that 'Besides a habitual neglect of the fact that the quality of a society is physically lowered by the artificial preservation of its feeblest members, there is a habitual neglect of the fact that the quality of a society is lowered morally and intellectually, by the artificial preservation of those who are least able to take care of themselves.'[45] Spencer's critique of equality was also a critique of charity and relief for the poor (social welfare); his argument being that when the 'feeblest members' of society are helped, they are prevented from dealing with the consequences of their own nature.

I evoke this longer history of eugenics-based arguments against equality because scholars and commentators are making similar arguments today, with EDI taking the place of welfare as the object of critique. There are many scholars today who claim that diversity initiatives deny some groups are inherently superior to other groups, and that they lower standards by artificially elevating inferior groups.[46] When diversity work is treated as forcing change, hierarchical institutions are approached as if they are organic bodies that came into being without artifice or intervention.[47] Jay

Timothy Dolmage notes how the steep steps that tell us of the elite nature of some institutions are not only an architectural feature but reinforce that elitism; they are 'a movement upwards – only the truly "fit" survive this climb'.[48] To listen to complaint is to learn the *mechanics* of how hierarchies are naturalized and enforced by being built into the machinery of institutions.

When assistance is 'built in', it tends not to be seen as assistance. As I mentioned earlier, Dolmage uses the term *retrofitting* to describe how institutions are made accessible – such as the placing of ramps adjacent to the stairs. The ramps are visible as a form of assistance, but the stairs are also a form of assistance for those who can use them. Even when the stairs are not seen *as* assistance, we can see them. Most forms of built-in assistance are not visible at all. The class system can function like steep stairs; each step of the way, the middle and upper classes are given assistance in going further or moving up. The steep stairs can be going to the right schools. Or knowing the right people. Or speaking right or looking right. The steep stairs can be fitting the criteria for this job or that promotion.

The steep stairs thus tell the story of merit: how some go higher because the structures were built with them in mind. Diversity is then framed as 'special assistance', which is how anyone who does not embody the norm will be called 'a diversity hire'. When diversity and merit are seen as separate tracks, diversity acquires negative associations for individuals (as evidence they are not there by merit), even when it is used as a positive brand for institutions. We are given incentives to disassociate from diversity and the baggage that comes with that term, leading to a phenomenon we can call *minority conservatism*: the door is opened to some of us as long as we shut the door right behind us, shut the door on others like us, shut the door by not thinking of ourselves as 'the others' (although, as we learnt from Penny, any wrong step and you can be quickly demoted to 'the others'). Perhaps you are more likely not to be stopped by barriers when you deny they exist. And then you can be used as evidence of what does not exist.

The progress of minorities through the narrow corridors of power is used as evidence there are no doors, no barriers to entry or progression. You don't have to disassociate yourself from diversity to be usable as evidence in this way. One time, after I gave a talk on diversity based on empirical data in which I used the term *institutional whiteness*, a white man in the audience responded, 'But you're a professor!' – as if my own individual trajectory contradicted the evidence I was presenting on institutions. Heidi Mirza described a very different response after her inaugural lecture as a professor: 'A white male professor leaned into me at the celebration drinks and whispered bitterly in my ear, "Well, they are giving chairs to anyone for anything these days."'[49] When 'the others' end up in senior positions, they are either treated as individuals (disassociated from diversity) or the positions themselves are devalued (associated with diversity). Diversity is treated as forcing institutions to meet our requirements and as lowering theirs. That is how diversity ends up being associated not only with the loss of value but with the potential loss of institutions (how they will become something other than what they are).

Hostility towards change is now typically channelled into critiques of EDI itself. At the Battle of Ideas Festival in London, in October 2023, mathematician John Armstrong offered one such critique: 'One of my hobbies is writing to the EDI team at the university to complain about the idiocies I have found in their training courses,' he said. 'Every email I get back is decorated with pronouns and a rainbow flag. Are they doing this to pull my chain? If they are, kudos to them. Sadly, I think it is just old-fashioned stupidity.'[50] Armstrong's speech about EDI was clearly meant to be funny. How people laughed. And when they laughed, the hostility filled the room. Armstrong was able to joke about Black history month, about trans people and disabled people, about suicide and self-harm, by channelling the humour into a critique of the 'stupidity' of EDI.

The use of the acronym might be how hostility towards 'the others' can be expressed because it evokes 'the others' without naming them. But if hostility towards 'the others' is sometimes masked, that mask is coming off. After the election of Donald Trump to his second term as President, a new era of exhilaration derived from an old freedom to be offensive has been ushered in; one banker told the *Financial Times*, 'I feel liberated. We can say "retard" and "pussy" without the fear of getting cancelled.'[51] Critiques of diversity treat it as the dominant order, as 'compelled speech', which is how offensive speech is articulated as 'liberating'. This is rather similar to how sexual harassment itself is framed as a refusal to comply with moral mandates.

We can now explain what might appear as a paradox: that free speech arguments are not only *not* made for all speech but made *against* some speech. Conservative commentators such as Christopher F. Rufo call for free speech whilst arguing that programmes such as Gender Studies should be 'shut down'. They manage the obvious contradiction between these positions by identifying such programmes as 'ideological capture'.[52] What they call *capture* we call *critique*. Gender Studies, an open and diverse field, is all about questioning sexism and other received wisdoms, including the very idea that sex is immutable, that it cannot be changed.[53]

Conservative commentators (rather like institutions themselves) typically confuse commitments to change with change itself. It is a strategic confusion. One conservative think tank found that elite institutions were more likely to use 'progressive terminology'. The headline of a newspaper stated in response that universities are 'peddling their woke agenda to students'.[54] The most elite, white institutions are described as 'woke' on the *basis of the existence of diversity programmes designed to make them less so*, less elite, less white.

It might seem, in the face of this withdrawal of commitments to diversity and equality, that it is time to abandon our own critiques of what diversity is not doing. I think these critiques will become, if anything, more important because they help us to explain what is going on. Let's return to the sign 'Birds welcome'.

Diversity as hegemony.

A conservative think tank could use that very sign, 'Birds welcome', as evidence that the birds are a powerful lobby who've pushed their way into our box. They might write letters about how wrong it is, 'how woke it is', that the birds are given special privileges. The birds help us to recognize something here: some of us are called powerful even when we cannot get into the damn box!

Woke can thus be understood not only as a counter-complaint but as hegemonic complaint. Hegemonic complaint works by identifying 'the others', those who have to push to be included, *as* the hegemony, framing a fight for survival as the formation of an industry. The point is, of course, that those who understand the box as theirs, that common sense we call ownership, are still using the box. By representing 'the others' as taking what is theirs, *they fill the box with that very claim.*

The identification of diversity and equality as 'woke' is an argument that change is being imposed or that beliefs in change are being imposed (that sex can be changed, or bodies, or marriage, or families, or institutions, or history). It is not simply that not all complaints are about changing institutions but that some complaints are made to resist that very change. How institutions resist change *is* how they reproduce themselves. To intervene in this reproduction requires doing more than complain or doing more with complaints, to stop what usually happens from happening, the same old letters from being posted in the same old box. And it is to 'doing more' with complaints that we now turn.

Part Three

Dismantling and World Building

To build a new world we need to dismantle the existing one. In saying no, or by saying it, we search for an alternative. *We complain for a more just world.* That *for* matters. We are more used to speaking of complaining *about* something or *against* it. Complaining *for* means we have to work against something to bring something else about.

The term *world building* is most often used with reference to speculative fiction, the imaginative creation of alternative worlds. My emphasis in this part of the book is different but related. The practical effort to dismantle structures is how we grasp the possibility of alternatives. We have to fight to make things possible, including, in some cases, ourselves. Queer theorist Jack Halberstam offers a powerful critique of the utopian impulse of world making. Rather than focusing on the future as the space of hope, he considers institutions that are collapsing and finds amidst the ruins a queer potential. Halberstam quotes from the Black lesbian artist Beverley Buchanan:

> My interest in walls involves the concept of urban walls when they are in various stages of decay, walls as part of a landscape. Often, when buildings are in a state of demolition – one or two structural pieces (Frustula) stand out that otherwise, never would have been 'created'. This state of demolition presents a new type of 'artificial' structural system piece that by itself (its undemolished state) would not exist. These 'discards' or piles of rubble can be pulled together to form new systems. These new systems are very personal statements to me. They are inspired by urban ruins but are created, 'in my own image' by me, in concrete and painted with dark paint. Deceptively, they appear to be black. (One of my dreams: to place fragments in tall grass where a house once stood but where, now, only the chimney bricks remain.) (Buchanan, n.d.).[1]

When the walls collapse, they can become part of a different landscape. What is discarded as rubble can amount to something else. When we encounter walls, the doors, in making complaints, they seem to be functioning rather well. They hold up. But when you make complaints within institutions, you often end up involved in the effort to change them, to stop them from working. The very effort to stop the doors and the walls from working is how we create a different landscape.

In *No is Not Enough,* author and activist Naomi Klein argues that 'the firmest of no's has to be accompanied by a bold and forward-looking yes'.[2] I understand my argument in *No Is Not a Lonely Utterance* as complementing rather than contradicting Klein's. We have to repeat *no* because of resistance to hearing it. When I used to give talks on racism, I would hear a 'but' typically turned into a question, 'But what can white people do?' Another question was, 'But what about resistance?' That latter question was repeated enough times for me to wonder whether the desire for resistance was itself a resistance to hearing about racism. People want to pass over a *no* quickly. We have to work to stop *no* being passed over or blocked or stopped. *No* is not just what we say; *no* is what we do. We learn what it will take to build alternatives from our refusal to reproduce more of the same.

We have been hearing of many defences against institutional change; anti-woke is just the latest version. It is not just some complaints that are blocked but the messages they contain, what I call **killjoy truths**. There are some very clear messages, we could even call them instructions: stop confusing brilliance with bullying! Or confusing collectivity with compliance! Stop protecting abusers! Or covering up complaints! Consider, for example, the resignation of Archbishop Justin Welby in 2024 after the publication of a 253-page report into child abuse perpetrated by John Smyth. Religious Studies scholar Linda Woodhead argued that his resignation would or should lead to an 'existential crisis', for the Church: 'It's been a very, very long time coming, like lots of crises,' she said, 'but this is a critical moment.'[3] We need institutions to have existential crises. Mostly, however, it is those who complain who end up having them.

Our work becomes to cause a crisis in the system. Changing the system can be our life's work. We could ask who can afford to make working to change the system their life's work? We could ask who can afford not to? We've heard already from people who complained, even though they could ill afford to, because they could *not* afford the conditions in which they were living or working *not* to change. Nevertheless, it is still worth thinking about the resources needed for complaint as part of our justice work. I certainly know of people who complained because they had the resources to do so (and by resources, I don't just mean money, but time and skills). Some people complain precisely because they are aware other people can't. Some people use their resources to help other people complain.

Behind the perception of the complainer-as-privileged lurks an assumption that principles are only for those who can afford them. And yet, and I think we know this, so many people who can afford principles don't have them. We have been hearing how people are rewarded by institutions for giving up principles. I doubt very much that radical change is going to happen because of the actions of those who can most afford to have principles. Those who can most afford principles might, after all, have most to lose from radical change. So, our question might be not *who* can afford to fight for change but *how* can we afford to fight for change. Thinking about complaint as activism and as a queer method is another way of reflecting on the possibility of radical change not as simply or only deriving from principled action but as a practical and collective task.

5/ Complaints as Activism

Complaints have long been used by activists to document the extent of social problems as well as to push for change. Take, for example, the 1967 'Summer Project' campaign by CARD (Campaign Against Racial Discrimination). This campaign was intended to address the limitations of the Race Discrimination Act (UK) (1965), which had placed housing and employment outside the scope of the legislation. Historian Kennetta Hammond Perry describes how the 'Summer Project' campaign, modelled on the US 'Freedom Summer', was designed to 'draw public attention to the quotidian realities of British racism as experienced by Black Britons and other communities of colour'.[1] In 1966, CARD sent a four-page leaflet, 'How to Expose Racist Discrimination', to 10,000 Black British people.[2] The leaflet begins as follows:

> No CARD member will need to be told that racial discrimination is spreading in Britain, especially in jobs, housing, insurance and credit services. But whenever CARD has called for laws against discrimination, the politicians have refused to accept what we know – that discrimination is respectable in

> many areas of British life. CARD urgently needs to build a case-by-case exposure of the extent of racial discrimination, so that the Press and Parliament can no longer pretend it does not exist.

CARD encouraged Black and brown people in the UK to make complaints about racial discrimination using their complaint form so they could collect these complaints and submit them to the Race Relations Board. They explained, 'The most obvious way of finding cases of discrimination is to ask people for them. This can be done in meetings, or in door-to-door canvassing'. In the leaflet they make clear that the process is about collecting information rather than taking any role in resolving the complaints:

> It is important that we have the information, even if the victim of discrimination does not want CARD to complain on his or her behalf to the Race Relations Board. Incidentally, we realize that the Race Relations Board has no power to deal with complaints of discrimination in employment, housing etc. It has no power anyway; but we want to make complaints to the board to educate members about the extent of discrimination and to push for it to be more effective.

CARD was able to gather evidence of discrimination because there was discrimination. By March 1967, CARD sent over 150 complaints gathered during the 'Summer Project' to the Race Relations Board. Approximately 90 per cent of these cases were outside the scope of the Race Relations

Act and were found in the areas of housing, employment and the issuing of credit.

The CARD campaign shows how complaints can be used to document the nature and scope of discrimination. That complaints can be repurposed by activists shows us what they can do when they are no longer kept internal to institutions. The stories shared in this chapter are about the repurposing of complaints. But there's a caveat: just as complaints can be directed against those who are fighting for equality and justice, so too can complaint activism. Those with vested interests in the status quo will borrow any tactics we use in fighting for change to fight against it. That makes the work harder. It is also another reason for doing it.

BECOMING COMPLAINT ACTIVISTS

The term *complaint activism* might seem counterintuitive. Activism sounds powerful – the work of refusing, intervening, protesting, marching, combining our forces, our energies. Activism sounds hopeful – you work harder for change when you believe it is possible, as well as necessary. Complaints can make you feel smaller, alone, apart. Complaint procedures are *designed* to make you feel that way. You might be told not to talk to anyone else about what is going on. You might not even know what is going on. It would not be surprising, then, if you experienced complaint as a lessening rather than an increase of power.

Many of the stories I've shared in this book seem to be

about pushing very hard not to get very far. There is sadness in these stories, without question. I noticed how often people expressed sadness, sometimes breaking down in tears, not so much when they were describing their complaints, but when they were telling me what they had loved doing before the complaint or before what happened that led them to complain. They expressed grief for what they had lost, not because of what the complaint did but because of what it did not do, probably could not do, which is allow a return to how it was before it happened, what led to the complaint being necessary in the first place.

In grief, there is grievance.

I too felt that grief, and I feel it still, for what I had to give up, a job I had loved, a job that I could not go back to even if I wanted to.

Even though I feel grief, I do not feel regret. I did not think of my support for the students' complaint as a choice, but what I had to do *given* my commitments. I am not sure I could have lived with myself if had not done whatever I could to support their complaint. It is not uncommon to understand complaint as how we can live with ourselves. Hana complained about bullying by her supervisor because otherwise, she said, 'I couldn't live with myself.' She turned that statement into a question: 'What can I live with? And what can't I?' Gina complained about bullying from her head of department: 'I wouldn't have been able to live with myself just coping with that situation and letting it happen,' she said. A complaint can be how you live with yourself because it is a refusal to cope with, or adjust to, a situation that is wrong.

When you complain about something wrong but hit that door or wall, you might expect you would be left rather discouraged. That might be true for some people, but it is not true for many others, including me. I left fighting. I am left fighting. Doing this research did not leave me feeling discouraged either. I was inspired by how hard people were willing to fight whether for their own jobs or for other people's. We heard this willingness to fight in the reasons people gave for complaining. We heard from Laura, who complained because 'a wrong had been done' and who said she would do it again not for herself but for others. We heard from Andrea, who complained because she did not want other students to 'have to go through the same practice'. We heard from Heather, who complained 'to fight them'. We heard from Jean Porcelli, who complained because she was 'fighting for her job'. We heard from Permila Tirkey, who complained because she wanted 'the public to know what happened to me as it must not happen to anyone else'.

Even when we complain to fight for our jobs, and our dignity, or other people's, we don't always know what we are fighting against. A complaint can be how we come to know. A professor, Jules, talked to me about what it was like to watch her institution protect a serial abuser. At the end of our informal conversation she said, 'I just want to put a flame under it.' She was not only politicized by complaint but ended up wanting to burn it down. And by it, I mean the system. It is the system that encourages us to complain *within* it rather than *about* it; to make a complaint about a faulty product rather than about consumerism or capitalism, or a complaint about an individual rather than an institution. Complaints made *within* a system can still be how we come to see *for whom* the system is working. The clarity that comes with complaint can be jarring, but it can also be energizing and enraging. Even if you don't make a complaint because you are trying to change the system or 'to dismantle the master's house', to evoke the title of an important essay by Audre Lorde,[3] that's where some of those who complain end up.

It is a rather hopeful trajectory. The hope of complaint might be rather weary, coming out of an intimate knowledge of how much we are up against. One student, Angela, described this weary hope rather well: 'You know the process is broken, but still, you know you must do it, because if you don't, more falls to the wayside. So, it's like a painful repetitive cycle where you do what you know is right, knowing it may not make a difference at that time, but you always hope, you always have that hope, that maybe because I did this, it paves the way for something else.' You keep complaining even if it's 'painful' and 'repetitive' because that's the only way something else can happen. You keep complaining not despite the consequences of complaint *but because of them.*

You might keep complaining to avoid the costs of not doing so. Heather, who retired early from her academic post in part as a result of a complaint, described 'not complaining' as being 'crushed'. She said she'd 'seen so many people crushed in many ways because they haven't gone to the union, they haven't gone to access-to-work; they'd just been so isolated that they just get crushed.' For Heather, that complaints bring you into contact with unions was key to how people can fight the system. She added, 'For me the tragedy was that I have seen so many other colleagues go under because they've been too scared to fight that fight. And I completely understand why they have been.' It might be fear that stops people from fighting that fight. But whatever stops people from fighting that fight, an effect of some being stopped is that there are fewer people left fighting. From complaint we learn about the costs of *not* complaining, of leaving problems unaddressed. These problems – such as harassment – can lead some to leave, 'to go under'.

As I was completing this book, I communicated with all the participants in my original study. When I got back in touch with Heather, she updated her complaint biography. Although she left her job because of a complaint, she did not leave complaint behind. She explained: 'Much of my time has been spent over the last two and half years representing the residents at the retirement flats where we now live against the shark-like property management company who run the building.' Complaining on behalf of other residents meant 'collecting and collating all the evidence of the wrongdoings'. Heather described the work as 'exhausting', not least because she experienced 'appalling harassment from the company'. Other participants also gave important updates on their complaint biographies. Rosie, who decided not to pursue an academic career in part because of what she learnt about universities from her complaint, also remained a complainer. Rosie's son has autism. She said she was 'living with a new kind of systematic violence'. Rosie described how her 'journey from complaining student' had 'morphed over time into becoming a complaining mother'.

The need to keep complaining, morphing from one kind of complainer to another, is a result of institutional failure and systematic violence. There is no doubt that this proximity to violence is exhausting. In that weariness is not just hope but practical wisdom. To become a complainer is to acquire skills that can be transferred across different settings. In my introduction, I mentioned that the term *complaint activism* came to mind when I was talking to Esther about the complaints she had made as a student. Esther used complaints to press against institutions, to demand from them what they should have given her: the time and space she needed to complete her degree as a wheelchair user with a chronic illness.

When Esther initially participated in my study, I anonymized her testimony. With her permission, I now share her full name: Esther Loukin. She agreed to be named so you could follow her story of taking what she learnt from complaining within one institution out into the wider public. Esther explained this transition into complaint activism in her testimony: 'I have started doing this activism using the law and in particular the part of the Equality Act

(2010) that only applies to disability regarding reasonable adjustments.' She made use of the law, however limited, as a tool to try to press many different organizations to become more accessible, to comply with existing legislation.

When complaints can lead you to learn how an institution works, you take that knowledge with you wherever you go, in work or in life. Esther took her complaint activism onto the streets, making complaints about shops that were not accessible to her as a wheelchair user. She was described in local media as trying to 'ruin' small businesses. One headline read: 'Panic in Cambridge's Mill Road: disabled woman sues seven shops and makes 25 complaints about access'.[4] The reports treated her as a serial complainer. But when she won her case, the owner of one business said, 'I didn't know that relatively small steps can be a complete barrier to getting into a shop for some wheelchair users. I believe that all high street shops should maximize access for all people, including wheelchair users. I believe there should be more guidance for business owners to know how to do this and where to get information. I hope that all shopkeepers are able to proactively make the same small adjustment.'[5] Complaining to overcome barriers can be how other people are made more conscious of them.

Complaining about inaccessibility led Esther to realize how hard it was to use the Equality Act to bring cases of disability discrimination to the courts. She co-founded the disabled-led campaigning organization Reasonable Access, which aims to 'empower other disabled people in the UK to assert and enforce their right to access through peer assistance and information provision'.[6] Complaint activism is often about advocacy; giving advice and practical support to others. It is not just that skills of complaint can be transferred from one setting to another but that skills can be transferred between people.

Complaint activism does not come from an optimism regarding the law or complaint procedures; if anything, complaint activism come from an intimate understanding of the difficulty of changing the system using these methods. From her advocacy, Esther realized that the main reason disabled people don't use the law to 'assert and enforce their right to access' is because of the potential costs incurred in making cases (any claimant is at risk of having to pay the defendant's costs if they lose the case). In 2020, Esther applied for a judicial review, taking on 'justice ministers in the high court over the ruinous costs disabled people can face when they take on disability discrimination cases'.[7] Complaint activism can involve moving complaints *out* but also *up*; to the High Court, in this instance. Svetlana Kotova, director of Campaigns and Justice for Inclusion London,[8] supported the application, agreeing that the potential costs incurred in making cases stops too many being made. She commented, 'This is why the Equality Act largely remains a dead letter; we experience discrimination on a daily basis, and organizations choose to adopt a "let's see what we can get away with" approach, instead of making their services accessible.'

Complaint activism can be an attempt to breathe life into the law. But when 'breathing life' into the letter of the law means changing the law, that is no easy task. Esther herself was treated as the problem as if she only brought the case because she was 'litigious'. Disability justice activist Natalya Dell stated, 'The government did not raise their "only Esther" argument in their expanded arguments. We clearly made an impact and showed that Esther is not alone.' Although Esther's case was dismissed, it did indeed have a lasting impact. In the judgment, 'the Court recognised the barriers faced when bringing cases under the Equality Act and acknowledged that the current costs rules were stopping people from enforcing their rights.'[9] Francesca Di Giorgio, another campaigner for Reasonable Access said, 'We are a step closer to justice.'[10] Four years later, on 27 November 2024, the government announced an 'open call for evidence', about cost protection for disability discrimination claims, citing Esther's application for judicial review as a key background to the call.[11]

It takes many steps to get closer to justice and not all of them succeed. Complaint activism teaches us that even when a complaint fails that failure is part of, rather than the end of, the story. Ellen Pao's *Reset: My Fight for Inclusion and Lasting Change* is about how she lost her lawsuit against her employer, venture capitalist firm Kleiner Perkins Caufield & Byers (KPCB) for sex discrimination. But rather than a story of institutional defeat, *Reset* offers a story of a political victory. The book 'draws back the curtain on this private, insular world' in order 'to show people what was really going on'. There can be nothing more politicizing than the truth when so many people are invested in keeping it hidden. Ellen became what I call a feminist ear: 'In the wake of my lawsuit people have told me they felt comfortable telling stories they hadn't shared before – so much so that I've become a kind of confessor for people who have faced workplace injustice.'[12] Becoming a feminist ear, a receiver of complaints about workplace injustices, is how one complaint gathers more.

Becoming a feminist ear is thus another trajectory into complaint activism. Ana Avendaño describes her book, *Solidarity Betrayed: How Unions Enable Sexual Harassment and How They Can Do Better* as a 'tough love letter to the labour movement'.[13] Ana had served as vice-president for labour engagement at United Way Worldwide, one of the largest charities in the world. In 2019, she learnt that union leaders 'were sexually harassing female labour liaisons'. Ana heard from other liaisons that 'they, too, had experienced sexual harassment at the hands of labour leaders but had not come forward for fear of retaliation and losing their jobs.' After she published 'two articles on the labour movement's failure to adequately address sexual harassment', she was 'falsely accused of bullying [her] staff' and fired. Ana fought back. She sued and won a substantial settlement.

Ana Avendaño does not end the story with that success because it is not just her story. *Solidarity Betrayed* is itself an important example of complaint activism. It brings many stories together, 'in the hope that women who were betrayed by their unions will find solace in knowing they are not alone'.

COMPLAINT COLLECTIVES

A complaint collective can be what we need to form given how hard it is to push for change as individuals. I introduced this book with reference to one such collective, the Grenfell Action Group, formed because of what happened – or did not happen – when residents of the Grenfell tower made individual complaints.

I also mentioned in my introduction that the students whose complaints I supported formed a collective. Leila Whitley, Tiffany Page, Alice Corble, Heidi Hasbrouck and Chryssa Sdrolia wrote later, 'There is no one story of how our collective came together.' They explain how they became a collective 'before we realized it'. A collective can be a story of many *nos*. Some of the students said *no*, quietly, by withdrawing or not participating in the department. A *no* can bring you together once you realize there are different ways of saying it: 'We were articulating our nos each of us on our own, but each of us knowing that our no was not the only one.' They kept each other going, 'never stopped talking to each other about what was happening'. They collected each other's stories and cared for each other: 'We gathered around each other. Care was always prioritized over complaint work.' Collectivity, for them, was a way to 'share the costs of complaint'.[14]

The point of a complaint collective can be the process of becoming one. Emily, a postdoctoral researcher, participated in a complaint about transphobia and bullying on a research project. She reflects on the nature of the process: 'I think the laborious part of it was trying to translate our individual and collective experience into something that institutionally made sense and [could] be recognizable as a complaint. In terms of what we did, we Skyped a lot and we emailed a lot and we swung back and forth between sharing our stories or being like, this awful thing happened and this awful thing happened and this awful thing happened, and then having to come back and work out how to put that on paper.'

To create a document that can be recognized as a complaint but is authored by a collective requires time as well as effort. You need to communicate with each other, swinging back and forth. And in that motion and movement, you find out about the 'awful things that happened' to others, just as they find out about the 'awful things that happened' to you.

If complaints procedures are designed to keep us apart, they don't always succeed. Let's return to Viola's experience of 'hitting all those doors'. She told me that if she hadn't complained she wouldn't have realized that she was not the only one: 'It was quite amazing actually to find that in my department there were more than a handful of staff who were there complaining about the same issues.' They had been complaining at the same time 'but in an atomized way', she discovered: 'None of us knew that we were all having similar problems and were making similar complaints.' Using the word *atomized* to describe a complaint process is to resist that process. The very labour of complaint is how we identify similarities in our experiences: *similar complaints, similar problems.*

To notice the door is to become conscious of the institutional effort to separate us from others. When that consciousness is achieved, the effort has failed. The classic scene of 'consciousness raising' is of a group sitting together sharing their reflections. Complaint gives us a rather different scene. The consciousness that comes from complaint is achieved not by withdrawing from action but by action. You raise consciousness of power in the process of trying to redress abuses of power.

But as we have been hearing, what comes back when you complain can be an increase of the violence that led you to complain. A collective can be what you need for violence to be *witnessed* by others. A collective can be what you need to *withstand* this violence. The more force is applied to stop a complaint from being made, the more people are needed to witness and to withstand that force.

The more we come up against, the more we need more.

The Guerrilla Girls showed us how we can create our own platforms to share our stories of complaint, as did political movements such as #MeToo. To get more people involved in a complaint can be to change its direction. We end up addressing each other as much as (or even rather than) the institution. In other words, when we create a complaint collective we change *the addressee*.

An example of this kind of change is offered by Grievance

Festivals. The Disability, Illness and Divergence Association (DIVA) hosted one such event in Adelaide, Australia, in 2022. In their event description, they acknowledged that for many neurodivergent and disabled students who have faced difficulties, registering a formal complaint 'can be overwhelming' and that 'the process of reporting an incident is also re-traumatizing'. Addressing students directly, they explained they were hosting a grievance festival

> *as an opportunity for you to speak to and hear from fellow students who understand what you've gone through. It can be cathartic to vent, and we invite you to scribble down on paper or on the whiteboard things you've experienced, large and small. There will also be the opportunity to anonymously submit your experiences to a Google form. The Disability, Illness and Divergence Association is committed to fostering spaces and community where students can speak about the difficulties and harassment and ableism they have faced, and where they can find comfort in each other. It is our responsibility to be in dialogue with the equity group we represent. It is clear to us that the solution to the problems of complaint procedures will not come from the institution: the solution will come from us, working together.*[15]

If institutions use venting as a technique to manage complaints, venting can also be what we do for ourselves, offering a kind of catharsis or release. A grievance festival is another version of a complaint collective: you create a space for people to speak of the difficulties they've faced with other people who've shared some of these same difficulties. To vent together can be to 'find comfort in each other'.

I have shared many stories of how people are retraumatized by entering formal complaint processes. Complaint activism can be about the creation of *safer spaces,* so that people can speak *from* trauma as well as *of* it. We need to build relationships of trust. Earlier I referred to Ana Avendaño's book *Solidarity Betrayed* as a form of complaint activism. She emphasizes how activists had to push unions to take sexual harassment more seriously as a labour issue. She explains, 'Unions have a poor track record of using grievance mechanisms or their power in the shop in favour of women who are harassed at work, especially if the harasser is a coworker.' Avendaño also gives examples of complaint activism coming out of unions. She highlights the United Service Workers West (USWW) chapter of the Service Employees International Union (SEIU) representing Californian janitors as a 'shining star'.[16] She ends her account with how that union broke with the 'harmful practice of sending survivors to HR' while they 'defended the harasser'.

Avendaño stresses that the procedural change came from cultural change. She spoke to Alejandra Valles, a senior Latina staff member of the union. Alejandra tells the story of how almost everyone stood up during a board meeting after a facilitator asked, 'Stand up, if you are a survivor of sexual violence.' Alejandra said, 'It was a huge moment: it shook everyone.' The union began to certify trainers (*promotoras)* who would 'go into workplaces to share knowledge and resources with fellow workers'. In 2016, they opened the Ya Basta Centre, 'which provides *promotoras* a space to engage with fellow workers, educate them on their legal and self-empowerment, and continue training the janitorial community to confront and eradicate sexual harassment on the job'. By creating spaces for workers to share their experiences, new practices within the union remained 'worker-led and trauma-informed'. Cultural change is slow. But it can be *made to happen*. As Avendaño herself puts it, 'Change is most surely necessary, but it requires confronting painful truths.'[17]

Earlier in this book I suggested that it can take a complaint not to reproduce an institutional legacy. It probably takes a complaint collective. We create spaces within institutions, so we can do things in another way, not just referring to the important people, as if they are the only ones who should have a say, not alluding to history as a reason for doing things in the same way. But the spaces we create within institutions are *not* freed from the histories we are trying not to reproduce. Shazia, whose complaint about racism led to her being reminded 'she was not one of them', talked about what happened when she contributed a paper to a special issue of a journal on decolonizing her discipline: 'The response of the editor was: "Needs to be toned down, not enough scholarly input to back up the claims they are making." Basically, get back in your box, and if you want to decolonize, we'll do it on our terms.' She ends up being given the same instructions by a white editor in the decolonizing special issue as she was given in any other issue; being tone-policed, asked to remove herself from the text. I think again of the birds who turned a postbox into a nest. So often when we turn up, trying to change the institution, we are told 'get back in your box' or 'this is not your box'. It helps to know that we can be told this even in groups set up to change institutions!

It can be difficult to create spaces to share our complaints, those painful truths, those **killjoy truths**, without them being coopted by the very institutions we are trying to change. I imagine (with some degree of horror, I confess) the setting up of a new committee within an organization called a 'complaint collective'. Of course, it would be a good thing if organizations created spaces in which people could collectivize their complaints. But a 'complaint collective' could easily become just another committee, another way organizations go about their business. The very structure of the committee brings with it a history, a way of doing things that can stop something more explosive from happening.

We have to work hard to keep doing things in our own way, using our own terms. I noted earlier in this book that transformative justice within institutions can be used to avoid accountability. Decolonial feminist Xhercis Méndez points to many tactics we can use to resist the co-option of transformative justice. She points out that the move 'to certify people to be transformative justice practitioners' or to create centres for transformative justice would not lead to lasting change. In fact, such moves would just 'generate more income for the institution that's problematic'.[18] If transformative justice becomes another means by which problematic institutions generate income, those of us trying to transform these institutions could end up investing in them rather than each other.

Transformative justice, and indeed complaint activism, means not letting the institution be the limits of our political horizons. We expand our horizons by addressing each other, widening our activities, asking what justice might look like, listening to other people so we can learn from them what they need to heal. As Méndez puts it, we are 'doing this on our own without hoping the institution is going to save us'. Méndez suggests we can 'rehearse ways of being in space together'. She adds, 'I can't have my healing be hostage to somebody coming to the table.' Instead, she says, we should 'try as many things as possible', and engage in 'a million tiny experiments', and 'knock on a lot of doors'.

Finding alternative ways to be in spaces or groups together involves bringing our whole being, our history, to every table. That's why creating a more accessible world requires much more than changing how we design buildings or administer access needs. Activist and writer Mia Mingus calls for 'access intimacy'.[19] Mingus explains, 'Access intimacy is that elusive, hard to describe feeling when someone else "gets" your access needs.' For Mingus, 'access intimacy', is 'ground-level, with no need for explanations', offering a way of holding 'the weight, emotion, logistics, isolation, trauma, fear, anxiety and pain of access'.

Those with more need to complain, who have to work harder to access spaces or institutions, have more knowledge of what to do and what *not* to do to create alternatives.

If you have an experience of 'hitting all the doors', or if you have to create a wall around yourself to protect yourself, you might be less likely to assume what other people need not just to access spaces but to breathe in them. That too can be what it means to be a feminist ear; lightening the load by listening to each other, staying attentive to our differences. Complaint collectives might be what we form not just to make formal complaints, or to withstand the effects of making them, but to lessen our need to keep making them.

RESEARCH AND ACTIVISM

I began this chapter with a reference to CARD and its Summer Project of collecting complaints in order to demonstrate the extent of racial discrimination and to challenge the resistance of policymakers to recognizing it. Complaints become activist tools in part because of how they involve research. Complaint activism also changes our understanding of the function of research. In their leaflet 'How to Expose Racial Discrimination', CARD stated that they were 'not going to carry out endless academic surveys. We do not want to study discrimination, but to end it.' They added, 'This leaflet describes what you can do about discrimination – CARD appeals to you to do it.' Research here is about generating knowledge not for its own sake, but to change the world.

It is not surprising that complaints are useful for activism given the research that goes into making them. Reflecting back on my own experience of supporting a formal complaint, I think understanding it *as* research helped me to handle the situation because it gave me a way to process the information. I remember one time I went to a meeting with the equality officer and a senior administrator. We were discussing the sexual harassment cases. The 'conflict of interest' policy, which I discussed in chapter 4, came up. I spoke of my frustration that the policy was still on the college website. The senior administrator said it was 'wishy washy'. The equality officer looked at me and said, 'It is not wishy washy: it is offensive.' We recognized each other recognizing that the senior administrator did not understand the problem. I began to collect evidence of how the problem was being obscured or made 'wishy washy'. I did not think of myself as a complaint activist at the time, but I was on my way to becoming one.

To complain we usually have to write and submit a form, the complaint itself. Many of my participants spoke of the length of their complaint. Drew described how she submitted 'hundreds of pages'. Andrea said that her complaint was longer than her MA dissertation, which was 10,000 words. To make a complaint is to write a history, your own history: and you can achieve a sense of power in doing just that. The complaint then ends up outside of oneself, in the world not just in your head.

Sonia, who made a complaint about bullying, described her relation to her complaint. She said, 'I am glad that it exists for me, and that if any questions are raised I have it, and also that I did lodge a grievance, I had a go, I did try.' She added, 'The record matters to me. It matters to me not that

I tried to seek justice, because I don't really believe the process can deliver that, but just to have some accountability and explanation in the hope of institutional change, which was, I think, all I was asking for in the end.' A record can be how you remind yourself of the effort you made. Even when an effort did not lead to institutional change, it matters to people that they made it.

You end up gathering more evidence about the institution in which you make the complaint. Black feminist activist and scholar Janine Francois, who I follow on social media, described her own practice as complaint activism.[20] I later spoke to her about her practice. Janine had made a complaint about racism at an organization where she had worked. That experience of complaint led her to develop a style of complaint activism in which 'the institution' itself became the research object. She consulted all the organization's policies: 'I am really going through all of the HR policies, again and again, highlighting things, highlighting the inconsistencies and going back to them and saying, I can tell you line to line what everything says.' She was conscious she was helping the organization: 'I became a free EDI consultant.' But she was also creating a map of the organization by 'reading the policy, seeing where it is not quite right'. Janine was 'going to meetings after meetings after meetings', which helped her to 'create a spread sheet', 'it was like pages and pages'. When she got involved in the Black, Asian and Minority Ethnic (BAME) network and became their note-taker in meetings, Janine was able to justify her participation as 'action research'.

Janine used the verb 'pop' a number of times. One time she said, 'And so, I used to pop up. And the same HR advisor who did not help me was the same HR advisor who did not help other people deal with their circumstances.' Another time: 'So I am constantly popping up in different people's meetings around discrimination. And they were like, shit, she's seeing us.' By popping up, Janine saw the structure; the same things happening; the same people doing those things. In other words, she saw them: the organization as it is enacted by people as well as policies. Eventually Janine was stopped from doing the research; she was told she was 'stepping out of [her] line as a researcher'. She explained to them how attending meetings was part of the research: 'Well, my whole thing was like, I was supposed to be an insider researcher and I was reminding them that my research was socially engaged, that it was active research, which means you are going into institutions, you are working with people, and we all agreed this, we all agreed this was the ethics behind it, is building professional intimate relationships with my colleagues.'

Janine knew what was going on. By working together as people of colour in a 'very white organization', they were not just 'seeing them' but 'pushing back'. She said, 'Four of us were like, we should have a meeting – a conversation. And we met and we unpacked all the things we had been told by other people. We came up with strategies and used the BAME network to push back against the institution.' But they quickly learnt that the organization did not want them to work as a collective: 'You are not meant to band together.' Janine added, 'We are saying, "Your story is made my story."'

Investigative research has been a useful way of addressing problems in workplace culture because it pulls stories of complaint out of the workplace without those who complain having to take the lead. On 8 June 2023, investigative journalists Madison Marriage, Antonia Cundy and Paul Caruana Galizia published an article in the *Financial Times* about sexual harassment and sexual assault claims against hedge funder Crispin Odey, head of the Odey Finance Management Company (OFC).[21] Odey has denied the allegations. The report itself created a complaint collective of many women, nine of whom had 'never told their stories publicly before'. Most women 'requested anonymity for fear of social, professional or financial retaliation'.

Investigative research, by protecting individuals from the risk of retaliation through granting them anonymity, allows more complaints to be collected. There is strength in numbers. But when a person is named publicly, or can be identified without being named, it is not just retaliation that is risked; it is defamation. Investigative research does not eliminate the risk of defamation but transfers that risk from complainers to journalists and publishers. That risk can also be transferred to those who cite that research (so when I cite such research, that risk is transferred to myself and my publisher). On 3 December 2024, Odey announced he was suing the *Financial Times* for damages to the value of 79 million pounds. The *Financial Times* made the following statement: 'Our investigative journalism about Mr Odey was carefully prepared and publication was in the public interest. We stand by our reporting and look forward to vigorously defending it.'[22] When defamation is not a threat but an action, research is essential to the defence.

Research is, of course, essential to the kinds of formal workplace investigations discussed throughout this book as well as to those conducted by regulative authorities, as it is to legal trials, both civil (complainant and defendant) and criminal (defence and prosecution). On 17 March 2025, the Financial Conduct Authority (FCA) published their decision to ban Crispin Odey from participating in regulated financial activities, claiming he was 'not a fit and proper person' to perform any such function. The FCA decision referred to internal investigations undertaken by OFC since 2020, prompted by numerous allegations of sexual harassment by women employees. It quoted from the Final Written Warning received by Odey on 4 February 2021, which stated that employees were reluctant to raise concerns, 'because of a desire not to *"ruffle feathers"* or because of concerns that nothing would be done, and that some employees would rather say nothing or resign instead of lodging a complaint'.[23] The decision also refers to how Odey had, on two occasions, disbanded internal committees that handled complaints, replacing them with himself. An appeal of the decision is likely. But the information contained in it *about* complaints, that some were made, why some were not made, how they were handled, that procedures were suspended, is now in the public domain.

Research on complaint processes helps to expose the mechanisms whereby complaints are suppressed. But research on these mechanisms can still be suppressed by them. On 19 September 2024, the BBC screened a documentary about sexual abuse and sexual assaults committed by Mohamed Al Fayed, owner of Harrods, from 1985 to 2010.[24] The documentary included testimony from twenty women who had been assaulted by Al Fayed, and five women who had been raped by him. How was it possible to screen the documentary without risking defamation? Because Al Fayed is dead and you cannot defame the dead.

A few days after the initial screening, on 24 September 2024, Henry Porter, former editor of the magazine *Vanity Fair*, published an article about what followed their exposé of Al Fayed as a serial abuser and racist in *Vanity Fair*'s September 1995 issue. Al Fayed sued for libel. Although they were not 'professional investigators', Porter and lawyer David Cooper had, by the summer of 1997, 'gathered enough evidence ... particularly on the sex abuse, to be confident of a good outcome at trial'. But, after the death of Princess Diana and Al Fayed's son Dodi on 31 August 1997, the libel case was settled. Porter writes, 'We agreed to place all evidence in locked storage. It seemed the right and humane decision in the immediate aftermath of the shocking deaths. But it wasn't, because of the countless women who have suffered since our case was settled, including many who were raped by a man who appeared unaffected by grief or regret.'[25]

Porter explained that 'in one respect' he did not 'go along

with the settlement'. Rather than handing over the boxes of evidence so they could be locked up where they could not be accessed, he placed them in a 'secure setting' that he controlled. He then allowed that evidence 'to be consulted by journalists, including the makers of this important documentary that finally, after 27 years, nails Mohamed Al Fayed and gives his victims the voice they deserve'. Justice can be a long time coming. I will return in chapter 6 to the time it can take to unbury complaints, to get them out of filing cabinets.[26]

When we research complaints, which themselves involve research, the product of that research, whether it is a story, a book or a report, is often treated in the same way that complaints are treated: as what must be stopped from circulating. If complainers are institutional plumbers, so too are researchers of complaint. That is why I have learnt so much about systems from sharing this research with different audiences, whether in person or virtually.

One time, I had a seminar with students the day after I gave a lecture on complaint. The students told me that some of them could not attend the lecture as it was given in the same theatre where the university had held a 'town meeting' to discuss sexual harassment cases. It would have been triggering for them to go into that room to hear this work. That is how I ended up *not* addressing the people most affected by the forms of institutional power and violence I was critiquing.

Sometimes it is the very air we breathe that makes it hard to complain, hard even to get into the room. History can be stale air. I think of Mia, who had to struggle through a meeting to discuss a new policy on bullying because she had been bullied. If we sometimes need to find another room to express our complaints, I needed to find another room to share the research.

Another time I was contacted by a student after giving a virtual lecture. She apologized for having left early and explained she had done so because she 'saw the name of her abuser in the chat'. Think about that: you have to leave a discussion of complaint because the person who abused you is in that discussion.

Yet another time, a woman of colour was due to give the land acknowledgement (an acknowledgement of the Indigenous custodians of the land) for a virtual talk. I was told at the last minute that she was not able to do so. She contacted me afterwards to explain why she had declined the invitation. She said, 'I found it disingenuous to do so under emerging and struggling work of the institution to decolonize, and to address white supremacy. Equity work is violent, as you know, and I have had many undermine my position and work. I wanted to share, not as the burden is yours, but for truth and awareness. Folks listened to your words. Then enacted institutional violence.' I ended up speaking *to* institutions about the violences they kept enacting.

Invitations to speak about complaint *to* institutions can be used *by* them. Yes, I was being *given the nod*. Institutions (and probably also individuals), by inviting me to speak on complaint, created an impression that they were willing to hear critiques of themselves. Another time I gave a lecture that included a discussion of nodding as a non-performative.

A number of senior managers were in attendance, seated towards the front of the lecture theatre. Afterwards some students came up to me. They had been seated behind the senior managers. The students observed that the senior managers had been nodding, even nodding during my discussion of nodding! The students were at the tail end of a long and difficult complaint. And they told me that the management had enacted the very tactics that I was describing in the lecture. Nodding can be about recognizing a problem insofar as the problem is safely construed as being about somewhere else or as coming from someone else. Even critiques of how our complaints are used can be used.

Another time, I was about to give a lecture in a university and was sent a direct message by someone on social media. It was a warning that the person who had invited me was using the invitation as a screen and that he himself had been the object of complaints about sexual misconduct. The message came to me just before the lecture. I went ahead with it, perhaps against my better judgement, otherwise known as my **killjoy judgement**, because I did not want to let people down who were coming to listen. After the lecture, there was a dinner. The professor began speaking to me, leaning on me, telling me how teaching was erotic, how students wanted to have sex with the professors, so what could they do. I felt the hand of a feminist colleague on my arm, not a disciplining hand, but a hand that said, I know you need to get out of here. I got out of there.

Yet another time I was contacted by students before visiting their campus. They told me that the head of their department, who had disciplined them repeatedly for complaining too loudly or in the wrong way, had shared one of my emails on PowerPoint. She did this without my knowledge or permission. Why? She seemed to be using my work as a way of performing something, giving herself credibility, perhaps, despite how much she had been complicit in the institutional violence against the students themselves. I thus had to ask for the seminar I was scheduled to hold in that department to be student-only. I found the whole experience triggering. It reminded me of what had happened at my own workplace, how they (managers, colleagues) kept trying to pull me away from the students with whom I was doing the work.

If institutions use our work, even our work that critiques how they use our work, so too do individuals. I talked to Samia about this problem. She described how white feminists would constantly refer to my own work, even mentioning my critiques of the non-performativity of anti-racism as if they were not themselves implicated in the critiques. She joked, 'We can ask them to put on a non-performative badge. That's you, we are talking about you!' Even then they would probably nod, and think we were talking about somebody else.

I communicated informally with another woman of colour who had shared on social media that white women had 'weaponized' my work on complaint whilst 'tirelessly harassing and targeting WOC [women of colour] in academia.' She added, 'Your insurgent and activist work has been weaponized by these women to give them the language of resistance and marginalization while they continue to inflict racist harm on BIPOC [Black, Indigenous and people of colour] in academia.' Earlier I mentioned Karen, that white woman who uses complaints to claim space for herself. I am well aware that Karen could be reading my work. She could be reading this book. You could be Karen! I am not addressing Karen, nor am I interested in stopping Karen from reading this work (even if I could). I am addressing other women of colour, those of you who recognize the problem with her name.

I have learnt from how my research on complaint has been used against people who have complained. One student who made a complaint about her supervisor wrote to me after attending one of my lectures. She explained what happened:

'One of the worst parts was the tribunal at the end, where we were cross-examined by my supervisor's lawyer, without any guidelines in place to regulate what could be asked. This turned out badly for many reasons. However, what I thought might be of interest was that me and the other complainants were asked by the lawyer, suspiciously, if we read "feminist theory" (!) and specifically whether we'd attended your lecture on complaint. The implication was that we'd somehow all got together after the lecture and workshop to plot a complaint, although the process had in fact begun far earlier. The university team had to collect other people's tweets about your lecture and work to demonstrate that my tweet was not unusual.'

To get a complaint through the system, we often have to become activists, by which I mean, we have to organize collectively. But then our complaints are dismissed as activism.

Even attending a lecture on complaint can then be used as evidence against a complainant; as plotting something, a feminist plot. Perhaps feminism is treated as infection, what causes a complaint to spread.

Become a feminist infection!

Maybe that, too, is what it means to be a complaint collective: the closer we get to each other, the more we catch. When we launched my academic monograph *Complaint!*, back in 2021, we created a complaint collective. It was during the pandemic, so it was a virtual launch. One woman wrote after the event, 'It is so comforting to know WE ARE NOT ALONE, thank you all for sharing this space of complaint.' Another shared that 'as a feminist killjoy', she was also a complaint collector who had 'accompanied other complainers for almost a decade'. She added, 'It does make a huge difference being part of a collective, feeling part of something larger.' Another woman said that even if she was 'thrown out', for complaining, she would, 'have no regrets, because now I know that I am not alone, there are many of us!' Complaint collectives: so many manys.

COMPLAINT TO PROTEST

I began this chapter by reflecting on different people's trajectories into complaint activism; and I conclude by considering the actions themselves. For some people, a complaint *is* a protest action, how they intervene in a situation or make a problem more visible. For example, in 2022, Tony Jones lodged a complaint with the Royal Commission in Australia after an airline refused to help him transfer from his custom electric wheelchair into an 'aisle chair' – a narrow wheelchair that Jetstar requires passengers to use to be taken to their seat on the plane. He explained: 'Going to the Human Rights Commission is really the only way I can get this properly addressed, because the first step is mediation and it brings you and the carrier together.'[27] Jones said he hoped his complaint would act as a test case to draw attention to the fact that 'air travel should be accessible to everyone and when airlines have a policy, they need to honour it.'

Jones's complaint, alongside those lodged by other disabled travellers, led the Disability Royal Commission engagement team to organize workshops for disabled people to share their experiences. Tamara Weaver, director of Community Engagement, commented: 'These workshops provided a valuable opportunity to hear directly from people impacted by inaccessible systems, procedures and infrastructure in the air travel industry and to discuss ways to improve it.' Disability advocate Zoe Simmons said, 'Our stories just get swept under the rug. We get told we are the problem. People don't realize how widespread the problem is.'[28] Actions can have knock-on effects; complaints can create platforms for other complaints.

Whilst some people understand their complaints as

protest, for others complaints lead to protest because of what the complaints failed to achieve. Academics and students based at Complutense University in Madrid were frustrated by how their institution treated complaints about sexual harassment rather like dirty laundry, as what should not be aired in public. Irene Blanco-Fuente, Marta Eulalia Blanco-García, Paula Martín-Peláez, Syra Peláez-Orero and Carmen Romero-Bachiller described how they created a 'rather ordinary clothesline at the entrance of the Students University Cafe'. They then 'invited all passers-by to peg their own stories of harassment on the clothesline, as a washing out display to give presence to situations usually identified as absent.' They said they wanted 'to wash out the silence'.[29]

Protests can be *about* complaints or at least how they have been handled. The point of a protest can be to make that complaint again but in a way that makes it more visible. Emma Sulkowicz's *Mattress Performance (Carry That Weight)* could be described as protest art. Emma carried a mattress around her campus to call attention to the campus sexual assaults, including her own rape by another student in 2012.[30] Journalist Roberta Smith called the piece 'symbolically laden yet drastically physical'. She said, 'It is so simple: a woman with a mattress, refusing to keep her violation private, carrying with her a stark reminder of where it took place.' Emma walked her complaint around the campus in protest at how the man who had assaulted her had been protected.

When bodies bear the weight of complaint, it is not

surprising they are how complaints become protests. In 2013, artists and practice-based researchers Jenny Richards and Sophie Hope, began a project, *Manual Labours*, about our physical relationship to work. They explored 'The Complaining Body', and the world of workplace complaints. The research, developed with artist Sarah Browne, choreographer Hamish MacPherson and writer Ivor Southwood, involved a series of workshops with call centre workers in a London borough council, commuters on a train station platform in Worcester and staff dealing with student complaints in a UK university. They observed, 'The emotional labour involved in listening to and managing complaints, the social and cultural conditions of complaining and the effect of not complaining all have repercussions on the body as a site of resistance, absorption and expulsion.' They concluded that 'the uncomplaining body is often in fact a sick body, having to perform a healthy body and happy self by internalizing and stifling our complaints.'[31]

To be a complaining body can be to protest the conditions in which we work. Ileana Jiménez describes how a group of high school students enacted a form of 'complaint activism' she calls 'embodied wilfulness'. The students at her school found out that the school did not have a policy on sexual harassment. There was an empty space where the policy was supposed to be. For the students, complaint activism was about filling the empty spaces: 'Within days of discovering the missing sexual harassment policy, the girls staged an assembly that revealed a screenshot from the school's online handbook where the policy should have been.

The screenshot laid bare exactly what was "missing", tucked between "theft" and "tobacco use" and other behaviours that the school does not condone, were the words "sexual harassment".[32] The students turned the absence of a policy into a performance. They assembled together, turning their bodies into a collective, making the absence of the policy present.

Jiménez discusses how one student's words related to the conduct of a senior administrator at the school. He was at the assembly. The student, Gabi, did not sit down after she said her words. She stayed standing. Jiménez was scared on her behalf: 'There was no policy to protect the girls at the school, and certainly not the girls on stage. There was no policy that would protect Gabi if the school realized that the "superior" she mentioned was actually in the room.' To complain of a person who is in the room is to become vulnerable to retaliation. Later, as they watched the performance together, Gabi asked, 'Why am I standing? Like the reason why it bothers me so much is because it's already such a vulnerable experience and, like, I do not have to be standing more than I have to. So literally why am I standing? Everyone else is going up and down like whack-a-moles. And I'm literally standing. Thank God Helen was standing too. I have stage fright, like I'm gripping on to my script. I think, honestly, I was scared.' Gabi had stayed standing not because she was being disobedient but because she was afraid; she forgot the script, her body swaying. It is not just that our bodies can express our complaints. When we get our bodies out there, on the stage, they tell us something about the situation that we might not have consciously registered.

Complaint activism can be about how we end up standing up. In chapter 2, I referenced Abigail Thorn's film about complaining as a trans woman to the NHS (and about the NHS) for the failure to receive the healthcare to which she was entitled. At one point in her film, which itself could be described as complaint activism, Abigail describes how she wrote those complaints on placards, demonstrating with them, outside the NHS headquarters. In chapter 1, I suggested that a complaint can be the sound of a transition from a private to a public domain. Some publics can be rather restricted. Complaint activism can be how you jump *between* publics – rather than making demands inside a building you make them outside it.

Complaint activism thus draws on old methods for direct action. In December 2021, trans and queer activists enacted a 'die-in' outside NHS headquarters, staging the deadly consequences of the failure to provide equality in healthcare. Queer activists had previously used die-ins to focus attention on the costs of the AIDS crisis. Actor David Montalvo notes, 'While AIDS activists weren't the first to simulate death to call attention to lethal threats, the action became a powerful tool to show that, because the epidemic was being stigmatized and ignored, bodies were piling up.'[33] To stage a die-in is to make many bodies immobile, as if dead, as if gone, to *enact* the consequences of unheard complaints. More recently, in July 2024, after the government imposed a temporary ban on the use of puberty blockers for trans youth, the activist group Trans Kids Deserve Better staged a public protest, scaling the NHS headquarters building and standing up on a ledge overhanging the street, displaying signs such as, 'We are not pawns for your politics.'[34] They staged yet more protests in December 2024, when the Labour government made that temporary ban on puberty blockers permanent.[35]

Bodies can say *no*, becoming tools, whether by lying down, standing up, sitting, marching, scaling, trying to force those with the power to make policy to witness how policies are deadly, that lives are at stake. A complaining body can also be striking. Take, for example, the strike action against sexual harassment by workers from McDonald's in 2018. That strike came about as a result of the failure of the company to respond to multiple internal complaints about sexual harassment. Reporter Alex Press commented, 'The employees say McDonald's ignored complaints about workplace sexual harassment, which included groping, propositions for sex, and lewd comments.'[36] In response, 'a McDonald's spokesman said the company had policies and training in place to prevent harassment and would continue to work with experts to "evolve" these practices.' Low-paid workers are more vulnerable to retaliation when they complain about sexual harassment. Press shows how this makes #MeToo 'a tense moment', because workers 'feel empowered to speak up about sexual harassment', at the same time that workers' collective bargaining power is being 'eroded'.

Complaint activism might require forming alliances between workers within and between different organizations and sectors, to push back against those protected by financial as well as institutional power. Consider the action undertaken by cleaners at SOAS, University of London, in 2017. They took action to stop the outsourcing of their work so they would keep having access to the benefits of being employees of the university. The cleaners were nearly all migrants, many of whom did not speak English. Journalist Aditya Chakrabortty described their motivation:

> The cleaners had one big goal – to be directly employed by the college they worked at, rather than through another company. Top of SOAS's values is 'promoting equality and celebrating diversity' – yet members of its own community suffered economic apartheid. Unlike direct employees, the cleaners got no sick pay, hardly any holiday pay and the minimum wage. They cleaned up after lectures on worker exploitation – a subject on which they were the experts.[37]

So many complaints about worker exploitation are made in organizations that pride themselves on their equality and diversity. You can be lecturing on precarious workers and still ignore the precarious workers in your own organization. Chakrabortty notes that the cleaners' complaints, 'however serious', would usually 'go ignored'. The cleaners succeeded in beating the system even though they were repeatedly told that they couldn't. They enlisted other members of the university, including professors and the student union, to put pressure on management to recognize their trade union. In June 2009, SOAS cleaners 'finally forced outsourcing firm ISS to recognize their trade union'. Chakrabortty again: 'Days later, they were summoned to an early-morning meeting on campus, ostensibly to discuss shift patterns. Doors were blocked and when ISS representatives mentioned the phrase "immigration papers", immigration officials in riot gear stormed into the hall. They checked everyone's status.'

Outsourcing had made the cleaners 'somebody else's problem'. The raid, that display of state force, 'made that untenable'. Through protest, the problem could no longer be somebody else's. It ended up displayed for everyone in the organization to see, 'student protestors were now occupying the director's offices; walls were covered in graffiti'. Chakrabortty concludes that the cleaners 'had effectively exhausted their employer'.

To resist the institution is to exhaust it.

Or to be more specific, to resist the institution requires exhausting its capacities to resist being changed. To complain can feel like being overtaken by the institution. Complaint activism is how you get more people involved in the complaint, so it overtakes the institution.

Complaint activism can sometimes be about getting a complaint out of the building. It can also be how we occupy the building. For example, students at Goldsmiths formed an action group, Goldsmiths Anti-Racist Action (GARA) in 2019 after their individual complaints about racism had been ignored. They occupied the main hub of the college, Deptford Town Hall, for 137 days, protesting the lack of commitment to anti-racism at the college. The college tried to force them out: they were granted a possession order for the building by a judge at the high court. This order was granted on the same day that the parties reached an agreement, with the university making 'some concessions', including a commitment to anti-racist training for staff.

Ethiraj Gabriel Dattatreyan and Akanksha Mehta, two academics of colour, noted how the university appeared to be listening to students at the same time as they engaged in a disciplinary process against them:

> *Just as GARA was coming to a final agreement with management, it found pinned on the door of Deptford Town Hall a large envelope with over 500 pages of documents charging trespass and filled with social media 'evidence' of GARA members' involvement in the occupation. Rather than a simple injunction, senior management threatened to prosecute core individuals involved in the occupation if they didn't vacate the building immediately.*[38]

That this institution, known for being radical and progressive, showed itself willing to use force mattered. When a complaint remains invisible, so does the force used against those making it. By turning their complaint into an occupation, the students *forced the force out*. Forcing the force out is how they peeled away the polish of the non-performative, the emptiness of the hearings that took place behind those doors. The documents that might have been filed away end up posted on the door.

When complainers become institutional plumbers, learning the different methods used to stop the complaints from getting through, they are on the route to becoming complaint activists. I suggested earlier that to persist with a complaint is to see a sequence: when one method does not stop the complaint, other methods are used. If it is politicizing to see the sequence, it can be even more politicizing to see through it. You learn how organizations give a nod to a complaint, appear to hear those who are complaining, *at the very same time* as they try to expel them with force. By turning the complaint into an occupation, activists demonstrated how participation in formal complaints is used to manage conflict and disagreement. As Dattatreyan and Mehta observed, 'Complaint and grievance, in the eyes of management, become the grounds to cultivate participation while dampening collective rage.' We need to be aware of the tactics used to manage our complaints. And we need to cultivate our rage against these tactics.

6/ Complaint as a Queer Method

The words we use for our complaints teach us about them. One lecturer, Eric, used the word *surreal* to describe his experience. He talked of how papers kept appearing and disappearing from his complaint file: 'I would bend towards the surreal, the situations have been so bizarre.' It was the surreal nature of complaint that led Eric to share his complaint with me: 'I want to believe there is some research value in that because it is so strange.' I agree there is a research value in telling stories of complaint precisely because of how strange they can be; how odd, how queer.

That complaints are such a queer experience might be why they offer a queer method. In her book *Feeling Backward: Loss and the Politics of Queer History*, Heather Love reflects on how queer critics have turned to the past for redemption: 'In attempting to construct a positive genealogy of gay identity, queer critics have found themselves at a loss about what to do with the sad old queens and long-suffering dykes who haunt the historical record.'[1] Love suggests those figures who haunt our history should not be abandoned. A queer method might then not be the motion of looking forward but 'feeling backward', going over what is hard and painful and difficult. Complaints too have a backward temporality. We go back over what isn't over but is often treated as if it is.

I have approached complaints as coming out stories. In this chapter, I show how we don't just come out with a complaint or in one. We also need to get complaints *out* of institutions. That's how we find out how much has been buried. Unburial can be revelatory. It can also be surreal.

FALSE POSITIVES

The word *queer* has been used, and is still used, as an insult, a smear or a slur for those whose sexuality is not straight. To embrace the word *queer* for our projects is to head towards what we are told would or should make us miserable, depriving ourselves of the safety of a brightly lit path. To complain, we are also told, is to head in a miserable direction, killing our careers as well as any hopes for happiness or inclusion. Complaints are often treated as contagious, as if we can catch negativity from them. To make complaint our queer method is to turn negativity into a tool. We direct the *no* that has been directed at us back to the institutions that do not accommodate us.

It is hard not to be pulled in by positivity. I ended the previous chapter with Ethiraj Gabriel Dattatreyan and Akanksha Mehta's argument that management uses participation in a complaint process as a way of 'dampening the collective rage' of those complaining. Participation sounds positive. It can also be how you are redirected by engaging in an institutional process. I think back to my experience of having my arm pulled by an administrator who wanted to tell me about the institution's 'side' of a story about racism that does not have sides. To be pulled into *that* dialogue would have been to be pulled *away* not only from complaint but from the other complainers, the students, my complaint collective.

I had to pull my arm away on another occasion. I had just given a talk on racism. A white woman came up to me after and put her arm next to mine. She said, very quietly, 'We are almost the same colour.' I looked at our arms, seeing how she wanted me to see them, how others too might see them, not different, in harmony, in solidarity even. When we speak of racism we are often met with denial. It might be hard to hear the aggression, but I felt it. I said nothing. I pulled my arm away, letting it do the talking.

I call such gestures *false positives*. They might appear to be positive, to open a door or a dialogue, but are not. Let's return to Laura's testimony. Laura had left one department where she had been racially harassed by a white woman who was her head of department. She ended up in another department where she was racially harassed by a white woman who was her head of department. When yet another white woman became head of her department, she said to Laura, 'I want you to reconcile with her because after all she is my friend and colleague and all she ever did was write you some long emails.' Her friend had done much more than write long emails: harassment is often minimized as a style of communication. An expression of desire for reconciliation might appear to be a friendly gesture. It is not. If Laura is not willing to smooth things over, she will be the one who breaks the connection by refusing to repair it.

Reconciliation can be the requirement that we reconcile ourselves not only to other people but to history, to injustices. We become ill adjusted, maladjusted, when we do not adjust to injustices.

Don't adjust to injustice!

We have to see through gestures that might seem on the surface conciliatory. Andrea, for example, who complained about 'an important man' received an apology from him. It was an unsolicited apology; it suddenly appeared in her complaint file. She said, 'I think it's a box-ticking exercise, oh, at least he apologized, but look at the words, think about what an apology really means then tell me you've apologized or whether you have got a lawyer and wrote a letter that you wanted to show.' To describe an apology as a box-ticking exercise is to suggest that the apology is fulfilling a bureaucratic function. Some apologies are made so they can be shown to have been made ('a letter that you wanted to show'). Andrea added, 'I didn't ask for any contact from that man. He is a bully. He already lives in my nightmares.' The apology allowed the professor to enter her complaint file in the same way he had entered her mind ('He already lives in my nightmares'). She said, 'I think they thought I would accept it as a real apology.' To accept his apology would be to accept how he had inserted himself, into her complaint, her file, her life. Finding that letter in the file is to be put under pressure to accept it, to move on with it, to get on with it. An apology might be offered as a way of drawing a line under the past. An apology can be how you are told it would be over if you got over it.

I am not willing to get over what is not over.

You might be told that time heals. That relationships heal. Sometimes they do, but sometimes they don't. Or won't. You might need to end some relationships to persons (or institutions) to have the time and space you need to heal. Feminists have long shown that ending abusive relationships is extremely difficult because of the dynamics of abuse. Some of this dynamic could be called *insistence on relation*. I use these terms precisely because they sound positive. Let's say you experience a person's conduct as hostile or abusive. If that person *insists on relation*, it means they will not allow you to end the relationship or to withdraw from it without entering further discussion. If you were to try to withdraw, the person may apologize, express regret, promise they will change. And then you end up back in relation.

Insistence on relation names a complex inter-personal power dynamic that can be reinforced by a complaint process. Jenny, an undergraduate student who was harassed by her tutor, was advised by a complaints officer to write him a letter. She said, 'I have no wish to reopen channels of communication with him as I have successfully cut myself off and I do not want to start a conversation with him or give him a chance to explain himself.'

In earlier chapters, I explored how some solutions to complaints about harassment and bullying make light of them. The problem with some solutions is also the expectation of communication. I talked to Gina, a woman professor who had been bullied by her head of department. She was invited to a mediation meeting: 'The deputy vice-chancellor then said, I am going to give you this gift, I have arranged for you to go to this hotel, and I have arranged for this person, a negotiator, to sit with you and sort this out. I had been bullied and called in so many times by this guy. I just thought, I am not going to a mediation meeting with this person.' Being asked to enter mediation is represented as a gift as if all that is needed to resolve the problem is time and proximity. To be asked to be in the room with someone who has bullied you is to be asked to witness a bully be given more opportunities for self-expression.

When some people try to withdraw from relationships with people who are abusive, the withdrawal will typically be framed as the beginning rather than the end of hostilities. Alex, a non-binary academic, wrote to me about their experience of being harassed by a professor who identified as 'gender critical'. They had found out from other colleagues that the professor was 'operating in anti-trans circles: groups invested in stripping rights from trans people'. Alex had no interest in stopping the professor from expressing her views. They just did not want to have to engage with them. 'I kept my head down,' they said, but 'she wouldn't leave me alone.' The 'gender critical' academic would not accept this refusal to engage. And so, Alex tried to have an email dialogue with her about sex and gender 'to see if we could find a way through, a mutual understanding of our differences'. But it did not work. Alex explained. 'The tone and level of disclosure in her emails made me uncomfortable.' The professor then accused them 'of silencing, threatening, no-platforming, and harassing', even though 'she seemed to have no problem finding various platforms on which to loudly proclaim her views.' Alex added, 'This was never about repair or resolution. It was about humiliation. Forcing me to engage with ideas that undermine my humanity in ever increasingly hostile spaces.'

You might be invited to participate in a conversation or debate that ends up undermining your existence. In 2020, journalist and political commentator Owen Jones published an article about homophobia, which he shared on Facebook. One person commented in response: 'We should be allowed to debate whether homosexuality is a mental illness.' This statement did not claim that homosexuality is a mental illness. It said we should be allowed to debate whether or not it is. One suspects that only a person who has such a viewpoint, that homosexuality is a mental illness, would articulate a desire to make that viewpoint debatable. If we were to reopen the debate as to whether homosexuality was a mental illness, gay people would have to defend ourselves against this claim, to say, we are not mentally ill, to give time to what undermines our existence.

Calls to debate are often *false positives*, requiring some people to be in proximity with views that undermine their existence. In chapter 4, I described sex-realist feminism as a thinly masked hostile environment. Sex-realist feminists often call for a debate about sex and gender. The call to debate functions as a claim that sex-realist feminists have not been allowed to have that debate, in other words, that they have been silenced (though reflecting back on Alex's testimony, this claim to be silenced might be another version of *insistence on relation*; a demand that other people listen). Sex-realist feminists, in calling for a debate, might be responding, in part, to the principle of 'no debate' that is typically identified with trans and trans-inclusive organizations such as Mermaid and Stonewall but is widely used by members of the LGBTQIA+ community. 'No debate' means trans people should not have to debate their existence. As actor Elliot Page puts it, 'There's no debate to trans people's existence – full stop.' He added, 'To debate our existence continuously over and over again, I think it's appalling.'[2]

'No debate' does *not* mean we should *not* debate terms such as sex and gender. Many feminists, especially trans and queer feminists, have, in fact, long been debating sex and gender. If you consult this critical literature, you will find feminist critiques of gender, feminist uses of the sex–gender distinction, feminist critiques of that very distinction, as well as feminist critiques of sex.[3] Returning to these debates is helpful as it reminds us that the terms *sex* and *gender* have always been disputed within feminism. Sex-realist feminists, however, tend to repeat the same point, that sex is fact, gender a fiction, *as if these terms had not been long disputed within feminism.*[4] Treating sex as an undisputed fact, and gender a disputed fiction, does something precisely because of who these terms are associated with. As I pointed out in chapter 4, apparently neutral statements such as 'sex is real' quickly slide into claims that trans people are *not* real; that they are both deluded and dangerous.

The call to debate *sex* and *gender* is thus not *really* about debating the terms themselves (that's the *false positive*). The

'Let's have a debate about sex and gender.'

call for debate is *how* the very existence of trans people is made debatable. Let's return to the 'Birds welcome' sign.

That sign 'Birds welcome' could be an invitation to debate about whether some people are *really* birds (birds is also slang for women and girls). You are being invited to enter the box to join a debate about whether you are entitled to enter it. That very debate leads to the posting of more and more letters in the box, more offensive statements about how you are not real, not who you say you are, imposing your beliefs on others, being dangerous or deluded. *A debate can be the requirement to be in proximity to such statements.* Were you to enter the box, to write letters to oppose theirs, those letters would end up in the same pile, dialogue as displacement. It can be exhausting to have to keep debating your existence. As Shon Faye describes in *The Transgender Issue*, borrowing terms from Toni Morrison, 'Such debates are time-consuming, exhausting distractions from what we should really be focusing on: the material ways in which we are oppressed.'[5]

A yes can be another 'exhausting distraction'. One method for dampening the energy of those committed to justice and freedom is to offer to negotiate. A false positive *is* a non-performative: a *yes* is how you are drawn into a situation that gives you more power, but only on condition you give up your will or capacity to say *no*. To resist being pulled in by false positives is to hold on to our complaints, both as a historical resource and as a source of energy and power.

INSTITUTIONAL CLOSETS

Complaints can be how we say *no* to violence. They can be why we say *no*. We might say *no* to get the violence out from behind closed doors, to bring the institution to account. But that violence can then be reburied by paperwork, as we learnt from Mia's experience of being assaulted by her head of department only for the report that followed her complaint to describe it as 'on par with a handshake'. Or the papers themselves can be buried, as we learnt from Viola, who said all the materials generated by her complaint ended up 'as a file'. A file can be a bin. One student, Drew, said her complaint was 'shoved in the box'. Or a file can be a grave. Another student, Kay, said her complaint went 'into the complaint graveyard'.

A filing cabinet can be where complaints go to die. Anne, who made a complaint about bullying comments: 'One of the things I talked about in those documents, I am very open, I was under such stress and trauma that my periods stopped. That's the intimacy of some of the things that go into it, bodily functions like this.' She told me of a senior manager who had read her complaint, with all its intimate embodied detail, but remained indifferent. Her mother, in contrast, said in sympathy, 'It must have been so awful.' A body has to bear it, what is 'so awful'. *That* body can stop functioning. *That* body can end up in a document. And *that* document can end up in a file. And that file can end up in a cabinet.

We can be buried with our complaints.
We can be buried by them.

I call filing cabinets 'institutional closets' to point not just to how but why information is buried. The word *closet* evokes a queer history, to be in the closet is to keep something secret about oneself. An institutional closet holds information that institutions intend to keep secret about themselves. Some of their secrets are our complaints. A complainer knows a burial has happened. And not just one. Anna describes how she came to realize how many complaints her institution had buried: 'The scale of the response was so extreme compared to what we were complaining about. Now on reflection I guess it was because there were hundreds of complaints they'd suppressed, so they did not want to have a lid lifted on it.' When an institution tries to stop one complaint, it might be because they are trying to keep hundreds of others in the closet.

When institutional closets succeed, we do not know about them. It is not just complaints that are buried, histories are too. The institutional closet thus offers another way of thinking about history itself. In 2011, an archive became public: a collection of documents, 8,800 files to be exact, from thirty-seven former British colonies. Among these documents were 'a handful which show that many of the most sensitive papers from Britain's late colonial era were not hidden away but simply destroyed'. These documents instructed that post-independence governments should not get any material that 'might embarrass Her Majesty's government', that could 'embarrass members of the police, military forces, public servants or others, for example, police informers', that might compromise intelligence sources, or that might 'be used unethically by ministers in the successor government'.[6] We have traces within an archive of the papers missing from it, destroyed because of what they would evidence.

The British empire was an empire of closets. So much of violence in that history has been buried, and not just by destroying documents. A story can be a closet. Empire is often told as a happy story; a polite story of well-mannered English colonizers that is so familiar because of how many times we have heard it before.[7] We learn not just from the story but *where* it is told and to whom. In the *Life of the United Kingdom*, a guide to citizenship tests, empire is referenced in primarily positive terms as what brought 'more regular, acceptable impartial systems of law and order' to the colonies.[8] There is mention of the devastating loss of life from two world wars but not from colonialism or slavery.

Citizenship might be the requirement to parrot that shiny, happy story of empire. Consider how India was described as a 'jewel in the Crown', a colony as a shiny stone, of value to the state and the monarchy. Perhaps those of us who come from countries colonized by Britain are supposed to gleam as well as be grateful, not just smile for their brochures but gloss over the violence that led many of us to be here. This might be another way of understanding diversity: as an institutional closet. Trevor Phillips, the former chair of the Commission for Racial Equality, gave a speech to the Conservative party in 2005. He described empire thus: 'We created something called the empire where we mixed and mingled with people very different from those of these islands.' Yes, the subjugation and enslavement of millions of people is described as a bit like a party.

Violence can be buried in a story of empire. Or by a story. That the empire is not far away in time or space is evidenced by the experiences many people of colour have within institutions. Mira shared with me what happened when she participated in a project on diversity. She had been instrumental in getting the project funded, only to be shut out once it was. She was the only person of colour on the team. She knew she had been *used* to get them the funding; she said she was treated as a 'mascot'. One of the directors of the project was a senior white woman. She was also a direct descendant of colonizers: 'she is high colonial British Raj . . . her grandmother's gravestone is in Calcutta and that's rare, you have to be really high up in the British Raj.' Mira added, 'We have to go back to understand what is happening, the colonial history of Britain, how we are still refusing to have a dialogue about South Asian and East Asian histories, because the relatives are still alive, the descendants are still alive, and reparations is a dirty word for these people; it means having to confront their wealth, the filth of their wealth.' To complain about racism in the present is to go back, to go over what they refuse to go over, a colonial history living on, in and through the inheritance of wealth.

The British empire *remains* an empire of closets. Consider Palestine. British imperialists had a key role to play in what happened to Palestine in the early twentieth century, in the form of deals made by government officials: the Sykes-Picot treaty of 1916, the Balfour declaration of 2 November 1917. Balfour's letter written on behalf of His Majesty's Government was no secret. Addressed to Lord Rothchild, it both 'declared sympathy' with Zionist aspirations and viewed 'with favour' the 'establishment in Palestine of a national home for Jewish people'. Ramzy Baroud describes how he heard the name Balfour as a child growing up in a Gaza refugee camp, because the anniversary of the declaration was a day of protest. He concludes: 'While Balfour cannot be blamed for all the misfortunes that have befallen Palestinians since he communicated his brief but infamous letter, the notion that his "promise" embodied – that of complete disregard of the aspirations of the Palestinian Arab people – is handed from one generation of British diplomats to the next, the same way that Palestinian resistance to colonialism is also spread across generations.'[9]

Letters do not need to be filed away to be hidden. Balfour promised that land away, with 'complete disregard' for the Palestinian people living there. But many of us living in Britain, and its former colonies, are not taught about it. And so, we need to learn to see through the history we were taught. What I was taught in the classes on the Holocaust at school will forever remain etched on my skin; the horror of learning what human beings were capable of doing to other human beings. I was taught that Israel came into existence because of that horror. I came home after one of these classes and spoke of Israel. My father said to me, 'It was Europeans taking that land.' I can now hear in what my father said something of his own history: as a child, he and his family were forced to leave their home because of another line created and enforced by the colonizer: Partition, the division of India and Pakistan in 1947. A line for some is memory, not map, a place where so much violence happened.

That was one time my father said something to me that hit a nerve, a spark of realization that there could be another truth, a **killjoy truth**. Such truths rattle around, unsettling us. I was unsettled by a question: could the solution be the problem, another story of empire, Europeans making 'the others' pay for their crimes against 'the others', crimes against Jewish people, crimes against humanity?

A few years later, when I was studying for my literature degree, I read Edward Said's classic book *Orientalism*. There was another sentence that struck me. It is the one time Said himself appeared in the text. He wrote:

> *Much of the personal investment in this study derives from my awareness of being an 'Oriental' as a child growing up in two British colonies. All of my education, in those colonies (Palestine and Egypt) and in the United States, has been Western, and yet that deep early awareness has persisted. In many ways my study of Orientalism has been an attempt to inventory the traces upon me, the Oriental subject, of the culture whose domination has been so powerful a factor in the life of all Orientals.*[10]

I followed Said's inventory, another archive of complaint. I read his critique of Zionism. Said shows, through painstakingly close readings of Zionist narratives, how Palestine was rendered 'a *whole* territory essentially unused, unappreciated, misunderstood . . . *to be made* useful, appreciated, understandable'. Said notes how to be 'made useful', however forcefully uttered, was written in the language of care. Palestine was treated as 'an empty and patient territory, awaiting people who show a proper care of it'.[11] Palestine became empty, waiting, rather like *terra nullius*, a 'territory without a master', how Britain justified the colonial conquest of Australia.

Palestine and Palestinians are emptied of 'meaning or life', to borrow terms from anthropologist Mary Turfah. She explains:

> *Zionism's solution for the 'problem' of the Palestinians is to empty them of any meaning or life that is not self-referential, such that they can be eliminated without triggering remorse, such that the decision to let them stay – on the land, alive, it doesn't matter – becomes an act of benevolence. If the Palestinians are allowed historical grievances (or anything beyond 'desires and prejudices'), a consciousness before Zionism, beyond Europe, Zionism collapses.*[12]

A historic grievance is evidence of an existence.

To remove a people, Zionism removed the violence of that removal. That framing is how a genocide against the Palestinian people by Israel is being conducted in full view of the world. It was living and writing during these genocidal times that led me to revisit the idea of **killjoy truths** and to reuse them in this book.[13] Remember: the blinds come down because the violence is seen. Ideology can be understood as an institutional blind, how violence is shut out.

In the violence that is seen, we see the violence that is not.

We see the violence of the Hamas-led attacks on 7 October 2023. But we also need to see the violence that came before, the violence of colonial occupation, in the violence that came after. When we hear how Palestinians have been talked about since that day, it is history we hear. 'Human animals.' 'Not a humanitarian crisis.' 'Not ethnic cleansing' because they are 'not humans'. 'Not civilians.' 'The children of darkness.' In the UK, those of us who call the actions undertaken by Israel 'genocide' are called extremists; another grievance not permitted. That so many people over the globe are protesting against Israel, naming genocide, also Israeli apartheid, tells us that what is not permitted can still be expressed. It can take a movement, a global movement, to get the truth out. It will still be way too late for way too many.

It is important to remember that institutional closets are temporary residences; what goes in will come out, one way or another, at one time or another. We have learnt this from the genre of complaints described as 'historic institutional abuse'. In 2022, minister for Northern Ireland Michelle McIlveen offered an apology to 'victims and survivors of historical institutional abuse; on behalf of the State'. She apologized to them that they had 'not been believed or protected'.[14] The Historical Institutional Abuse Inquiry (HIA) had examined complaints about twenty-two homes run by the state, churches and charities between 1922 to 1995. This inquiry into the abuse of children took place in 2017, almost a decade after survivors began lobbying. It revealed a pattern of abuse of children in homes in Northern Ireland. It also revealed a long history of cover-ups of complaints and allegations: 'When boys complained about the abuse they experienced there is evidence that their accounts were ignored or not taken seriously or were not adequately investigated by the Belfast Welfare Authority or the Eastern Health and Social Services Board.'[15]

Inquiries into historic institutional abuse in care and residential homes for children have taken place in numerous countries. Kathleen Daly, in her account of institutional abuse in Canada, refers to how the story began to leak:

On Monday, 13 February 1989, St John's Radio Host Bill Rowe received a call to his morning talk show programme 'Open Line'. It was from Steve Neary, a colleague of Rowe's during their year together in politics. On air, Neary said that in a 1979 inquiry, testimony was given of a cover-up in 1975 when the police investigated the sexual and physical abuse of residents at Mount Cashel, a school for boys in St Johns, Newfoundland.

Interviewed later, Neary said he had no idea that the phone call would 'set up such a chain reaction'.[16]

There is happenstance in how complaints come out so many years after the abuse happened. A leak is how we learn of a closet. It can take just a small opening, a call on a radio show, for so many complaints to come out. An institutional closet is not then a singular object where history is hidden. Each person who is silenced for complaining, for saying *no* to abuse, becomes another closet; memories becoming burdens, passed down over generations. For that history to come out, for the institution to be 'outed', those who were abused have to provide evidence of what they suffered, to testify, to bear witness, to keep doing so, to relive the violence by giving it form.

Histories can come out because they are in the materials we share. One time, I was speaking at a conference on race and racism in Canada. I read out the Grimm story of the wilful child. Maria Campbell, a Métis writer, was in the audience. At the end of my talk, she stood up and told me that she had heard the story before because the nuns in her residential school used to tell it. It was the arm she remembered, how it kept coming up until it was beaten down. She did not know where the story came from. We can hear something else in that Grimm story, once we know where it travelled. The residential schools in Canada were tools of assimilation; one school's motto was 'Kill the Indian, save the man'. The story of the wilful child was delivered as a warning to Indigenous children, to make them obey, to remove wilfulness from themselves, to identify with the rod, the school, the nuns, with whiteness, the imperial project.

There is so much violence in this history, so many graveyards, complaint graveyards, actual graveyards, too.[17] Wilfulness might persist, then, as refusal, a refusal to remove one's people from oneself. That is how complaint becomes a life project: *we try to catch the arm as it is still rising.* When Maria stood up to tell me she recognized the story from the arm, she thanked me for sharing it. If it helped her to know the origin of the story, it helped me to know it was helpful to know. It is a lesson that is repeated, one I keep learning: to know a history is to be given a handle. Perhaps that is what we are doing, finding a way to handle histories, the violence of them, creating spaces to share our stories.

Maybe that's another way of thinking about the complaint graveyard, not just as where complaints go to die, but where we gather to bring our stories to life. I shared with Anne the image of a complaint graveyard given to me by Kay. Anne said, 'You have to think about the impact of doing this. Because having yet another complaint, it means that you give more credibility to the one who comes after you. When you talk about haunting, you are talking about the size of the graveyard. And I think this is important. Because when you have one tombstone, one lonely little ghost, it doesn't actually have any effect; you can have a nice cute little cemetery outside your window, but when you start having a massive one, common graveyards and so on, it becomes something else; it becomes much harder to manage.'

In becoming a complaint collective, we become harder to manage, lending each other a hand, giving each other credibility. We become something else, something more explosive. To be buried together is to haunt together. That too is a hope: that our complaints will return to haunt the institutions, a reminder of what has not been dealt with. Complaints tell us another story about time, queer time, how complaints that have been filed away, buried, made to disappear, have not gone.

Complaints have not gone because of what goes on.

Unburying the past is not always possible. One time, Anne was invited by another woman who had been involved in the complaint to meet up. When she was deciding whether to go, disturbed even by the difficulty of having to decide, her husband said to her, 'This is like veterans' reunions.' She explains, 'Whenever you meet, you go back, and you talk about the past and how it is haunting all of you. So, for my own protection, I needed distance, because we would invariably go back, and it would upset me. It would destabilize me. It would pull me back. I need to put all my energy in rebuilding everything they destroyed: self-esteem, self-belief, self-worth.'

We can be haunted not just by the past but by each other. Some people have told me that they could not bring themselves to read my work on complaint because it would be triggering, bringing up a history that was still too hard for them to handle. It is important for me to say: take all the time you need. You might never read this sentence because you are taking the time you need. Killjoy solidarity to absent readers!

COMMUNICATING COMPLAINTS

Sometimes, we might have to shut the door of consciousness to violence in order to focus or function. We shut out what institutions shut in. That is how our complaints, our data, our **killjoy truths**, end up under lock and key. And that's also why opening the doors of institutions requires opening the doors of our consciousness. Even when that opening is painful, it can be how we breathe the past in a little more easily. Heidi Mirza wrote about her experiences of being sexually harassed when she was a student; experiences that were 'so painful' that they 'lie deep in [her] soul in the place of shame'. She describes writing about it now as 'unlocking the doors of shame', so that she 'can begin to exhale'.[18]

It is not simply that our truths, when spoken, so they are 'out there', will change institutions. Even **killjoy truths** don't have the power to do that. But when we unlock a door, and a *no* comes out, *something shifts*. Andrea, who said *no* to a professor only to be warned he was an 'important man', felt something shift. She did not start out by saying *no*; it took her time to say it because of how she doubted herself.

But then she said, 'I was like, *no, no, no, no*, things are wrong not just in terms of gender, things are desperately wrong with the way he is teaching full stop.' Once one *no* came out, others followed, *no, no, no, no*; an army of *nos*. Maybe that is why complaint is an *activist affect*, you feel that release.

Get a *no* out so that others can follow!

Others can be a reference to other *nos*. Or *others* can be a reference to other people who in hearing your *no* might be encouraged to express their own.

This proliferation of *nos* is possible even when *no* shuts a door. It might even be made possible by a shut door. Andrea had wanted to pursue an academic career before that door was shut. But the shut door was not the end of her story. Andrea shared with me recently that she is now teaching at another university and is considering doing a PhD. Having had one door shut, she eventually found her way 'to a much more supportive and kinder environment'. When I first introduced you to Andrea, she expressed some regret for complaining. Now, many years later, she reaffirmed her *no*. She said that by saying *no*, shutting that door, she had 'honoured [her] values'. A *no*, even after it has faltered, can, with more time, become even bolder. She explained, 'I refused to walk to the beat of the institution, to bend to patriarchal abuses of power in order to get ahead on a particular path.' She added, 'I'm so, so glad I shut [that] door.' When you say *no* out of integrity, you don't just lose a path, you make it possible to find another one. And not just for yourself: I think of the feminist values Andrea is now able to pass on to her students, the different paths she might lay for them.

No is a small word with a lot of work to do. Or we might have a lot of work to do to keep it going. Let's return to Stephanie's experience of being assaulted by a lecturer when she was a student, over twenty years ago. She did try to say *no* at the time, writing a letter that was sent to a dean who told her to think of her career and have a cup of tea with the man who assaulted her instead. I communicated with Stephanie along with Kate and Tina who, having been students together, were harassed by lecturers from the same department. I asked Kate and Tina if they had complained at the time. Kate answered, 'No, it was part of the course; it was something you had to put up with. It was almost: that's what they do.' Tina expanded, 'We knew it was really bad, what happened to us. But we didn't know anything about complaint procedures. And I was embarrassed. It didn't feel I had any route, anywhere to go.' When culture is the reason people don't complain, or when people don't know how to complain or don't feel they can, it is not only that the culture is reproduced, but that violence is buried.

A history can be buried without complaint.

Kate, Tina and Stephanie ended up in conversation about their experience as students many years later. How? When a story had broken about sexual harassment at their former institution, Tina had posted a link on Facebook, commenting, 'No surprises there.' Kate responded, 'Some things don't change.' They arranged to meet up. Tina described the process: 'We kind of disclosed everything to each other, what had happened.' They lifted a lid by talking to each other. Tina said, 'It was all very bizarre.' Stephanie shared what they came to know: 'It turned out that between us we had knowledge and firsthand experience of harassment and/or assault from five male members of staff within one department.'

There should have been four of them participating in these conversations. I first learnt of who was missing when Stephanie told me more about the lecturer who'd assaulted her: 'He was a known harasser; there were lots of stories told about him. I had a friend who was very vulnerable, he took advantage of that, she ended up taking her own life.' Their friend committed suicide as a result of a relationship with the same man who'd assaulted Stephanie. I am glad to know the name of their friend and to have learnt more about her since. She is part of this story. That she is not here to tell it is a reminder of just how devastating sexual misconduct and sexual harassment can be. We are not just talking about missing data. We are talking about missing people.

When people are not held to account for abuse, they keep moving, not just on but up. Stephanie said the lecturer who assaulted her kept moving jobs despite the 'black cloud on his record'. When he was retired, his record was clean. She knew this because she looked him up: 'It appears to have had no impact on his career, even though he is a known harasser.' Many people have shared with me such stories of looking up 'known harassers' only to find they had no blemishes on their record. When records are cleaned, there is so much we do not know.

We do not know how many said *no*.

Tina, Kate and Stephanie decided to make a formal complaint, a 'historic complaint'. And they decided to do so because they found out from current students that one of the other professors who had harassed and assaulted them was still 'at it'. They complained not just because history was buried, but because it was being repeated. Still. The scale of abuse in this department should have been a scandal. But no, it wasn't. The institution found a way to bury their complaint, making it history again, quietly retiring the professor; another record cleaned. Stephanie wrote a letter to the university, complaining about how they had 'scaled down the problem to one rogue member of staff who has recently retired'. A *no* can take a long time to come out. That *no* can be reburied.

A *no* in the present can unbury an earlier one. Esther, who inspired the term *complaint activist*, was not getting anywhere with her complaint about the failure of her university to make reasonable adjustments. After a very difficult meeting, a file suddenly appeared: 'A load of documents turned up on the students' union fax machine, and we don't know where they came from. They were historical documents about students who had to leave.' The documents included a handwritten letter to a human rights charity by a former student who had cancer and who was trying to get the university to let her finish her degree part time.

Esther had her own theory about who had sent the file: 'My best theory is that someone in admin cared about it for some personal reason, like they are disabled, their kid is disabled, and decided to carry [out] their own little bit of direct action.' The word *secretary* derives from secrets, the secretary is the keeper of secrets. It would not be surprising that a secretary might become a saboteur; those who do administration, institutional housework, know what is in the files (or even just that there are files). They know how to get the files out. Esther described how, whilst she was making her complaint, administrators had been 'personally supportive' even though they 'weren't allowed to be publicly supportive'. She explained, 'They would say things to me like "I can't give you any advice on this, but I know somebody who used this lawyer" or "Can't give you any advice on this, but have you checked the statutory code on education."' Advice too can be subversive: given by how some people say they can't give it.

Whoever released the file, it helped Esther to keep going with her complaint. She was not the first person to complain. Nor the only person. She had companions. We do not know the name of the student who wrote that handwritten letter. Yet we know that she existed, because of a story of communication in which the file is just a part; she wrote a letter, it ended up in a file, which somebody pulled out, which Esther read and told me about. And now I am telling you.

We can meet in an action without meeting in person.

Communicating complaints is a kind of *time travel*. What is left behind by one generation can be picked up by another. Writing matters because it is how we leave something of ourselves behind. A formal complaint is written in a document. An informal complaint might be scribbled in a book. Or it can be graffiti on a toilet door or a wall. Or a leaflet pressed into other people's hands. After I left my post, students put posters with words from my work on the wall; killjoy sentences including 'When you expose the problem you become the problem.' Yes, they were taken down. But no one can stop them from having been there.

There are so many ways to get the word out. Even to speak of being silenced is to make some noise. Complaints that are filed away, pulled out of circulation, can still be the topic of conversation. One student, Erin, told me that her complaint about sexual harassment ended up in a file. Some years later, she was contacted by two research assistants from the department: 'They told me that my complaint became an influence on many in the faculty, it stirred discussions and uneasiness.' Complaints can stir up conversations. They can be conversations.

We might whisper quiet words in each other's ears about

who to avoid in order to protect yourself. A whisper network is an old-style feminist communication network. In recent times, whisper networks have been semi-formalized by being available electronically. An example is the 'Shitty Media Men' list, which began as a Google spreadsheet by Moira Donegan. It was initially anonymous. Donegan only came out as the author after rumours she was going to be doxed.[19] Dalit feminist Raya Sarkar compiled a list of alleged abusers in Indian universities only to be chastised by feminist academics for not using the 'systems of transparent and just procedures of accountability' they had 'worked to establish'.[20] Of course, there are risks in such lists. Names can end up on there for the wrong reasons (such as retaliation or 'false accusations'[21]). But we can still ask why these tactics become necessary. Emma's description of procedures suggests they too become closets: 'The attempt to do things in a proper way is not necessarily effective; it just becomes how things get buried.'

You can use procedures to escalate complaints. Recall the complaint made against the anthropologist John Comaroff. A letter was signed by his colleagues presenting him as harshly disciplined by the institution. That letter said all he had done was warn a student about the risks of sexual assault. It was only because students from his department, Margaret Czerwienski, Lilia Kilburn and Amulya Mandava, had sued Harvard University that the complaint file was released into the public domain. The file detailed information about how complaints had been handled or mishandled internally.[22] For us to learn what was *not* in the letter, it took three graduate students, risking the doors being shut on their careers.

To release the data of complaint, that missing data, you can conduct your own research, interviewing complainers, buffering them with anonymity. I discussed in chapter 5 how such reporting does not bypass the risk of defamation but transfers it from complainers to researchers and publishers. That risk can be transferred back again; because even when stories of complaint are anonymized, complainers can be recognized. There are some stories I have not shared in this book, which I have removed from it, to avoid the transfer of this risk. To unbury some *no*s is still to leave others buried. Maybe they will come out at another time, in another text.

To release the data of a complaint, you might become a whistle-blower. Even when there are laws protecting whistle-blowers, to blow the whistle is to risk so much and to act in a way that contradicts what you have been taught about professionalism (to be professional is to become an institutional closet, willing to keep the institution's secrets). Whistle-blowers thus have long complaint biographies, of being blocked from getting the information *to* the institution about what is going on *within* it.

Take, for example, Susan Fowler's memoir about her experience of blowing the whistle about sexual harassment at Uber. Susan published a blog post titled, 'Reflecting on One Very, Very Strange Year at Uber'. It was an account of sexual harassment that was also a 'meticulously, cautiously, deliberately crafted portrait of the company,' written with 'excruciating care, every sentence backed up by documentation'. Susan describes how the story was picked up by the media; she began to receive thousands of stories from other people who had had similar experiences at Uber. She says, 'I couldn't wrap my head around the fact that so many powerful people inside the company had known about how terrible Uber's culture was, yet none of them had taken their stories to the public until I had.'[23]

Lifting the lid can loosen other people's tongues.

Communication might matter more precisely because of how complaints can leave us feeling rather isolated. Viola, you might remember, used the word *faded* to describe how she felt when she left – her colleagues did not speak to her out of politeness. Viola read her resignation letter out loud to her dean. But she wanted to do more. She wanted to put her resignation letter on the wall: 'I just thought, I am not the kind of person who would put my resignation letter on the wall, but I just wonder what it is that made me feel that I am not that kind of person because inside I am that kind of person, I just couldn't quite get it out.'

Perhaps we have to help each other get our complaints out. Viola came to a lecture in which I shared words from her testimony. The words she gave to me I gave back to her. 'It was only after the lecture,' she wrote, 'that I realized how undignified these complaint processes are, and how, yes, my dignity was stripped. In my dealings with the union, they had advised me at the time that my dignity at work had been breached, but that word did little then for me, as it felt like another procedural piece of jargon – but when I felt a swell of pride at the lecture, indeed, when I felt a sense of dignity about it all, I realized that this must have been somewhat lost.' Words can be emptied of meaning, becoming polish, how we are removed from our own stories. When we share our complaints with each other, giving them to each other, they acquire a different meaning and value.

We hear each other scratching away, 'little birds'. To hear with a feminist ear is to hear that sound as labour. Complaint activism, I suggested in chapter 5, can involve *changing the addressee*: we address each other. Sometimes we do so literally, by writing each other letters or postcards. I think of actions undertaken by Time's Up Ateneo (TUA), which was a coalition of students, faculty and alumni from Ateneo de Manila University in the Philippines, that began with an on-campus protest against sexual violence and impunity on 15 October 2019. Three years later, TUA honoured the protesters by offering flowers at the protest site and distributing postcards to the Ateneo community and inviting them to write to survivors of sexual abuse. These postcards were published on social media and read out loud. One, from Jasmine, begins with: 'One day you will celebrate a victory. It won't be exactly what you want it to be, but it will be enough. It will fill your life with meaning.'[24]

Words sent out come back to us. And when they do, they mean something different. They sound different. Sound matters because of how it travels. Remember Serena's story, how in the middle of a meeting, when she received another harassing email, she let out a sound, *eehhhhh*, that alerted other people to what was going on. Serena's queer complaint was a non-intentional, guttural sound. It was the sound of frustration.

Frustration is a feminist record.

However involuntary, that sound was an action. If bodies are key to how complaints become protest, so too is sound. The *eehhhhh* tells us that she could not take it anymore. Nor would she. The sound of complaint can be sharp and piercing. Or dull and low. Zehay Liva Bocretsion wrote to me about how she turned her complaints about racism into songs, which she sent to cultural institutions such as museums. She explained, 'I got the idea because in Danish *klagesang* (complaint song) carries both the meaning of elegies, the retelling of a tragedy, and a more sarcastic meaning, like someone who is just wailing on about all the things not going their way.' Zehay sings her complaints with a 'monotonousness' which 'becomes a point in itself', as a way 'to express the matter-of-fact ways in which a lot of people try to disregard the complaints I have had'.

We can turn the sound of frustration, of not getting through, into another way of expressing our complaints. In chapter 5, I referred to the art project 'The Complaining Body' on the emotional labour of workplace complaints. In a follow-up piece, 'The Uncomplaining Body', Ivor Southwood describes, with reference to his own experiences cleaning offices, how small sounds can be refusals:

Even the slightest involuntary gesture can communicate insolence; a sigh or a way of walking can be read as insubordination. Although barely registering in the organization's consciousness, these bodily complaints, by their very inarticulacy, are in a way more radical than a list of demands; in their negations, they do not propose alternatives or improvements; they reject the work-relation itself. They are forms of refusal where refusal is impossible.[25]

An uncomplaining body is a body that complains in another way, a complaint that is barely a sound and yet is one. Resistance is not always loud. It can be barely audible. A friend wanted to become a citizen to avoid the exhausting bureaucracy of living and working in the UK without being one. She had to pledge allegiance to 'the Queen and her heirs'. She did not want to make any such pledge. She had no such allegiance. And so, she pledged allegiance to 'the Queen and her hairs'. That barely audible difference, delivered solemnly, was on its way to being shared as a humorous story, a queer subversion.

Many of the smallest complaints, the slightest gestures, the tiniest of deviations, are not audible to every ear. They might need to be inaudible to be sayable. They can still be extended. Collective protests are sonic extensions of the bare sounds of refusal; the snap of a slogan; the repetition of a chant on a demo. I hear the sharp sound of the direct-action group Sisters Uncut setting off 1000 rape alarms to mark the anniversary of the Clapham Common Virgil for Sarah Everard, murdered by a police officer in 2021. The police had beaten and arrested many women on the day, coming down because of who came out.²⁶ I hear the rallying cry of feminists in Argentina, saying *Ni una menos* (Not one less), a 'collective scream against *machista* violence',²⁷ words that spread to other places, other collectives, repeated, echoed, amplified, passing between bodies, travelling across time and also space: transgenerational; transnational.

We might hear anger in that *no*, that refusal, but also a lament, the sound of grief. Chicana-Palestinian feminist Sarah Ihmoud writes of speaking through grief. She shares exchanges she has with Mona Ameen, a young Palestinian scholar in Gaza. She asks Mona if she has any messages for women and feminists around the world. Mona answers, 'Keep posting and posting and posting about us . . . keep us in your prayers.' Ihmoud invites us to break out of 'this غصة/ *ghassa*, this lump in our throat that keeps us from speaking, and to speak loud and courageously into the wind'.

What makes it difficult to speak is why we need to do so.

When people use the expression 'shouting into the wind', they usually mean it is pointless to make a noise against the flow of air. But when the situation is urgent, there is always a point. We might need to shout *no* now, so we can hear each other over what Ihmoud calls 'the noise of complacency'. Time can be like the wind: a *no* is blown about. We don't always know when it will be heard. Or how.

Remember: we are louder not just when we are heard

together but when we hear together. Sound moves. Sound builds. A complaint collective can be the sound we hear when we bring stories from different times and different places into the same text or room. They jostle around, become noisier, keeping each other company. I smiled when I wrote this. I smiled with affection even though these stories have been difficult to share and might have been difficult to read.

SURVIVAL AS COMPLAINT

Some of us have to complain because otherwise we would not survive and, by this, I mean not just keep ourselves alive but our projects. To keep our complaints alive, we share them, so that other people can become our feminist ears, hear what went on or what we did to go on. That is why the story of communicating complaints can be retold as a story of survival.

I recall a conversation I had with Sally, an Indigenous student. She was the only Indigenous student in her Indigenous Studies class. She ended up having to listen to 'constructions of Indigenous people in the classroom that are very colonial'. And so, she wrote a letter to the professor, which took the form of an informal complaint about white supremacy in her classroom. Sally did not go to the next class. One of the students told her, 'The professor came to class today and he read out the email you wrote about us.' Rather than respond to Sally, the professor printed out her letter and read it out to the class without her permission.

**A complaint about what is taken
from you can be taken from you.**

Sally became, to use her word, 'a monster' and had to complete her PhD off campus. But then, she said, 'an unexpected little gift', was how other students could come to her: 'They know you are out there and they can reach out to you.' She used that expression twice, 'an unexpected little gift'. Even though her complaint led her to leave, by complaining she left enough of herself behind for other people to find.

**A complaint can open the door
to those who come after.**

I think, too, of a conversation I had with Mary, an Indigenous academic whom I introduced you to earlier. Mary tried to complain when a senior manager sabotaged her case for promotion (as he did against other Indigenous academics). Her complaint was blanked. And she knew that there was an expectation, even hope, that she as an Indigenous woman would just give up or go away. She decided she would do what she had to do to get her promotion. For her, thriving was surviving, another way of taking the institution on: 'I took everything off my door, my posters, my activism, my pamphlets. I smudged everything all around the building. I knew I was going to war; I did a war ritual in our tradition. I pulled down the curtain. I pulled on a mask. My people, we have a mask. And I never opened my door for a year. I just let it be a crack. And only my students could come in. I would not let a single person come into my office who I had not already invited there for a whole year.'

Closing a door can be a survival strategy. Mary took herself off her door, the posters, pamphlets, her commitments, traces of where she had been. The door is easier to shut when it is just the institution's door. She still does her work; she still teaches her students. But she uses that door to shut out what she can, who she can. And she pulls down those blinds and she pulls on a mask, the mask of her people, connecting her fight to the battles that came before, because, quite frankly, for her, this is a war.

The battle to survive an institution can be the same as the battle against colonial occupation. It was Mary's people she needed in her fight for survival; it was her people who came with her. Early on in her testimony, Mary evoked another door, a door she said she was yet to open too widely: 'There's a legacy, a genealogy, and I haven't really opened that door too widely as I have been so focused on my experience in the last seven years.' We can inherit closed doors; a trauma can be inherited by being made inaccessible, all that happened that was too hard, too painful, to reveal. Black feminist work, Indigenous feminist work, feminist of colour work is about opening these doors, the doors to what came before, colonial as well as patriarchal histories, harassment as the hardening of *that* history, of who is entitled to whom.

A complaint can open the door to those who came before.

It might seem that doing what we can to thrive or survive – whether by withdrawing our formal complaints or our labour– is how institutions remain hostile. But survival can be how we transmit different messages and values. When some of us are told to identify with the institution to increase our chances of progression, we are told to separate ourselves from our people or our projects or our politics. Survival might require refusing that instruction, not allowing ourselves to be remade in the institution's image, holding as much of ourselves as we can back. We put our people first, those who came before us, who travel with us.

Doing what we can to survive institutions gives us a better chance of transforming them.

I think of Chelsea Watego's account of walking away from a complaint she had made about sex and race discrimination as an Indigenous woman in Australia, walking away, also, from her tenured position in a sandstone university. She recognizes how her action could be framed by others: 'Some might frame it as one of loss and a lesson on the futility of race discrimination processes, the racism inherent in calling out racism, while others might tell of this story as one of winning and the power of white supremacy prevailing.'[28] Citing the work of Mohawk scholar Audra Simpson, Watego writes, 'Refusal is indeed a most powerful stance in the fight against race, and my decision to walk away from UQ [University of Queensland] and the complaint process marked a refusal to allow them to exercise any more power over me than they already had.'

From Watego I learn that to complain using their processes can be to lose a battle for our own. 'In vesting my power in this process,' she says, '[I] had 'handed my story over to a process that refused to see me fully, including the full extent of the injuries I and my family had sustained.' Watego teaches us that complaints can sometimes become more forceful by being withheld from the institution; it can be how you demand more, demand sovereignty, a demand kept alive by your people in the story of their survival.

A story can be of survival. And yet, many do not survive the violence that brings them to complaint or to protest. A story, then, can be what survives or what we have to keep alive for those who have not survived. I think of the words given to us by Refaat Alareer, a Palestinian writer, scholar and poet assassinated by the state of Israel on 6 December 2023. His poem 'If I Must Die' begins, 'If I must die, you must live to tell my story.'[29] A poem can be the gift of an image. Alareer gives us an image of a piece of cloth and some strings, becoming a kite, 'flying up above', so that a child 'somewhere in Gaza' might see it and 'thinks for a moment an angel is there, bringing back love'. That cloth, those strings, words strung together, becomes a story we live to keep telling. So many activists and freedom fighters have carried Alareer's words onto the streets; a poem, a story, the snap of a slogan, a *no*, repeated; a collective refusal.

Complaint as survival: each fragment, each sharp piece, brought together. We have to find ways to tell these stories, of violence, of resistance, also existence, without turning ourselves into a spectacle. I think, for instance, of Christina Sharpe's *Ordinary Notes*, which, through note form, documents how quickly memorials become spectacles; films that depict violence against Black people, shown to Black people, reenacting the violence.

One note:

> *The architecture of the memorial stages encounter.*
> *Spectacle is not repair.*[30]

By weaving together what she has learnt from encounters with violence, with lessons from her mother, lessons from love, Sharpe tells another story of survival, of finding beauty in relation. I learn from her that if we are to repair violence, it is not the institutions that caused it that will do the work. We will. I hear the sound of Sharpe's many notes, rising above the dull notes and noise of everyday racism. Such clarity. Such beauty. Such survival.

Also, such creativity; in every note. Receipts gathered, more notes. Palestinian writer Sara M. Saleh keeps her receipts. Saleh, writing about the brutality of the Israeli occupation of Palestine, has many to collect: Palestine removed from the map, complaints directed against Palestinian people for speaking out; Palestinian people prevented from speaking. Saleh ends her piece, 'Every Palestinian I know is forced to become a bookkeeper. One day, our receipts will come in handy.' To keep a record is to keep alive the hope that justice will happen 'one day'. As Saleh describes, 'Freedom of speech is stuffed in the back of a cupboard when we seek to speak.'[31] By complaint as a queer method, we point to these unofficial collections, to what we find, who we find, stuffed in the back of the cupboard.

Another lesson from complaint: consciousness depends upon materials. If to be conscious is to be conscious *of* something, some things get in the way of consciousness. So much violence is hard to see because of how institutions are built (the backs of cupboards, the closed doors, the windows with blinds that come down; the narrow corridors). We have more than enough materials despite that (or even because of it): the complaints we have made; the ones we haven't made; the complaints made about us because we complained. We assemble a complaint archive, necessarily incomplete.

There is so much stuff. Data. Records. Matter. Straw in the nest, bits and pieces gathered together and brought back to the same place. Yes, I am thinking of the birds, our queer kin, who made a nest out of a postbox. They turned an opening intended for letters into a door, a queer door perhaps, a way of getting in and out of the box. The birds have more to teach us. Disrupting usage and creating a shelter can refer to the same action.

Disruption can be about stopping activity. From our complaint activism, we know all about being stopped.

Disrupting usage.

When complaints are stopped, the engine of an organization keeps running. So, one way to get complaints moving again is to stop the engine of the organization running. We might have to stop other people's movements, block the doors to the building, becoming as inconvenient as possible.

I am willing to be inconvenient.

But in that commitment is another, to take time out from what you might be doing, where you might be going.

We learn our commitments, whether or not they are genuine, when they are inconvenient.

I am willing to be inconvenienced.

I learn from Audre Lorde's commitments. She tells us of one time when she was driving her car and heard on the news that a white police officer had been acquitted of the murder of a black child, Clifford Glover, in 1973. History is what gets repeated. Too many unheard complaints. Lorde stopped the car, to let it in, the violence of the police in, of white supremacy. She stopped the car and a poem, 'Power', came out, with its electric line, not to let our power 'lie limp and useless as an unconnected wire'.[32] If there is something poetic in complaint, in the manner or form of its expression, a complaint can be a poem. What Lorde let in, what she gets out, we read.

Sometimes, we need to stop the car, stop what we are doing, *whatever* we are doing, not just to let the violence in but to express our refusal of it. A *no* can be an occupation, we occupy the buildings, taking up as much time and as much space as we can. Hence many student protests against the genocide in Gaza have taken the form of solidarity encampments.[33] Students across the globe have used occupations to demand institutions recognize their complicity and divest from Israel and other imperial-war machines, saying *no* to business as usual. To force institutions to recognize their complicity in violence is another way of *forcing the force out.*

Resistance to change is also about force; force is turned back on those who complain, forcing them out. Complaint can be what we do in the gap, that time of suspension, before we are forced out. We fill that gap. We feel it fill. I felt it fill when I gave a lecture on complaint and common sense entitled 'Changing Institutions' at Oxford University on 7 May 2024. It was a couple of days after students had set up a Palestinian solidarity encampment on campus. It was an uncanny experience. I was talking about changing institutions whilst feeling that change in the room. The solidarity of the encampment leaked into the lecture theatre; that space, so often solemn, heavy with hierarchy and history, was full of energy and electricity. I had a sense of: another university is possible. I was reminded of another event that took place almost a decade earlier, on 11 November 2015. Trans of colour performers Janani Balasubramanian and Alok Vaid-Menon brought their 'It Gets Bitter' tour to the Centre for Feminist Research, in London. Oh, the killjoy joy and laughter![34] Afterwards a visitor to the campus said to me, 'I did not know a university could look like that.'

Or feel like that, I thought. The feeling in the room when I talked to the students who were trying to change the institution at Oxford was of an expansion of possibility. When I visited the encampment after the lecture, to express my killjoy solidarity with the students, with everyone fighting for a free Palestine, I was asked if I wanted to speak. I did not. I wanted to listen and learn. And I listened and learnt. I learnt how the students were working out how to look after each other, how they were negotiating differences and conflict with a shared consciousness of who does the work and who gets to speak. I learnt from how they were looking after the camp, the mundane, necessary work of caring for the grounds, including disposing of waste; organizing activities, teach-ins, assemblies, speeches, stalls; organizing the tents, for cooking, welcoming, reading, quiet times, wellness, for shouting 'No to business as usual whilst our institutions profit from and facilitate genocide'.

Remember again the birds' lesson: disrupting usage and creating a shelter can refer to the same action. We create spaces so we can find each other, openings, however small, where we can assemble without being displaced by the letters in the box or displaced too quickly. I added 'displaced too quickly' as spaces created by self-assembly are always precarious. To assemble, to say *no*, to do *no*, throws so much open. We throw ourselves into projects that are urgent and necessary, doing what we can, when we can, however we can, in the wear and the tear, for as long as it takes. This is not just about doing what we can to survive ourselves. It is doing what we can so others can survive. 'Survival can be a promise', to quote from Black feminist poet Alexis Pauline Gumbs quoting Black feminist poet Audre Lorde, one we make to each other.[35]

And so, we address each other. Little ghosts, little birds, a complaint graveyard, a queer nest. To make a nest possible, to make it possible to nest, we have to stop what usually happens happening; more letters being posted, piling up, taking up space. So many of our efforts, our complaints, our protests also, end up buried in the same pile, leaving us with less air. We have to fight, then, to breathe, creating pockets within institutions, or outside of them, so we can keep doing the work, using whatever we have handy.

We end up with so many materials. What a mess. Yes, that mess can be a picture of our complaints, a picture of our lives. That mess can also be a queer map, telling us where we have been, our comings and goings.

It can be heavy going, each line, labour. But think of this. Each line can be a conversation, one that you had to have, a conversation that can open a door, just a little, just enough, so that someone else can enter or hear something. Each line can be time, the time it takes to get somewhere, to do something, time as a queer line, going round and about as how you find things out. Each line can be a path, the places you go, the unlit rooms, the shadows, the doorways, who you find on your way there. Each line can be a trace, how we go back, how we come to know more, hear of others who complained before. Each line can be a promise, a leak

A queer map.

as a lead, how those who came after can pick something up, because of what you tried to do, even though you did not get through, even though you just scratched the surface. The scratches that conveyed the limits of what we can accomplish can sometimes be enough. To scratch a record can stop it from going around, making the same old sound.

A scratch can be testimony. Even when our complaints have disappeared, that disappearance leaves a trace. I think of Queering the Map, a community project for digitally mapping LGBTQIA+ experiences.[36] Queer Palestinians used this digital map to share their stories before they disappeared under the rubble. One Palestinian wrote, 'I just want this to be my memory here before I die.'[37] Queer Palestinians, queer Muslims, brown queers; we are not supposed to exist. A queer map can be created by saying, *we are here*. Or we *were*. We disturb the picture even with our grief. That we have lost each other; how we recognize each other. What we tried to make possible for each other. That's a **killjoy truth**, alive to possibility.

To make something is to make it possible.

We might complain to make our lives or our work possible. And so, when our complaints are buried, possibility might seem to be buried, too. Perhaps a burial is a possibility. I hear here the beautiful words of the Greek poet Dinos Christianopoulos, 'They tried to bury us, they didn't know we were seeds', echoed by so many activists, the world over.[38] A complaint as a seed, buried in the ground or deep in a pile, to come up later, plucked by those who come after.

Yes, possibility can be a plant. We still have to fight for it. It might seem we are not getting very far. But we don't know what our complaints will do or where they will go. We don't know when one complaint might dislodge another or when our complaints, piled up, will become too much, spilling out of that box, those containers, spilling all over the place. It helps not to know. Because it is not only that we can do more with complaints, but that complaints can do more than we know. And I also want you to know this: however small you feel, however lonely, a little bird, a little ghost, scratching away, you are part of this history, of how we are making each other more possible; and other worlds, too.

A Complainer's Survival Kit

We might complain to survive. But we also have to survive our complaints. To complain is often to encounter what you complained about but even more forcefully. So, in this survival kit are some tips for surviving a formal complaint process.

Although my focus is on surviving formal complaints, one of my core recommendations is not to think of complaints as distinct actions but as part of our life's work. Just as stopping complaints is not some separate level of institutional activity, making complaints is not some separate level of your activity. In other words, by complaining you are expressing the values and commitments as you work them out: what you bring to the world. You are modelling the world you wish for.

A complaint about a wrong does not make any of us right. It is not only 'other people' who need to keep questioning their investments in institutions. We all need to keep questioning ourselves. We remain implicated in the institutions we critique – even when our complaints lead us to leave institutions. Not all complaints or complainers are motivated by a desire for justice or a concern to redress harm. I offer some survival tips for those who are complaining for a more just world. None of these tips presume we have justice on our side.

1. *FIND* OTHER COMPLAINERS

Formal complaint procedures work to isolate those who complain. The doors that are shut to protect our confidentiality might be how we do not hear about other people who are facing similar problems. Isolation can make us feel smaller and makes it harder to challenge abuses of power or discrimination. So, do what you can to find other people in your organization who share your complaint or your politics. If you have been told not to talk to anyone about your complaint, treat that instruction for what it is: a management technique. You do not have to be managed by obeying the instruction. It might be that your complaint does raise issues that you feel need to be kept in confidence. You can still talk to people in the way that respects these confidences. You might find talking to people outside your organization helpful because of how hard it can be to untangle conversations from institutions when we are in them.

2. *REFUSE* TO ATTEND MEETINGS ON YOUR OWN

This is my most specific suggestion. But it is also very important! Many people are invited to 'informal meetings' to discuss their complaints. Often these meetings, by being designated informal, are not minuted nor witnessed. These meetings can be used to intimidate people to drop their complaints. Go with a person – whether a friend or a colleague or a member of your union or professional network. If you are told you cannot have someone with you, refuse to meet.

Another tactic used to stop the creation of a record is to avoid written communication by switching to phone-calls. Ask to record any phone calls relating to your complaint. If that request is refused, refuse the phone-call. The implication of all of these suggestions: complaints whenever they are made, however they are made, need to be *witnessed* by others. Don't let them make you smaller. Let other people in.

3. REMEMBER THE COMPLAINT IS YOURS

I am using the language of ownership to resist ownership. Let me explain. To complain formally can be to have your complaint taken away from you. You have to follow the institution's instructions, use their language and observe their rules. The complaint remains yours in the sense that it relates to something that happened to you. You have more knowledge of it than anyone else. The institution does not own you or your complaint. Given a formal complaint is just one way you are making your complaint, it helps to differentiate between the complaint you have and the one you make. The complaint you have remains yours whatever happens to the complaint you make. You take it with you wherever you go. You can file it away if you need to.

Making our complaints *ours* is how we resist the institution's demand for access to our personhood and our politics.

4. *LISTEN* TO WHAT DIFFERENT ACTORS ARE SAYING

When you are making a formal complaint, you have to attend different meetings with individuals who have official roles. They are acting on behalf of the institution and might be following explicit directives. A complaint can require becoming an institutional plumber – you have to work out how it gets stopped by the system. So, by listening, I mean system work: finding out how what is being said is doing something (or not doing something). Listen for warnings, threats and bribes. Listen for non-performatives – yeses and nods that are too weak to oblige any further actions. When a commitment is expressed to follow up with an action, get that commitment in writing. If it is not followed up, at least you have evidence they are not doing what they are saying.

5. *KNOW* YOU ARE NOT OBLIGED TO COMPLAIN

Some people complain in order to try and stop something from happening. Some people complain because they do not want what happened to them to happen to others. However, complaining is exhausting and demanding. It is important not to feel you are obliged to complain, at least formally. By saying this, I do not mean we do not have a responsibility to address abuses of power. If you feel you cannot complain because you are too institutionally or materially or psychically vulnerable, find another way to work with others, to redress the situation differently.

6. *WORK* WITH UNIONS OR EQUALITY NETWORKS IF POSSIBLE OR PRACTICAL

One of the primary ways we can gather institutional strength in making complaints and grievances is through unions. Use the power they give you. Not everyone has access to unions. And some people are let down by them. Some people of colour have found that unions do not understand or support complaints about racism. I know of examples when union representatives have not supported complaints about sexual harassment because they were friends with the harassers. You might consult Ana Avendaño's *Solidarity Betrayed,* which offers a critique of how unions can be complicit in reproducing the problem of sexual harassment whilst insisting on their value and necessity in pushing for rights and protection for workers. Unions can help you to politicize the complaint, not least because of the deep knowledge they hold of institutional and organizational culture. They can sometimes function as complaint collectives (or help you to find one).

Equality networks can also be useful as support systems – such as women's networks, BAME networks or LGBTQIA+ networks – because they bring together people who have experienced similar problems. Try and find out what networks and support systems are available.

7. KEEP RECORDS

This is very important. One benefit of making a formal complaint is that it creates a record. We have to record what we do not want to reproduce! You also have to resist how institutions stop that record from being created. When the institution claims ownership of complaints, they often claim ownership of the records. I know people who were told to destroy documents. Don't destroy any documents! Keeping a record does not mean always being suspicious. It means recognizing that you do not know what will happen. You might need evidence of what has been said and done. So, do what you can to have what you might need.

Create a folder (virtual and actual) in which you gather all your documents. Keep a record of everything that is sent to you. Send it to that file. Keep a record of all your emails and letters – the ones you write as well as those you receive. The more stuffed the file, the more work you have done. Be proud of that work. It shows what you know.

8. *TREAT* COMPLAINT AS RESEARCH

This point follows directly from the one above. It helps to think of a complaint made within an organization as researching the organization. By collecting a record, you are also learning about the organization, often finding a gap between what it says it is doing and what it does. It is thus really helpful to collect evidence of what organizations say they are doing: look at all the policies and procedures, consider how they are talked about or where they are located. (On the website only? Do they get given to new members of staff?) Approach every meeting as part of your research: jot down notes about what is being said and by whom, even comments that seem minor.

Approaching the complaint as research helps because it gives you another sense of point and purpose. It is also potentially empowering: when complaints procedures are designed to make complaints smaller, treating them as research makes them bigger, allowing you to make connections and reminding you of just how much you know.

9. *SEARCH* FOR DIFFERENT WAYS TO EXPRESS YOUR COMPLAINT

Let me stress again: the complaint is yours. A formal complaint is just one way you make the complaint. Formal complaints often end up in filing cabinets: the place complaints are buried (albeit temporarily). Be creative! Try different methods of expression. And learn from other creatives – from complaints turned into grievance festivals, or performances or songs or graffiti on walls.

10. *CREATE* A COMPLAINT COLLECTIVE

It helps to do this work as a part of a team, to be a complainer who has found other complainers. A complaint collective can be a group formed within an organization to lend support to a complaint or a complainer. There are different ways people work together – in-person meetings,

WhatsApp groups, by writing a shared complaint. Some groups have given each person a secret name so they can communicate without using any identifying details. A complaint collective can also be a research network or a social network that gives each member room to express and share their complaints. It can be another way of thinking about what we are doing when we form collectives. A complaint collective can be what we need to be if we are to persist with our complaints – or just to persist. They are also another way of thinking about time, how we can inherit complaints from those who came before us, and how others can inherit our complaints.

A Complaint Curriculum

Complaint can be a kind of life learning, a way of reflecting on our changing relationship to the world. I invite you to think about your own complaint biography, the times you did complain, the times you didn't, and what you learnt along the way.

When we worked together as a complaint collective in my former institution, we also read books together, kick-ass feminist books. Reading alongside complaining helped us to relate the administrative work, which can be tedious and overwhelming, to an intellectual and political project. It helped us to connect our struggles with earlier feminist struggles.[1]

This book is full of practical lessons. And yet, it does not offer any simple solutions. It is easy to confuse what is practical with simple solutions. In fact, it is easier to offer simple solutions when we work more abstractly, by pulling our stories away from our struggles. You might say, for example, if you have *this* problem, just do *that*. It would be simpler if I just told you this: just do *that*! In this book, you have heard from people who did just *that* but then came up against another problem. To approach a problem practically is how we realize that solutions to problems are often part of the same situation as the problems. I think it helps to know this: that working out what to do requires 'knocking on a lot of doors' to quote from Xhercis Méndez.

We can, however, practise knocking! In this complaint curriculum, I include contributions that have helped me to think more creatively about complaints, what we can do with them, what they can teach us to do. The curriculum includes a range of activities, which can be done in order or not. I suggest you begin by writing your own complaint biography – or at least part of one. For those of you who are not working in groups, you can do almost all these activities on your own. This book is a complaint collective. We are yours.

1. *START* A COMPLAINT BIOGRAPHY

Communication is key to how we survive our complaints. We can write about our complaints. We can also speak about them. So, begin with the following exercise: can you remember your first complaint or an early complaint? What happened? How did it affect you? Can you recall a time you decided not to complain. What happened? How did it affect you? You could write down these thoughts or record or video yourself voicing them out loud. I found that once you start thinking about complaints made in childhood or early life, you start remembering so much more.

If you are working as a group, you might like to share your complaint biographies with each other or talk together about the process of beginning one.

2. *BECOME* A FEMINIST EAR

What do you hear in the word 'complaining'? In this book I pick up on some of the ways different people describe complaints – from 'little birds scratching away at something' to 'one lonely little ghost'. What do you hear in some of the imagery surrounding complaint? What kind of images would you use?

We can be heard and supported in making complaints in unexpected ways, by unexpected people and in unexpected places (and also not be heard or supported by the people we expected to hear and support us). I think of how many people told me they were warned not to complain by colleagues they expected to support them; or of how an administrator gave support in subversive ways in Esther's story. Reflect back on who has heard or supported you, the unexpected as well as the expected.

I suggested that my task in the book was to become a feminist ear, to listen to other people's complaints. Have you ever had this role? Reflect back on how that listening was learning. I am not just thinking here about formal roles but of the ways in which we might lend our ears to our companions so they can express their complaints.

Those working in groups, you might like to consider how you are becoming feminist ears for each other and the challenges of taking up this role.

3. *COLLECT* EXAMPLES OF WORKPLACE GRIEVANCES

One of the main issues or difficulties in writing about complaints is that they are made confidential. Once a grievance is submitted to a court of law, it mostly enters the public domain. The law is thus how many complaint files get released. Search for workplace grievances that have entered the public domain. Compare and contrast them. Look out for any references to policies and procedures, for details about how the organization handled the original complaint, and uses of key terms such as 'hostile environment'.

4. *QUESTION* HOW COMPLAINTS OR GRIEVANCES ARE REPRESENTED IN PUBLIC CULTURE

I have suggested that 'woke' can be understood as a counter-complaint (a complaint about those minorities who complain) as well as a hegemonic complaint (how those with power frame 'the others' who are fighting for room as taking what is theirs). Once complaints are hegemonic, they are often not heard as complaints but are instead treated as neutral reports or common sense. Whole fields of study have been dismissed as 'grievance studies'. These dismissals could also be called hegemonic or counter-complaints. Find examples of how complaints and grievances are represented in public culture. Analyse them. Does a consideration of hegemonic complaints and/or counter-complaints change your understanding of your own complaints? What do you think about the figure of Karen, the white woman who complains about racism?

5. *READ* COMPLAINT MEMOIRS

Complaint memoir is not an established genre and yet there are a number of texts that would be well described by such a formulation. One of my favourites, which I have cited throughout the book, is Ellen Pao's *Reset*. I particularly like how Pao shows how her complaint led her to become a feminist ear, to receive other people's complaints. Catherine Mayer makes some similar observations in her important book, *Attack of the 50 Ft Women: How Gender Equality Can Save the World!*. I also highly recommend Ana Avendaño's inspiring *Solidarity Betrayed*, which shows how women workers have organized and combined forces to address sexual harassment within the workplace.

Whilst these are examples of feminists using memoir or life writing to describe their experience of complaint, we could also think about how complaint might allow us to read other feminist memoirs. How useful is it to think of 'feminist complaints', or feminism as a complaint? Are there problems with such formulations?

6. *FOLLOW* THE FIGURE OF THE WHISTLE-BLOWER

The figure of the whistle-blower is probably the best-known complainer, the one who 'blows the whistle' on institutional corruption by releasing confidential files or secrets. What images do you have of the whistle-blower? You can follow up your reading of complaint memoirs by reading stories by whistle-blowers. Famous examples include Daniel

Ellsberg, Edward Snowdon, Chelsea Manning and Susan Fowler. Each has written a book about their experience. Read as many of these as you can. Also find out about the protections given to whistle-blowers in your organization/country and follow that figure in public culture.

7. *ENGAGE* WITH CRITIQUES OF INSTITUTIONAL POWER

This book has shown that (also how) complaints are blocked because of who holds power within an organization. I have also shared examples of how those with power can use complaints. But institutions, too, can use complaints to direct our attention and energy. It is thus useful to engage with some strong critiques of how formal complaints are used by institutions to encourage participation and stifle dissent. I am including below the two pieces I have found most useful. One is by Chelsea Watego, 'Always Bet on Black Power' (cited in chapter 6). This is one of the most powerful essays I have read on complaint, which explains why not proceeding with a formal complaint can sometimes be an act of claiming power. Watego notes, 'In the fight against race as told by them, the Black complainant will always be cast as the troublesome protagonist in the institution.' She explains her decision to 'walk away' from the complaint as 'not walking away from the fight against race, but instead [. . .] choosing a battle more worthy of my time.' Watego's *Another Day in the Colony* (2021) is also highly recommended for all complainers.

My other recommendation is Ethiraj Gabriel Dattatreyan

and Akanksha Mehta's 'Problem and solution: Occupation and collective complaint' (cited in chapter 5). It offers a powerful analysis of how management can channel complaint so that it ceases to cause institutional trouble by encouraging participation in certain formal processes. I am still learning from how they expose the uses of dialogue as a non-performative tool. They write:

> In this essay we discuss one lesson that we've learned – the ways in which participants in GARA's actions [Goldsmiths Anti-Racist Action] have been individualized and positioned between being/offering potential solutions to issues of racism in the university and being intractable problems precisely because they/we participated in generating a collective complaint that publicly shamed the institution and its staff.

Read both of these essays slowly and carefully. How do their critiques of formal complaints also offer theories of institutional power as well as of resistance?

8. *GATHER* EXAMPLES OF COMPLAINT ACTIVISM

There are many examples in this book of how those involved in making formal complaints become complaint activists. Esther Loukin, who inspired the term, went on to work with a disability justice group to support complaints about disability discrimination. The students I worked with, for example, went on to form a lobby group, the 1754 group, to press for change in how universities handle student complaints about sexual misconduct and sexual harassment. Gather examples of complaint activism in your organization/institution. What do we learn from different methods used?

9. *FIND* DIFFERENT WAYS TO EXPRESS YOUR COMPLAINTS (AND LEARN FROM THE CREATIVITY OF OTHER PEOPLE'S EXPRESSIONS)

We can be very creative when it comes to expressing our complaints, sometimes out of necessity, because we were stalled during the formal complaint process, at other times as an alternative, to avoid that institutional process, complaint as DIY. I have shared examples of how people have turned their complaints into songs or performed their complaints by reading them out loud during meetings or standing up in assemblies.

Artists and practitioners have found many different ways to express complaints. One example is Lee Mokobe's spoken-word poem 'Surviving Blackness' a powerful complaint about racism and transphobia that highlights words such as 'grief' and statements such as 'how we lament'.[2] Creative projects can be about performing complaints as well as showing the art or artifice, the spectacle and drama, in the most banal of administrative processes. That was key to the art activism of the Guerrilla Girls, mentioned in my preface. Given one of the meanings of the word complaint is a minor ailment or condition, we might also think of how bodies perform complaints, sometimes intentionally, sometimes not. Could an object be a complaint? Or a building?

Consider the many different ways complaints can and have been expressed. Find some examples of your own and bring them together to form an archive. What does it do to a complaint to change its form or medium? Who is the audience for more creative complaints? Then: create your own complaint!

10. *WRITE* A COLLECTIVE COMPLAINT

The students I worked with on calling out sexual harassment told their story of complaint as a story of how they became a collective. I highly recommend reading 'Collective Conclusions', the chapter by Leila Whitley, Tiffany Page, Alice Corble et al. in my book *Complaint!* They begin:

> *There is no one story of how our collective came together. In part, this is because our collectivity took shape slowly, drawing on relationships and trust built over years. There is no single turning point which marked the shift from working alongside one another as peers and fellow students, towards friendship, towards collectivity. Instead, by the time we knew we had formed a collective together, it had already happened.*

What do you learn about collectives as well as complaints from this account of forming a collective to make a complaint? For those working in groups, having read their piece, write a collective complaint. If you do not have a group, feel free to write your own complaint and share it with me (complaintstudy@gmail.com). I will be your feminist ear.

In killjoy solidarity with everyone complaining for a more just world!

Sara xx

Acknowledgements

Little did I know when I met with a group of students on 3 November 2013 that so many years later I would still be writing about lessons learned.

I wouldn't have it any other way.

With so many thanks:

To Tiffany Page, Leila Whitley, Alice Corble, as well as Chryssa Sdrolia, Heidi Hasbrouck and others I cannot name, for becoming my complaint collective, and for teaching me what it means to be one.

To everyone who shared their stories of complaint, whether you spoke to me, wrote to me, or put your story out there in your own way, for that work, for that painstaking labour, for fighting for each other.

For each *no*, precious, not alone; sharp pieces, together.

To all the people who complained before.

For a more just world.

And to those who are to come.

To the Guerrilla Girls and all the other creative complainers out there.

To Judith Butler, for inspiring confidence in taking up the task of critique.

To Angela Y. Davis and Gina Dent, for comradeship and alliance.

To dear killjoy sisters for travelling with me every step of the way, especially Rumana Begum, Sirma Bilge, Heidi Mirza, Aliya Mirza, Aileen Moreton-Robinson, Fiona Nicoll, Fiona Probyn-Rapsey, Sandra Peel and Elaine Swan.

To Jonathan Keane, for being a comrade in queer worldmaking for almost a lifetime.

To my editor, Josephine Greywoode, for the solidarity and enthusiasm and helping me to see that the poetry in complaint is part of the point. To Claire Péligry, a brilliant copy editor, for help with getting the words right and to Sophia Rahim for super helpful feedback on an early draft.

To everyone at my agency, David Higham Associates, especially Nicola Chang and David Evans, for support in bringing these two books, *No is Not a Lonely Utterance* and *The Feminist Killjoy Handbook* out into the world. I am especially grateful to have become more involved in translations of my work.

Thank you to all the killjoy translators! And killjoy publishers and editors!

To my mother and wise sisters, Tanya Ahmed and Tamina Levy, and their beautiful families, for all you bring to my life, even from afar. I know you are always there.

To cottage, for being a nest.

To Poppy and Bluebell, your warmth and companionship helps me to breath and to step out into the world.

To Sarah Franklin, for your curiosity and ideas and imagination that make our walks and our lives so entertaining. I could not do this without you. I know at times the stress of this work has come out in ways that have made life harder for both of us. Thank you for bearing witness and for helping me through it, and for the humour and wit and the warmth and love.

Whilst this book was in production, the Supreme Court in the UK 'clarified' that, for the purposes of the Equality Act (2010), sex means 'biological sex'. I consider this disastrous for feminism (many of us have long critiqued biological models of sex) and for the LGBTQIA+ community, especially trans people. My solidarity with everyone complaining about and protesting against this judgment, along with many other judgments that have made, and will continue to make, so many lives harder. We say *no*, not alone, but together.

Notes

1 This description of the Guerrilla Girls is from their website: https://www.guerrillagirls.com/about. Last accessed 29 January 2025.

2 Sarah Urist Green, 'How to Turn Your Complaints into Art According to the Guerrilla Girls', https://www.artsy.net/article/artsy-editorial-turn-complaints-art-guerrilla-girls, 14 April 2020.

3 See 'Complaints Department Operated by Guerrilla Girls', https://www.tate.org.uk/whats-on/tate-modern/tate-exchange/workshop/complaints-department. Last accessed 16 January 2025.

4 Q&A with the Guerrilla Girls, Zara Afthab for BUILDHOLLYWOOD https://www.southlondongallery.org/journal/interview-guerrilla-girls/, 19 April 2024.

5 Sara Ahmed, *Complaint!* (Durham: Duke University Press, 2021).

6 This is the second time I have mentioned my father. The first time was when I set the scene for the feminist killjoy

and referenced how he would make sexist comments. As a feminist of colour, I am well aware that many people want to hear stories of sexism as being about a 'foreign' culture. The desire to project sexism onto the foreigner is not only a form of racism but how sexism in our culture is obscured. There will be one more reference to my father in chapter 6, for how he sparked a realization that there was another truth, a **killjoy truth**, about Israel and Palestine.

Introduction: A Feminist Ear

1 Peter Apps, 'What Has the Grenfell Tower Inquiry Taught Us about Resident Engagement?', *Inside Housing*, https://www.insidehousing.co.uk/insight/what-has-the-grenfell-tower-inquiry-taught-us-about-resident-engagement, 29 July 2022.

2 Edward Daffarn, 'Second Witness Statement', Grenfell Tower Inquiry, 21 April 2021, available here: https://assets.grenfelltowerinquiry.org.uk/IWS00002109_Phase%202%20witness%20statement%20of%20Edward%20Daffarn.pdf.

3 Peter Apps, *Show Me the Bodies: How We Let Grenfell Happen* (London: Oneworld Publications, 2022), pp. 1, 3.

4 Gaby Hinsliff, 'What Happens to Women Who Complain about Sexual Harassment: You Are Branded a Troublemaker', *Guardian*, 8 November 2017, https://www.

theguardian.com/world/2017/nov/08/women-complain-sexual-harassment-branded-a-troublemaker

5 Azeem Rafiq, Written Evidence for the Sports Governance Inquiry, https://committees.parliament.uk/publications/33242/documents/179913/default/, 12 December 2022.

6 Hattie Williams, 'Clerics Fear to Take Racism Complaints Further in the CoE, BBC's *Panorama* reports', *Church Times*, https://www.churchtimes.co.uk/articles/2021/23-april/news/uk/complainants-fear-to-take-racism-complaints-further-in-c-of-e-bbc-s-panorama-reports, 20 April 2021.

7 The tablet is housed by the British Museum. You can find details here: https://www.britishmuseum.org/collection/object/W_1953-0411-71. Last accessed 17 January 2025.

8 Mark Ingram, 'Fire at Yarl's Wood Detention Centre Highlights Plight of Refugees', https://www.wsws.org/en/articles/2002/02/yarl-f21.html, 21 February 2022.

9 Harmit Athwal, 'Yarl's Wood Trial: A Miscarriage of Justice', https://irr.org.uk/article/yarls-wood-trial-a-miscarriage-of-justice/, 2 September 2003.

10 Cowburn, Ashley and Ben Glaze, 'Suella Braverman Sparks Furious Backlash after Branding Migrant Crisis an "invasion"', *Mirror*, https://www.mirror.co.uk/news/politics/suella-braverman-sparks-furious-backlash-28374323, 31 October 2022.

11 Musa Okwonga, 'The Ungrateful Country', https://bylinetimes.com/2020/04/10/the-ungrateful-country/, 10 April 2020.

12 Cited in Aina Khan, 'Why are Ethnic Minorities More Vulnerable to Coronavirus?', https://www.aljazeera.com/features/2020/4/17/why-are-ethnic-minorities-more-vulnerable-to-coronavirus, 17 April 2020.

13 You can see the poem performed here: https://www.youtube.com/watch?v=gXGIt_Y57tc. Last accessed 15 January 2025.

14 Sarah Franklin, 'Sexism as a Means of Reproduction', *New Formations*, 86 (2015), p. 26.

15 Shirley Anne Tate, 'How Do You Feel? Well-being as Deracinated Strategic Goal in UK Universities', *Ethnicities*, 16:1, p. 69.

16 As a literary genre, the complaint is often described as not just about loss but holding on to it. Literary critic David Mikics explains, 'When a poet writes a complaint, he or she uses the poem to prolong the experience of loss, not, like the elegist, to frame the loss and put it into perspective.' *A New Handbook of Literary Terms* (New Haven, CT: Yale University Press, 2010), p. 67.

17 Leila Whitley et al., 'Collective Conclusions', in Sara Ahmed, *Complaint!* (Durham: Duke University Press), p. 262.

18 Whitley et al., 'Collective Conclusions', p. 268.

19 For information about the group, currently led by Anna Bull, Tiffany Page and Adrija Day, see https://1752group.com/. Last accessed 17 January 2025.

20 This post, 'Sexual Harassment', is available on my blog, https://feministkilljoys.com/2015/12/03/sexual-harassment/, 3 December 2015.

21 In chapter 4 I use the term *non-performativity* to describe statements such as these. They are made because they have no force.

22 I have not provided locations for participants to ensure they are not identifiable. In addition to the UK, I interviewed people based at universities in the following countries: Turkey, Portugal, India, Australia, Lithuania, the United States and Canada. I have also communicated about complaints informally with people based in South Africa, Argentina, Spain, Poland, Chile, Italy, the Netherlands, Pakistan, the Philippines and France.

23 See for examples the reports into sexual harassment produced by the Women and Equalities Committee, which put many quotes from participants in boxes and then numbered the boxes: https://committees.parliament.uk/work/6032/sexual-harassment-in-the-workplace-inquiry/publications/, 25 July 2018. I am not saying these reports are not valuable. I am just pointing to the different ways we work with the data we collect.

24 Angela Y. Davis, *Freedom is a Constant Struggle* (Chicago: Haymarket, 2022), p. 3.

25 Carrie N. Baker, *The Women's Movement Against Sexual Harassment* (Cambridge: Cambridge University Press, 2018), p. 69.

26 Jamie Grierson, 'Hostile Environment: Anatomy of a Policy Disaster', https://www.theguardian.com/uk-news/2018/aug/27/hostile-environment-anatomy-of-a-policy-disaster, 27 August 2018.

27 The Tory government even used 'go home' as an example of racist hate crime despite having sent that same message out on a van. May Bulman, 'Home Office Using "go home" as Example of Racist Hate Crime – Despite Emblazoning Same Message on Vans', https://www.independent.co.uk/news/uk/home-news/home-office-go-home-vans-racist-hate-crime-campaign-a9161196.html, 21 October 2019.

28 The term 'moral mission' was used by former British prime minister Rishi Sunak in a speech delivered on 19 April 2024. The current Labour government has extended attacks on disabled people with the announcement of massive cuts to disability benefits, primarily by raising the threshold for people to qualify for Personal Independent Payments (PIPs). See John Harris, 'Labour's Historic Attack on Disabled People is Already Wrecking Lives', https://www.theguardian.com/commentisfree/2025/mar/30/labour-attack-disabled-people-benefits-cuts, 30 March, 2025. For a useful article on how welfare reform is an extension of a hostile environment,

see Sophia Siddiqui, 'The Attack on Welfare: From Disability Benefits to Asylum Support', https://irr.org.uk/article/the-attack-on-welfare-from-disability-benefits-to-asylum-support/, 18 July 2024. In earlier work, I analysed how the figures of the asylum seeker and the welfare recipient were connected by the judgement of fraudulence. I wrote then, 'The effort to establish that you are not a fraud has life consequences: a system becomes a hammer directed against those who are perpetually being rendered dubious because of their origins, because their bodies, their story, their papers, are not in the right place.' See: https://feministkilljoys.com/2015/06/14/some-striking-feature-whiteness-and-institutional-passing/, 14 June 2005. My arguments about how complaint processes are exhausting and extend to other forms of administrative violence pick up from this earlier work. See also my book *The Cultural Politics of Emotion* (Edinburgh: Edinburgh University Press, 2004), for a discussion of the figure of the 'bogus asylum seeker'.

Part One: Making Complaints

1 Harry Davies, Dan Sabbagh and Rowena Mason, 'Sixty Women at MoD Complain of Widespread "toxic" and "hostile" Behaviour', *Guardian*, https://www.theguardian.com/uk-news/2023/nov/16/sixty-women-at-mod-complain-of-widespread-toxic-and-hostile-behaviour, 16 November 2023.

1. Complaints as Coming Out Stories

1   Sarah Wildman, 'I was Harassed at the New Republic. I Spoke Up. Nothing Happened.', https://www.vox.com/first-person/2017/11/9/16624588/new-republic-harassment, 9 November 2017. In writing about those who share stories of complaint in the public domain, I have chosen to use first names to match my use of first names for participants in my research.

2   Kara Fox and Jan Diehm, '#MeToo's Global Moment: The Anatomy of a Viral Campaign', https://edition.cnn.com/2017/11/09/world/metoo-hashtag-global-movement/index.html, 9 November 2017.

3   Angela Onwuachi-Willig, 'What About #UsToo?: The Invisibility of Race in the #MeToo Movement', *Yale Law Journal*, https://www.yalelawjournal.org/forum/what-about-ustoo, 18 Jun 2018.

4   The quote is from Andrea Garcia Giribet, 'Tarana Burke: The Woman behind Me Too', Amnesty International, https://www.amnesty.org/en/latest/education/2018/08/tarana-burke-me-too/, 21 August 2018.

5   I interviewed Stephanie first and then Tina and Kate together later. You can read about how Stephanie, Kate and Tina made a 'historic complaint' about sexual harassment in chapter 6.

6   Lucy Siegle, 'If the Guardian Can Behave Like This, How Much Impact Has #MeToo Really Had?', https://www.theneweuropean.co.uk/lucy-siegle-nick-cohen-guardian-complaint/, 4 August 2022.

7   Cited by Maitrai Agarwal, 'Repeating One's Truth: Why Coming Out is a Never-ending Process, not a One-time Event', *Mid-Day*, 22 June 2023.

8   Reference is from here: https://dictionary.cambridge.org/dictionary/english/in-the-thick-of?q=in-the-thick-of-it. Last accessed 15 January 2025.

9   Sarah Wildman writes: 'As far as I know, the entire incident was never spoken of again. I hadn't yet heard the word "gaslighting", but I think of it now. The very few people who learned of the incident from me were left with only one clear takeaway: Silence was infinitely preferable.' Some of the processes I describe in this book could be called 'gaslighting', a word that is now in common use to describe psychical manipulation leading people to doubt reality. The term has been extended from interpersonal to institutional dynamics. I have chosen not to use the term *gaslighting* not because it is not helpful for capturing very real dynamics but because I am exploring how the practices that lead to complainers being doubted (or doubting themselves) are built into institutions through norms of conduct. See especially the section 'Loyalties and Legacies', in chapter 3.

10 In my discussion of 'the melancholic migrant' in *The Promise of Happiness* (Durham: Duke University Press, 2010), I

discuss this 'odd temporality' of grief, suggesting that for a person mourning a death, recognizing death precedes it. I was building on the important work of David Eng and Shinhee Han, 'A Dialogue on Racial Melancholia', in *Loss: The Politics of Mourning*, ed. David L. Eng and David Kazanjian (Berkeley: University of California Press, 2003), pp. 343–71.

11 Kafka's door is a reference to Kafka's famous fable, 'Before the Law'. A man seeking the law arrives at a door. He asks the doorkeeper if he can enter. The doorkeeper says it is possible but not now – and keeps saying the same thing over the man's lifetime. When the doorkeeper sees the man is finally dying, he says, 'Here no one else can gain entry, since this entrance was assigned only to you. I'm going now to close it.' The story is often read as a parable on bureaucracy, and can be found here, https://www.kafka-online.info/before-the-law.html. Last accessed 11 April 2025. Judith Butler, 'Imitation and Gender Insubordination', *Inside/Out: Lesbian Theories, Gay Theories*, ed. Diana Fuss (New York: Routledge, 1991), p. 16.

12 'Examining the Complexities of Sexual Misconduct and Power', posted 3 May 2018, https://sites.gold.ac.uk/cfrblog/2018/05/03/cultures-consent/. Last accessed 6 November 2024.

13 For a brilliant discussion of the relation between paranoia and complaint, see Jennifer Doyle's *Shadow of My Shadow* (Durham: Duke University Press, 2024).

14 Sally in HR has her own insta page: https://www.instagram.com/p/CMPXIpBgtxW/. See Nicola Rollock, *The Racial Code: Stories of Resistance and Survival* (London: Allen and Unwin, 2022), for a very helpful discussion of Sally in relation to institutional racism.

15 In the UK, complaints are a 'protected act' and retaliation by employers against those who complain about discrimination or harassment is called *victimization*. See Section 27, the Equality Act (2010), https://www.legislation.gov.uk/ukpga/2010/15/section/27. Last accessed 6 April 2025. In the book I will primarily use the term *retaliation* rather the *victimization* as it captures how being punished for complaining can be carried out by multiple parties, not just employers. In Laura's case, the action justified as protecting her 'from further victimization' was itself victimizing. Laura also said her colleagues just stopped talking to her; some would even put their arms up when they saw her walking down the corridor as if to say 'danger approaching.' Retaliation can be how you end up at a distance from colleagues, pulled out of the rooms in which the most important business is discussed. I turn to how retaliation is usually hard to evidence in chapter 3, and also how, in some cases, it is purposely evidenced.

2. A Complainer as an Institutional Plumber

1 Ashley Kosak, 'At SpaceX, We're Told We Can Change the World. I Couldn't, However, Stop Getting Sexually

Harassed', https://www.lioness.co/post/at-spacex-we-re-told-we-can-change-the-world-just-don-t-try-to-stop-the-sexual-harassment.

2 The Duracell Bunny was such a popular campaign that it has its own Wikipedia page: https://en.wikipedia.org/wiki/Duracell_Bunny. Last accessed 14 March 2025.

3 Some complaints lead to counter-complaints, which I discuss in the middle part of the book. Administration can involve handling not just many complaints but the collisions between them.

4 Quotes are from the Acas website, https://www.acas.org.uk/dealing-with-a-problem-raised-by-an-employee. Last accessed 26 May 2025.

5 Ellen Pao, *Reset: My Fight for Inclusion and Lasting Change* (New York: Spiegel and Grau, 2017), pp. 150–51.

6 Lucy Siegle, 'If the Guardian . . .'.

7 Peter Apps, 'Grenfell is Simply Explained: Firms Chased Profits, Ministers Sat on Their Hands, Innocents Paid with Their Lives', *Guardian*, https://www.theguardian.com/commentisfree/article/2024/sep/04/grenfell-is-simply-explained-firms-chased-profits-ministers-sat-on-their-hands-innocents-paid-with-their-lives, 4 September 2024.

8 Vickie Cooper and David Whyte, 'Grenfell, Austerity and Institutional Violence', *Sociological Research Online*, 27:1

(2022), 213–14. Cooper and Whyte choose not to use the term 'structural violence', developed by sociologist Johan Galtung because of how it shifts from an interpersonal to impersonal approach on forms of harm that are 'imposed on its victims at a distance'. They use the term 'institutional violence' to denote violence that is directly experienced by victims and involves acts and decisions made by individuals but is still shaped by complex institutional processes.

9 For important elaborations of how 'slow violence' as well as 'slow death' work in relation to poverty and population see Ron Nixon, *Slow Violence and the Environmentalism of the Poor* (Cambridge, Mass.: Harvard University Press, 2013) and Lauren Berlant, 'Slow Death (Sovereignty, Obesity, Lateral Agency)', *Critical Inquiry*, 33:4 (2007), 754–80.

10 China Mills 'Understanding State Violence', https://healingjusticeldn.org/methodology/calling-some-people-a-burden-provides-a-cover-story-for-welfare-state-violence/, 6 June 2023.

11 Abigail Thorn, 'I Emailed My Doctor 133 Times: The Crisis in the British Healthcare System', *Philosophy Tube* (https://www.youtube.com/watch?v=v1eWIshUzr8), 11 November 2022.

12 Dean Spade, *Normal Life: Administrative Violence, Critical Trans Studies and the Limits of the Law* (Durham: Duke University Press, 2015), p. 11.

Part Two: Changing Institutions

1. Institutions are not just about work or the public sphere: feminists have long shown how 'the family' operates as a social institution with a central role in transmitting norms and values as well as organizing intimate life. It is also hard to complain within families (or about them). So much family violence has been treated as 'just domestic', or what must be kept 'in house'. In chapter 3, I explore how some workplaces are managed 'like' families.

2. Timothy Snyder, *On Tyranny: Twenty Lessons from the Twentieth Century* (London: The Bodley Head, 2017), pp. 17, 22. Snyder's example under 'defend institutions' is National Socialism. But the context is the election of Donald Trump to his first term as US president (he refers to 'the President' throughout). I came to read *On Tyranny* after the election of Donald Trump to his second term as President. During this time, many people shared on social media Synder's critique of 'anticipatory obedience' with its necessary and vital instruction, 'do not obey in advance'! History, Snyder states, 'does not repeat, but it does instruct' (p. 9).

3. Complaint as Feminist Pedagogy

1. Louise Jackson, 'Making Sexual Harassment History: The UK context', https://www.genderequalitiesat50.ed.ac.

uk/2021/06/24/making-sexual-harassment-history-the-uk-context/, 24 June 2021.

2   Jean Porcelli, 'Fighting Sex Pests Made Me Ill', *Mirror*, https://www.mirror.co.uk/news/uk-news/exclusive-fighting-sex-pests-made-628954, 13 June 2006. All quotes from Jean are from this article.

3   Jacob and Wilhelm Grimm, *Household Tales: Volume 2*, trans. Margaret Hunt (London: George Bell, 1984), p. 125.

4   The common Indo-European root for *complain* and *plague* is *plāk* (to strike, lament). See https://www.etymonline.com/search?q=complain. Last accessed 14 March 2025.

5   When I read the story out loud in lectures, I began to raise my own arm, turning it into a feminist point. That was how my own lectures came to include a more performance element: the wilful arm led me there. One person called a lecture I gave, 'a call to arms'. She was using the phrase in its usual sense of an incitement or encouragement to fight. But I heard the arms in the phrase, which led me to make the arm into my subject, to think about how arms and hands are used in political resistance – that clenched fist, that raised fist.

6   Leila Whitley and Tiffany Page, 'Sexism in the Centre: Locating the Problem of Sexual Harassment', *New Formations*, https://doi.org/10.3898/NEWF.86.02.2015, p. 40.

7   Alice Miller, *For Your Own Good: The Roots of Violence in Child-Rearing* (London: Virago Press, 1987).

8   For a very clear summary of feminist theories of power which also explains the contrast between 'power over' and 'power to', see https://plato.stanford.edu/entries/feminist-power/. Last accessed 15 January 2025.

9   If you become willing to do what you had been under pressure to do before, you might, in time, no longer experience yourself as being forced. Hence being willing can be experienced as being freed from pressure, a feeling that is easily confused with being free. For further discussion, see my book *Willful Subjects* (Durham: Duke University Press, 2014).

10 Amber Heard, 'I Spoke Up Against Sexual Violence – and Faced Our Culture's Wrath. That Has to Change', *Washington Post*, 18 December 2018. https://www.washingtonpost.com/opinions/ive-seen-how-institutions-protect-men-accused-of-abuse-heres-what-we-can-do/2018/12/18/71fd876a-02ed-11e9-b5df-5d3874f1ac36_story.html

11 For a description of the harassment directed towards Bahar Mustafa, see my blog post, https://feministkilljoys.com/2015/05/26/a-campaign-of-harassment/, 26 May 2015.

12 You can listen to Said's Reith lecture, 'Representation of the Intellectual' here: https://www.bbc.co.uk/programmes/p00gxr1s, 23 June 1993.

13 Isabella B. Cho and Ariel H. Kim, '38 Harvard Faculty Sign Open Letter Questioning Results of Misconduct Investigations into Prof. John Comaroff', https://www.thecrimson.

com/article/2022/2/4/comaroff-sanctions-open-letter/, 4 February 2022. The link to the open letter is included in this article.

14   Heard, 'I Spoke Up . . .'.

15   Bryce Covert, 'Years After #MeToo, Defamation Cases Increasingly Target Victims Who Can't Afford to Speak Out', https://theintercept.com/2023/07/22/metoo-defamation-lawsuits-slapp/, 22 July 2023.

16   Ali Medina, 'How Defamation is Used to Silence Survivors', https://journals.law.harvard.edu/crcl/how-defamation-is-used-to-silence-survivors/, 14 March 2024.

17   Charlotte Proudman, 'Speaking Up', *Counsel*, https://www.counselmagazine.co.uk/articles/speaking-up-charlotte-proudman, 10 July 2023.

18   Katherine Franke, 'Columbia University Collaborates With Enemies of Academic Freedom, Says Professor Who Quit', https://thewire.in/world/columbia-university-collaborates-with-enemies-of-academic-freedom-says-professor-who-quit, 11 January 2025.

19   A whole book could be devoted to how complaints are used to stifle the speech of Palestinians and their allies. We could consider the ways in which anti-Zionism is conflated with antisemitism, thereby erasing the contributions of anti-Zionist Jews. See John Agnew for a discussion of both the history and function of this conflation, 'The language of intractability and the Gaza War: Conflating anti-Semitism

and anti-Zionism is historically problematic and misses how much contemporary Israel has become a role model for ethno-nationalists worldwide', *Human Geography*, 17:2 (2023). Jonathan Hafetz and Sarah Aziz explore how 'the very definition of antisemitism offered by the IHRC [International Human Rights Commission] has been used to silence criticism of Israel.' They explain, 'Some pro-Israel groups, however, increasingly use the IHRA [International Holocaust Remembrance Association] definition not to address antisemitism but to silence critics of Israel. While attempting to define antisemitism is a laudable goal, the IHRA's version includes two examples, out of a relevant eleven, that have been exploited to censor speech. Specifically, the first example is "denying the Jewish people their right to self-determination, e.g., by claiming that the existence of a State of Israel is a racist endeavour"; and the second is "applying double standards by requiring of [Israel] a behaviour not expected or demanded of any other democratic nation". These examples are often interpreted, including by government and university officials, as allowing the penalization of speakers, including Jewish groups critical of Israel's anti-Palestinian policies, laws, and practices', *Nation*, 27 December 2023. See https://www.thenation.com/article/society/ihra-definition-antisemitism/.

20 For a discussion of how counter-terrorism tactics were an extension of Neighbourhood Watch see Sara Ahmed, *The Cultural Politics of Emotion* (Edinburgh: Edinburgh University Press, 2004, 2014).

21 Gurpal Virdi, *Behind the Blue Line: My Fight Against Racism and Discrimination in the Police* (London: Biteback Publishing, 2018), pp. 2–3.

22 Paul Foot, 'The Met is Guilty', *Guardian*, https://www.theguardian.com/world/2000/dec/12/race.uk, 12 December 2000.

23 Vikram Dodd, 'Race Case Met Officer Wins Victimisation Claim', *Guardian*, https://www.theguardian.com/uk/2007/oct/10/race.ukcrime, 7 October 2007.

24 Caroline Mortimer, 'Cecil Rhodes Statue to Remain at Oxford Despite Student Campaign, Oriel College Says', *Independent*, https://www.independent.co.uk/news/uk/home-news/cecil-rhodes-statue-will-stay-at-oxford-despite-student-campaign-oriel-college-says-a6840651.html, 28 January 2016.

25 Quoted by Leah Asmelash, 'How Karen Became a Meme, and What Real-life Karens Think About it', *CNN*, https://edition.cnn.com/2020/05/30/us/karen-meme-trnd/index.html, 30 May 2020.

26 Helen Lewis, 'The Mythology of Karen', *Atlantic*, https://www.theatlantic.com/international/archive/2020/08/karen-meme-coronavirus/615355/, 9 August 2020.

27 Victoria Smith, 'Censorious Sadism', https://thecritic.co.uk/censorious-sadism/, 2 May 2023.

28 Helen Lewis does acknowledge racism but then states 'that' is a US problem.

29 Joanna Williams, 'Kate Clanchy: No one is Safe from the Woke Mob', https://www.spiked-online.com/2021/08/12/kate-clanchy-no-one-is-safe-from-the-woke-mob/, 12 August 2021.

30 Tanya Sweeney, 'Aoibhinn Ní Shúilleabháin: I was Told Reporting My Harasser Would Damage His Career', https://www.irishtimes.com/culture/aoibhinn-ni-shuilleabhain-i-was-told-reporting-my-harasser-would-damage-his-career-1.4528343, 3 April 2021.

31 See Stephanie Riger, 'Gender Dilemmas in Sexual Harassment: Policies and Procedures', *American Psychologist*, 46:5, 213, 219–21.

32 Mariame Kaba, *We do this 'Til We Free Us: Abolitionist Organizing and Transforming Justice* (Chicago, Haymarket Books, 2021), p. 9.

33 Wendy Brown, 'What Exactly is Neoliberalism?', conversation with Tim Shenk, https://www.dissentmagazine.org/blog/booked-3-what-exactly-is-neoliberalism-wendy-brown-undoing-the-demos/. 2 April 2015.

34 Lauren Berlant, *The Female Complaint* (Durham: Duke University Press, 2021).

35 Mary Peterson, 'On Cancelling and Repair', https://www.thephilosopher1923.org/post/on-cancelling-and-repair (2024).

36 Moira Donegan, 'Oh Mercy', Book Forum, https://www.bookforum.com/print/2704/two-new-books-argue-

for-a-more-forgiving-stance-on-sexual-violence-24258 (2021).

37 Erin R. Shannon and Anna Bull introduce the term 'unwilling trust' to explain why some students complain about sexual misconduct at universities even though they do not trust the institution. See their 'Unwilling Trust: Unpacking the Assumption of Trust Between Sexual Misconduct Reporters and Their Institutions in UK Higher Education', *Sociology Compass,* March 2, 2024, https://compass.onlinelibrary.wiley.com/doi/full/10.1111/soc4.13197.

38 John Hutnyk, 'The Corporate Menagerie', *Thesis Eleven*, https://journals.sagepub.com/doi/10.1177/0725513620949009, 12 August 2020. Earlier, I mentioned the letter written on behalf of John Comaroff by his colleagues. In the letter he is described not only as a good colleague but as somebody who has been treated harshly by the institution, 'We are dismayed by Harvard's sanctions against him and concerned about its effects on our ability to advise our own students.'

39 Literary scholar Madeline Lane-McKinley notes that if to complain is to be 'put on trial', you will also be told you are 'putting someone else on trial'. Lane-McKinley, Madeline, 'Of Complaints and Apologies: Feminist Theses Against Carceralism', https://www.glass-bead.org/research-platform/of-complaints-and-apologies-feminist-theses-against-carceralism/?lang=enview

4. Complaint as Diversity Work

1 Margaret Price, *Crip Space Time: Access, Failure and Accountability in Academic Life* (Durham: Duke University Press, 2024), p. 1.

2 Tanya Titchkosky, *The Question of Access: Disability, Space, Meaning* (Toronto: University of Toronto Press, 2011), p. 61.

3 Jay Timothy Dolmage, *Academic Ableism* (Ann Arbor: University of Michigan Press, 2017).

4 Sara Ahmed, *What's the Use? On the Uses of Use* (Durham: Duke University Press, 2019).

5 The Chartered Institute of Personnel and Development offer a definition of EDI on their website. See https://www.cipd.org/uk/knowledge/factsheets/diversity-factsheet/, last accessed 27 March 2025. For a definition of DEI see, Nick Barney, 'What is DEI? Diversity, Equity and Inclusion Explained', https://www.techtarget.com/searchhrsoftware/definition/diversity-equity-and-inclusion-DEI#:~:text=Diversity%2C%20equity%20and%20inclusion%20is,religions%2C%20cultures%20and%20sexual%20orientations. Last accessed 27 March 2024.

6 Judith Levine, 'It is Clear why Trump Blames DEI for everything', *Guardian*, 4 February 2025, https://www.theguardian.com/commentisfree/2025/feb/04/trump-dei-judith-levine.

7   Acts of compliance in the US reported thus far include the removal of Black, Hispanic and women veterans from the website of Arlington Cemetery Brandon Drenan, 'Arlington Cemetery Strips Content on Black and Female Veterans from Website', (https://www.bbc.co.uk/news/articles/cz03gjnxe25o, 15 March, 2025). The power to tell the story of the past follows on from other kinds of institutional power. Official history is thus often *narrow*, rather like a corridor you have to go down. The contributions of some groups have to be explicitly referenced for them to be included in history (hence the need for women's history or Black history). To remove explicit references to their contributions is to return history to a narrow group of white men. One suspects this is not just the effect but the intent of the withdrawal of commitments to DEI. Note as well that the contributions of some groups who have had to fight for their rights have also been erased. An example is the removal of references to transgender people from New York's Stonewall National Monument website (Brajesh Upadhyay, 'Transgender references removed from Stonewall monument website', https://www.bbc.co.uk/news/articles/cglywwn29n6o, 14 February 2025). Some have to fight to be included in history. Some fights are not included in history.

8   Sophie Wingate, '"Woke" Diversity and Equality Jobs in the Civil Service to be Axed', *Independent,* 12 May 2024, last accessed 19 March 2025. This initiative is currently under review by the Labour government.

9   Before EDI, other terms that were used included 'widening participation', 'social justice', 'equity' and then 'diversity'. Before I began my research, there was already a substantial critique of the 'turn to the diversity'. I drew on the work of educational scholars such as Rosemary Deem and Jenny Osga, who showed how the word 'diversity' invokes difference but does not necessarily evoke commitment to action or redistributive justice in 'Women Managing for Diversity in a Postmodern World', *Feminist Critical Policy Analysis: A Perspective from Post-Secondary Education*, ed. Catherine Marshall (London: Falmer, 1997), pp. 25–40. I also drew on critiques of diversity within management studies such as offered by Yvonne Benshop, who suggested that diversity came to be used more because it was less associated with 'our sense of social justice' in 'Pride, Prejudice and Performance: Relations between HRM, Diversity and Performance', *International Journal of Human Resources Management*, 12:7, 1166–81. My work is deeply indebted to critiques of diversity offered by Black feminists and feminists of colour. For important examples of such critiques, see Jacqui M. Alexander *Pedagogies of Crossing: Meditations on Feminism, Sexual Politics, Memory, and the Sacred* (Durham, NC: Duke University Press, 2006); Chandra Talpade Mohanty, *Feminism Without Borders: Decolonizing Theory, Practicing Solidarity* (Durham: Duke University Press, 2003); and Heidi Mirza, 'Decolonizing Higher Education: Black Feminism and the Intersectionality of Race and Gender', *Journal of Feminist Scholarship*, 7:7, 1–12, 2015.

10 Heidi Mirza, '"One in a Million": A Journey of a Post-Colonial Woman of Colour in the White Academy', in *Inside the Ivory Tower: Narratives of Women of Colour Surviving and Thriving in British Academia*, ed. Deborah Gabriel and Shirley Anne Tate (London: IOE Press, 2017), p. 44.

11 Kay Inckle, 'Unreasonable Adjustments: The Additional Unpaid Labour of Academics with Disabilities', *Disability and Society*, 33:8 (2018), p. 1373.

12 Arlie Hochschild, *The Managed Heart: Commercialization of Human Feeling* (Berkeley: University of California Press, 2nd edn 2003), p. 4. See also Elaine Swan, 'Commodity Diversity: Smiling Faces as a Strategy of Containment', *Organisation*, 17, 1 (2010), pp.77-100 for an important discussion of the politics of diversity smiles.

13 Richmond Pharmacology v. Dhaliwal, https://www.bailii.org/uk/cases/UKEAT/2009/0458_08_1202.html, Judgment delivered 12 February 2009.

14 Weeks v. Newham College of Further Education (2012). The decision can be read here: https://employmentcasesupdate.co.uk/content/weeks-v-newham-college-of-further-education-ukeat-0630-11-zt.ae57593818394d2aab876633c85b5af4.htm. Last accessed 15 January 2025.

15 Annika M. Konrad, 'Access Fatigue: The Rhetorical Work of Disability in Everyday Life', *College English*, 83:3 (January 2021), 179–99.

16 Amy Marvin, 'Philosophy Meets the Gendertrash from Hell', https://blog.apaonline.org/2024/10/16/philosophy-meets-the-gendertrash-from-hell/, 16 October 2024.

17 Dan Irving, 'Gender Transition and Job In/Security: Trans* Un/der/employment Experiences and Labour Anxieties in Post-Fordist Society', *Atlantis: Critical Studies in Gender, Culture and Social Justice*, 38:1 (2017), 168–78.

18 Sarah Jaffe uses Joshua Clover's notion of 'an affirmation trap', where 'labour is locked into affirming its own exploitation under the guise of survival'. Sarah Jaffe, *Work Won't Love You Back: How Devotion to Our Jobs Keeps Us Exploited, Exhausted and Alone* (London: Hurst and Company, 2022), p. 9.

19 Rod Liddle, 'Are You Transphobic? No, Me Neither. We're Just Worried about our Children', *The Times*, https://www.thetimes.co.uk/article/are-you-transphobic-no-me-neither-were-just-worried-about-our-children, 19 November 2017.

20 https://www.etymonline.com/word/hostility. Last accessed 18 May 2025.

21 Some 'gender critical' feminists might be reluctant to use the term 'sex realism' because of the resonance with 'race realism' that is understood by many progressive intellectuals as code for work that justifies and denies racism. Sex realism is however increasingly being used and is probably more accurate, not least because an argument that

sex is immutable tends to lead to a conservative rather than critical stance on gender. See my post 'Gender Critical = Gender Conservative' for further discussion: https://feministkilljoys.com/2021/10/31/gender-critical-gender-conservative/, 31 October 2021. I have thus decided to use sex realism to describe the agenda of this movement.

22   Charles C. W. Cooke, 'How to Defeat a Mass Delusion', https://www.nationalreview.com/2023/06/how-to-defeat-a-mass-delusion/, 27 June 2023.

23   Jo Phoenix in conversation with Maya Forstater, 'Sex Matters in Universities' webinar, https://www.youtube.com/watch?v=AR8fJH7BBlc, 19 October 2021.

24   James Ames, 'Black Cleaner Wins Payout Over "Cheeky Monkey" Slur', *The Times*, https://www.thetimes.com/article/black-cleaner-wins-payout-over-cheeky-monkey-slur-0v7tjkcf9, 6 September 2022.

25   April Glaser and Char Adams, 'Google Advised Mental Health Care When Workers Complained about Racism and Sexism', https://www.nbcnews.com/tech/tech-news/google-advised-mental-health-care-when-workers-complained-about-racism-n1259728, 7 March 2021.

26   Leila Whitley et al., 'Collective Conclusions', in p. 265.

27   The Macpherson Report (1999), produced by the Stephen Lawrence Inquiry, can be found here: https://assets.publishing.service.gov.uk/media/5a7c2af540f0b645ba3c7202/4262.pdf. Last accessed 11 April 2025.

28 Pao, *Reset*, pp. 134, 141.

29 Owen Bowcott, 'Woman Awarded £184,000 in UK's First Caste Discrimination Case', https://www.theguardian.com/law/2015/sep/22/woman-awarded-184000-in-uks-first-caste-discrimination-case, 22 September 2015.

30 Ms R. Taylor v Jaguar Land Rover Ltd: 1304471/2018 (21 September 2020). https://www.gov.uk/employment-tribunal-decisions/ms-r-taylor-v-jaguar-land-rover-ltd-1304471-2018. Last accessed 19 March 2025.

31 Adam Cooke and Oscar Davies, 'A substantive Review of the Landmark Decision in *Taylor v Jaguar Land Rover Limited* and the Protection it Provides for Those Who Identify as Non-binary and Gender Fluid under the Equality Act 2010', https://www.lambchambers.co.uk/latest-news/taylor-v-jaguar-land-rover-limited/. Last accessed 15 January 2025.

32 Yomi Abdi describes 'performative activism' as 'activism done to increase one's social capital rather than because of one's devotion to a cause' in 'A Tale of Performative Activism: How Black Lives Matter Became Just a Trend', https://yaledailynews.com/sjp/2020/09/05/a-tale-of-performative-activism-how-black-lives-matter-became-just-a-trend/, 5 September 2020. Such critiques of 'performative activism' are very important. I understand my model of institutional commitments as non-performatives as a supplement to this body of work.

33 A performative utterance is not a description of a state of affairs but an action. So, when a person with appropriate authority says to two people (a man and a woman, or in some places a man and a man or a woman and a woman), 'I thee wed', that speech act is not describing a married couple but marrying them. For performative to be successful (or to use Austin's own term, *happy*), certain conditions have to be met. Although performatives bring things about, they still depend on histories or conventions to succeed.

34 Judith Butler, *Bodies that Matter: On the Discursive Limits of 'Sex'* (London: Routledge, 1993), p. 3.

35 Cited in Sara Ahmed, *On Being Included: Racism and Diversity in Institutional Life* (Durham, Duke University Press, 2012), p. 145.

36 As reported here: https://news.sky.com/story/suella-braverman-attacks-progress-pride-flag-as-she-blames-liberal-conservatives-for-losing-election-13175447, 9 July 2024.

37 For a history of the Pride Progress flag, see https://youth-worktipperary.ie/lgbti-information/history-of-pride/. Last accessed 15 January 2025.

38 See, for just one example, Ewan Summerville, 'Prisons Ordered to Remove Pride Flags that "promote gender ideology"', https://www.telegraph.co.uk/news/2023/11/21/prisons-remove-pride-flags-hmp-pentonville-wandsworth/, 21

November 2023. Much of this panic about Progress flags is directed towards trans people. As most people in the LGBTQIA+ community know, transphobia is recycled homophobia.

39 *Out at Cambridge: Investigating LGBTQ+ Identity Disclosure at the University of Cambridge*, https://www.lgbtq.sociology.cam.ac.uk/projects/out-at-cambridge, October 2019, p. 21.

40 Madeline Grant, 'If James Bond has Gone Woke, he Might As Well be Cancelled', *Telegraph*, https://www.telegraph.co.uk/news/2020/03/11/james-bond-has-gone-woke-might-cancelled/, 11 March 2020.

41 Marcus Wratten, 'Scandal-hit *Strictly Come Dancing* Reportedly Ditching Same-sex Couples to Return to "traditional roots"', https://www.thepinknews.com/2024/09/02/strictly-come-dancing-ditch-same-sex-couples-scandal/, 2 September 2024.

42 The definition is from here: https://www.merriam-webster.com/dictionary/complaint. Last accessed 15 January 2025.

43 Gareth Bacon, 'What is Wokeism and How Can It be Defeated', *Common Sense Thinking for a Post-Liberal Age* (2021), p. 22.

44 The word *woke* has a complex political genealogy. Author Ishena Robinson reflects on how woke turned up in everyday conversations as well as the Black power movement in the mid-twentieth century. She explains, 'It's perhaps this

very context – Black people's awareness of their history and their power to resist injustice – that made woke so ripe for the pernicious mutation it has now undergone. Indeed, the forced transformation of the colloquialism echoes how countless other Black ideas and intellectual contributions have been maligned.' 'How Woke went from Black to Bad' https://www.naacpldf.org/woke-black-bad/, 26 August 2022. When woke is turned into a counter-complaint, it is also about rejecting that struggle for equality and freedom of many formerly enslaved and colonized peoples.

45 Herbert Spencer, 'The Study of Sociology', *Popular Science Monthly*, 3 (1873), np.

46 Scholars making these kinds of arguments are now typically defended with reference to free speech. Consider the example of Nathan Cofnas, a postdoctoral fellow at Cambridge, who published a post titled 'A Guide to the Hereditarian Revolution', which argued that 'Harvard faculty would be recruited from the best of the best students, which means the number of black professors would approach 0%. Blacks would disappear from almost all high-profile positions outside of sports and entertainment', https://ncofnas.com/p/a-guide-for-the-hereditarian-revolution, 5 February, 2024. A number of scholars have in an open letter defended Cofnas on the grounds of academic freedom and free speech (without reference to the complaints made against him by students). See Wilf Vall, 'Academics Call for Cambridge to Drop Investigation into "race realist" Fellow', *Varsity*, https://www.varsity.co.uk/news/27524, 2 May 2024.

47 When Chairman Andrew N. Ferguson announced that DEI was 'over at FTC' (the Federal Trade Commission), he claimed it violated 'natural law'. https://www.ftc.gov/news-events/news/press-releases/2025/01/ftc-chairman-ferguson-announces-dei-over-ftc. Last accessed 18 March 2025.

48 Dolmage, *Academic Ableism*, p. 44.

49 Mirza, 'One in a Million', p. 43.

50 Armstrong folds feminism into his anti-EDI rant. He does so by equating feminism with sex-realist feminists, thereby positioning feminists who are queer and trans inclusive as well as trans activists as being concerned with 'men's feelings'. John Armstrong, 'Inside the EDI Idiocracy', Battle of Ideas, 2024, https://www.youtube.com/watch?v=A58PFmGLkEk. Last accessed 18 March, 2025.

51 Steff Chávez, 'Corporate America Embraces a New Era of Conservatism under Donald Trump', *Financial Times*, https://www.ft.com/content/973421a3-c96a-4038-96c6-725af5aa6124, 14 January 2025.

52 Christopher F. Rufo, 'Shut Down Activist Academic Departments', https://www.city-journal.org/article/shut-down-activist-academic-departments, 15 May 2023.

53 It is worth noting here that 'sex realist' feminists who share this conservative view of sex have also written and spoken against EDI and 'woke politics'. See for example, Kathleen Stock, 'Turn of the Woke Tide Will Leave Many Stranded', *The Times*, https://www.thetimes.com/uk/society/article/

turn-woke-tide-leave-many-stranded-transgender-cass-report-3xh5kwm6x, 22 April 2024. In an interview on the podcast *Savage Minds* given in 2021, Jo Phoenix argues that all employees of an institution are 'by definition' included and that inclusion is just about 'feeling included', thus ignoring decades of feminist anti-racist, disability justice as well as LGBTQIA+ research on the means and mechanisms whereby organizations exclude some people from participation. The managerial misuse of diversity and inclusion (long documented by feminists of colour) is thereby conflated with the political struggle to build more accommodating institutions by minoritized groups ourselves. See https://savageminds.substack.com/p/jo-phoenix, last accessed 6 February 2024.

54 Connor Stringer, 'Half of Our Universities Peddle their Woke Agenda to Students: League Table Reveals "dark shadow" has Fallen on Elite Institutions', https://www.dailymail.co.uk/news/article-11638389/Half-universities-peddle-woke-agenda-students.html, 15 January 2023.

Part Three: Dismantling and World Building

1 Jack Halberstam, 'Unbuild the World', https://blogs.law.columbia.edu/revolution1313/jack-halberstam-2/, 20 February 2022.

2 Naomi Klein, *No Is Not Enough: Defeating the New Shock Politics* (London: Allen Unwin, 2017), p. 2.

3. Quoted in Harriet Sherwood, 'John Smyth Abuse Report Triggers "existential crisis" in Church of England', *Guardian*, https://www.theguardian.com/world/2024/nov/16/john-smyth-abuse-report-triggers-existential-crisis-in-church-of-england, 16 November, 2024.

5. Complaints as Activism

1. K. H. Perry, *London is the Place for Me: Black Britons, Citizenship and the Politics of Race* (Oxford: Oxford University Press, 2015), p. 230.

2. Document 3: Leaflet, 'How to Expose Racial Discrimination', distributed by the Campaign Against Racial Discrimination (CARD), 1966. Archived at the Institute for Race Relations, London. Thanks to the archivists for help in finding CARD materials.

3. Audre Lorde, 'The Master's Tools Will Never Dismantle the Master's House', in *Sister Outsider* (New York: Crossing Press, 1984).

4. Raymond Brown, 'Panic in Cambridge's Mill Road: Disabled Woman Sues Seven Shops and Makes 28 Complaints about Access', https://www.cambridge-news.co.uk/news/cambridge-news/panic-cambridges-mill-road-disabled-12674450, 2 March 2017. Please note that the article refers to Esther Leighton, but she has since changed her name to Esther Loukin.

5   Nicola Gwyer, 'Agreement Reached in Row Over Mill Road Disability Access', https://www.cambridge-news.co.uk/news/cambridge-news/carlos-disability-access-agreed-settlement-16058033, 1 April 2019.

6   https://www.reasonableaccess.org.uk/. Last accessed 30 January 2025.

7   The judicial review challenge was over an asserted decision of the Lord Chancellor not to extend Qualified One-Way Costs-Shifting (QOCS) to discrimination claims in the County Court and/or the failure to extend QOCS to such claims. Quotes from Esther Leighton and disabled justice activists are from John Pring, 'Support for "amazing" Campaigner Whose Vital Legal Case could Help Thousands',https://www.disabilitynewsservice.com/support-for-amazing-campaigner-whose-vital-legal-case-could-help-thousands/, 30 January 2020.

8   https://www.inclusionlondon.org.uk/. Last accessed 30 January 2025.

9   https://dpglaw.co.uk/disability-campaigners-call-on-justice-minister-to-protect-people-discriminated-against-under-the-equality-act-following-high-court-judgment/. Last accessed 30 January 2025.

10 John Pring, 'Disabled Campaigners "one step closer to justice" Despite Court Setback', https://www.disabilitynewsservice.com/disabled-campaigners-one-step-closer-to-justice-despite-court-setback/, 20 February 2020.

11 https://www.gov.uk/government/calls-for-evidence/costs-protection-for-discrimination-claims/costs-protection-for-discrimination-claims-call-for-evidence. Last accessed 30 January 2025.

12 Pao, *Reset*, pp. 4, 165.

13 Ana Avendaño, *Solidarity Betrayed: How Unions Enable Sexual Harassment and How They Can Do Better* (London: Pluto Press, 2025), pp. 1, 3, 12.

14 Whitley et al., 'Collective Conclusions,' pp. 262, 267.

15 Event archived here: https://m.facebook.com/photo/?fbid=206158015068300&set=ecnf.100069838526501&locale=hi_IN. Last accessed 12 January 2025.

16 Avendaño, *Solidarity Betrayed*, pp. 15, 75–9.

17 Avendaño, *Solidarity Betrayed*, p. 2. It is useful to know that spaces to share our stories of sexual harassment, to confront painful truths, to pass on the knowledge in, as well as skills of, complaint can be created by workers unions. We might expect unions to do this: after all, they are meant to bargain collectively for workers by pushing against institutional power. But the point of *Solidarity Betrayed* is to show how women workers (especially women of colour workers) often had to push unions (or push against them) before they would take on this kind of work.

18 'Organizing Transformative Justice Responses to Gender-based Violence and Campus Sexual Violence', Barnard

Centre for Research on Women, 27 April 2022; Xhercis Méndez in conversation with Dean Spade, https://www.youtube.com/watch?v=9fBLrCKG_Vo. See also Angela Y. Davis, Gina Dent, Erica R. Meiners, and Beth E. Richie's discussion of how institutions 'manage and contain' the radical demands of abolitionist feminist and other radical networks by adding 'yet another "diversity committee" or another "equity officer"', in *Abolition. Feminism. Now* (Chicago: Haymarket Books, 2021), p. 159.

19 Mia Mingus, 'Access Intimacy: The Missing Link', https://leavingevidence.wordpress.com/2011/05/05/access-intimacy-the-missing-link/, 5 May 2011.

20 On social media, Janine described her complaint activism as 'advocacy work for BIPOCs in the arts & academia, supporting mainly race-based complaints/grievances'. In another tweet Janine elaborated, 'This means co-writing complaints letters, attending meetings, explaining policy, providing advice & strategy. I don't charge for this labour. I do this for: 1) better working conditions for oppressed folks 2) structural/policy/procedural change & have been successful in doing so.'

21 Madison Marriage, Antonia Cundy and Paul Caruana Galizia, 'How Crispin Odey Evaded Sexual Assault Allegations for Decades', https://www.ft.com/content/e5d14398-e866-44b3-8ecb-4e6371167c6d, 8 June 2023.

22 PA Media, https://www.theguardian.com/media/2024/dec/30/crispin-odey-ft-libel-case, 30 December 2024. You

can read the decision in full here: https://www.fca.org.uk/news/press-releases/fca-decides-fine-and-ban-robin-crispin-odey, last accessed 20 March 2025.

23 Kalyeena Makortoff, 'Crispin Odey Banned from City and Handed £1.8m Fine by FCA', https://www.theguardian.com/business/2025/mar/17/crispin-odey-banned-from-city-fine-fca, 17 March 2025.

24 Information about the documentary *Al Fayed: Predator at Harrods* is available here: https://www.bbc.co.uk/programmes/m0023ff5. Last accessed 20 March 2025.

25 Henry Porter, 'My Battle to Expose Mohamad Al Fayed,' https://www.theguardian.com/global/2024/sep/22/remorseless-ruthless-racist-my-battle-to-expose-mohamed-al-fayed, 22 September 2024.

26 We need changes to the law so that we don't have to wait for people to die to stop abuse. One bill currently being discussed by Parliament in the UK is to prevent the use of SLAPPS (Strategic litigation against public participation) defined by the government as 'an abuse of the legal process, where the primary objective is to harass, intimidate and financially and psychologically exhaust one's opponent via improper means' (cited by Victoria Moffatt, https://www.lawsociety.org.uk/topics/business-management/slapps-and-reputational-risks, 25 January 2025). Given the primary point of the bill would be to prevent the misuse of litigation to suppress freedom of speech, it has the potential to be used to stop stories of sexual harassment being

suppressed by retaliatory litigation. See https://bills.parliament.uk/bills/3544, Last accessed 7 April 2025. Legal scholars Tejal Jesrani and Daimiris Garcia describe what they call 'gendered SLAPPS'. They explain, 'In the wake of the #MeToo movement, criminal cases lodged by those accused of SGBV [sexual and gender-based violence] have targeted, retraumatized, criminalized and silenced those who have spoken out about sexual harassment and abuse. Many women who spoke out were then subject to private criminal prosecutions by powerful figures to silence and discredit their allegations. As a result, women have faced criminal proceedings merely for speaking publicly on social media.' See 'Gendered SLAPPs: Addressing criminal prosecutions against exposers of sexual and gender-based violence under international human rights law', *International Journal of Law, Crime and Justice*, 80, https://doi.org/10.1016/j.ijlcj.2025.100729, March 2025.

27 Elias Visontay, 'Passenger Kept from Boarding After Jetstar's Refusal to Assist with Wheelchair Makes Discrimination Complaint', https://www.theguardian.com/law/2022/aug/05/passenger-kept-from-boarding-after-jetstars-refusal-to-assist-with-wheelchair-makes-discrimination-complaint, 4 August 2022.

28 'Workshops Find People with Disability an Afterthought in Domestic Air Travel', https://disability.royalcommission.gov.au/news-and-media/media-releases/workshops-find-people-disability-afterthought-domestic-air-travel, 24 November 2022.

29 Irene Blanco-Fuente et al., 'Violet Spots Against Sexual Harassment in the University: An Activist Collective Response from Spain', https://easst.net/easst-review/373/violet-spots-against-sexual-harassment-in-the-university-an-activist-collective-response-from-spain/, July 2018.

30 Lauren Gambino, 'Columbia University Student Carries Rape Protest Mattress to Graduation', *Guardian*, https://www.theguardian.com/us-news/2015/may/19/columbia-university-emma-sulkowicz-mattress-graduation, 19 May 2015.

31 *Manual Labours: The Complaining Body*, with Sarah Browne, Hamish MacPherson and Ivor Southwood, https://www.theshowroom.org/projects/manual-labours-the-complaining-body, 5–10 April 2016.

32 Ileana Jiménez, 'Embodied Wilfulness: #MeToo Girls' Activism, Affects, and "Complaint as Feminist Pedagogy"', in *Gender in an Era of Post-Truth Populism*, ed. P. J. Burke et al. (London: Bloomsbury, 2023), pp. 160, 163, 166.

33 David Montalvo, 'How AIDS Activists Used "Die-Ins" to Demand Attention to the Growing Epidemic', https://www.history.com/news/aids-activism-protests-act-up-die-ins, 2 June 2021.

34 Sophie Perry, 'Trans Teens Occupy Ledge at NHS England Headquarters: "Lives are at stake"', https://www.thepinknews.com/2024/07/01/trans-teenagers-nhs-england-protest/.

35 https://www.instagram.com/p/DDeZ46UoPDW/?hl=en&img_index=1, 1 July 2024.

36 Alex Press, 'What's next for #MeToo? The McDonald's strikes have an answer', https://www.vox.com/the-big-idea/2018/9/18/17876024/mcdonalds-strikes-walkout-me-too, 19 September 2018.

37 Aditya Chakrabortty, 'College Cleaners Defeated Outsourcing. They've Shown it Can be Done', https://www.theguardian.com/commentisfree/2017/sep/12/college-cleaners-outsourcing-soas, 12 September 2017.

38 Ethiraj Gabriel Dattatreyan and Akanksha Mehta, 'Problem and Solution: Occupation and Collective Complaint', *Radical Philosophy*, 208 (Autumn 2020), pp. 66–72.

6. Complaint as a Queer Method

1 Heather Love, *Feeling Backward: The Politics of Loss in Queer History* (Cambridge: Harvard University Press, 2007), p. 32.

2 'Elliot Page Says the Trans Community is "not a debate": "We're real"', https://abcnews.go.com/GMA/Culture/elliot-page-trans-journey-relationship-mom-abc-pride-special/story?id=99840880, 7 June 2023.

3 As I pointed out in *The Feminist Killjoy Handbook* gender-critical feminists have erased the feminist critiques of the

category of sex for a reason. It enables the identification of feminism with sex and sex-based rights.

4 As a result of employment tribunals, gender-critical beliefs are now protected. A criterion for a belief to be protected is that it has to be so certain that it would not be amended by any new developments or information. The fact that they are protected is evidence that they are not, as it were, 'up for debate'. For further discussion, see Keith Patton, 'Protected Beliefs Under the Equality Act', *Industrial Law Journal*, 3:2 (June 2024), https://doi.org/10.1093/indlaw/dwad033. See also my post, https://feministkilljoys.com/2024/05/10/some-observations-on-the-use-of-protected-beliefs-and-the-misuse-of-employment-tribunals/ for a development of the argument (5 October, 2024).

5 Shon Faye, *The Transgender Issue* (London: Allen Lane, 2021), p. 15.

6 Ian Cobain, Owen Bowcott and Richard Norton-Taylor, 'Britain Destroyed Records of Colonial Crimes', *Guardian*, https://www.theguardian.com/uk/2012/apr/18/britain-destroyed-records-colonial-crimes, 18 April 2012.

7 For a longer discussion of how empire is told happily, see *The Feminist Killjoy Handbook*, especially pp. 127–8. We become feminist killjoys when we refuse to bury the violence. Feminist killjoys are not just cultural critics, philosophers, poets and activists, as I described in the handbook; feminist killjoys are also archivists.

8 *Life in the United Kingdom: A Journey to Citizenship* (London: Stationery Office, 2007), p. 33.

9 Ramzy Baroud, 'How Britain Destroyed the Palestinian Homeland', https://www.aljazeera.com/features/2018/4/10/how-britain-destroyed-the-palestinian-homeland, 10 April 2018.

10 Edward Said, *Orientalism* (London: Routledge, 1978), p. 25.

11 Edward Said, 'Zionism from the Standpoint of Its Victims', *Social Text*, 1 (Winter 1979), pp. 28–31.

12 Mary Turfah, 'Running Amok', *The Baffler*, https://thebaffler.com/latest/running-amok-turfah, 18 June 2024.

13 I wrote a blog post in solidarity with Palestine with the title 'Killjoy Truths' on 16 October 2023. See https://feministkilljoys.com/2023/10/16/killjoy-truths/.

14 'Apology to Victims and Survivors of Historical Institutional Abuse – Ministerial Statements', https://www.executiveoffice-ni.gov.uk/news/apology-victims-and-survivors-historical-institutional-abuse-ministerial-statements, 11 March 2022.

15 'Kincora: Sex Abuse Victims Failed by Police, Ombudsman Says', https://www.bbc.com/news/uk-northern-ireland-63006208, 23 September 2022.

16 Kathleen Daly, *Redressing Institutional Abuse of Children* (London: Palgrave Macmillan, 2014), p. 1.

17 In May 2021, archaeologists found 200 unmarked graves in just one school in Canada. See Anderson Cooper, 'Canada's Unmarked Graves: How Residential Schools Carried Out "cultural genocide" Against Indigenous Children', https://www.cbsnews.com/news/canada-residential-schools-unmarked-graves-indigenous-children-60-minutes-2023-02-12/, 12 February 2023.

18 Mirza, 'One in a Million', p. 48.

19 Jaclyn Peiser, '"Media Men" List Creator Outs Herself, Fearing She Would Be Named', https://www.nytimes.com/2018/01/10/business/media/a-feminist-twitter-campaign-targets-harpers-magazine-and-katie-roiphe.html?_r=0, 10 January 2008.

20 Ayesha Kidwai et al. 'Feminists Uneasy Over Facebook Campaign to "Name and Shame"', https://sabrangindia.in/feminists-uneasy-over-facebook-campaign-name-and-shame/, 25 October 2017.

21 I place 'false accusations' in quote marks not because they do not happen but because the amount of attention given to false accusations *far exceeds* the amount they happen. This has the effect of attaching 'falsity' to complaints especially those made by women. For a discussion of that doubting of women's testimony see Leigh Gilmour, *Tainted Witness: Why We Doubt What Women Say about Their Lives* (New York, Columbia University Press, 2017).

22 Carmon Irin, 'What's Actually in the Harvard Sexual Harassment Complaint', https://nymag.com/intelligencer/2022/02/whats-actually-in-the-harvard-sexual-harassment-complaint.html, 9 February 2022.

23 Susan Fowler, *Whistle-blower: My Journey to Silicon Valley and Fight for Justice at Uber* (London: Penguin, 2021).

24 Information about the protests and postcards can be found at https://timesupateneo.org/. Last accessed 29 May 2025.

25 Ivor Southwood, 'The Uncomplaining Body', https://www.manuallabours.co.uk/wp-content/uploads/2014/11/Ivor-Uncomplaining-body-report-final.pdf, October 2015.

26 Press release, https://www.sistersuncut.org/2022/03/12/release-sisters-uncut-set-off-1000-rape-alarms-outside-charing-cross-police-station/, 12 March 2022.

27 '#NiUnaMenos: ¿Quién fue la autora de la consigna que une a miles contra la violencia de género?', https://web.archive.org/web/20170911065319/https://www.minutouno.com/notas/365815-niunamenos-quien-fue-la-autora-la-consigna-que-une-miles-contra-la-violencia-genero, 3 June 2015.

28 Chelsea Watego, 'Always Bet on Black Power', *Meanjin*, https://meanjin.com.au/essays/always-bet-on-black-power/, Spring 2021.

29 For the poem and discussion, see '"If I Must Die", A Poem by Refaat Alareer', https://inthesetimes.com/article/refaat-

alareer-israeli-occupation-palestine, 27 December 2023. See also Refaat Alareer, *If I Must Die: Poetry and Prose* (New York: OR Books, 2024), for an inspiring posthumously published collection.

30 Christina Sharpe, *Ordinary Notes* (London: Daunt Publishing, 2023), note 22, p. 36.

31 Sara Saleh, 'The Long List (of Receipts)', https://www.fineprintmagazine.com/articles/33-the-long-list-of-receipts, November 2023.

32 Audre Lorde, *A Burst of Light: Essays* (Ithaca, New York: Firebrand Books, 1988), p. 131.

33 You can visit an interactive map of these protests, *Palestine is Everywhere*. At the time of writing, the map lists 174 encampments globally, 247 solidarity actions, twelve universities destroyed in Gaza, 44+ sites of police repression, 2644+ arrests and thirty-five countries in solidarity: https://www.palestineiseverywhere.com/. Last accessed 17 January 2025.

34 One of Balasubramanian and Vaid-Menon's favourite quotes perfectly encapsulates the liberatory combination of humour and truth-telling about white cis patriarchy: 'Make them laugh and then stick the truth in their mouths while they're open.' As quoted in Interview with DarkMatter: 'If You Are Not Happy, Then You Are a Bitch', https://www.migrazine.at/artikel/if-youre-not-happy-then-youre-bitch, 2015. Vaid-Menon and Balasubramanian explicitly

link their performances to the art of being the killjoy in Kevin St John, 'DarkMatter: Be the Kill-Joy', https://www.guernicamag.com/be-the-kill-joy/, 2 May 2016.

35 Alexis Pauline Gumbs, *Survival is a Promise: The Eternal Life of Audre Lorde* (London: Allen Lane, 2024).

36 https://www.queeringthemap.com/, last accessed 13 January 2025. See also my discussion of artists Paul Harfleet's Pansy Project as a queer map in *The Feminist Killjoy Handbook*, p. 213.

37 Sarah O'Neal, 'Gaza's Queer Palestinians Fight to Be Remembered', https://www.thenation.com/article/world/gaza-queering-the-map/, 16 November 2023.

38 A. X. Mina, 'On the Origins of "They Tried to Bury Us, They Didn't Know We Were Seeds",' https://hyperallergic.com/449930/on-the-origins-of-they-tried-to-bury-us-they-didnt-know-we-were-seeds/, 3 July 2018.

A Complaint Curriculum

1 All the books we read together are in the Recommended Reading List shared at the end of *The Feminist Killjoy Handbook*. Please return to that list for some inspiration!

2 See https://fineacts.co/surviving-blackness. Last accessed 17 January 2025.